*Dedications:*

To my lovely wife who continues to accept my longing to write.

To everyone who has read my first book, I hope you enjoy this one as much as you said you did the last.

To Thimblemill library

# ILONA

## Wolf Queen

### The

# CIVILIS SAGA

## Part 2

# PETER BAGGOTT

# PROLOGUE

## Autumn 31AD. A forest hut, Germania

### Inferior

Rosevetha sat before the crackling fire; she felt winter's cold playing on her old injuries. The man who was to be her daughter's future was now unwittingly heading towards his destiny. She reflected on her own past and how the one and only man she had ever loved met his fate just as she told him he would. Then came Rome's retribution, breathing death and destruction on all those that had taken part. She had been young and beautiful then, until the Cherusci took their revenge on any who had fraternised with Rome.

Ilona stirred, woke, and watched her mother intently focused on the flames, as if in a trance. Rosevetha reached into a small bag, tossing some of its contents into the fire. It crackled and spat red flames.

'What is it you see, that I can't?' enquired Ilona.

'Yours is the greater gift, but you will have what I possess in time. For now, it is best that you don't. Prepare yourself, daughter – the weather brings your man to our door. His life is about to change forever, and painfully so. Only you can repair his tortured soul and give him hope. Of those that will seek him when he is lost, one will betray him to the devil that still seeks revenge on his family and friends.'

'What will happen to us?' enquired Ilona.

'Unity; even your pets must play their part in our defence. Friends will stand shoulder to shoulder, but the bloody tally will be heavy. Where there is no man in your life now, soon there will be three. Your world will change, forever.'

Ilona stared at her mother and felt an icy wave sweep over her. Beside her mother stood an unknown Roman officer, his arms wrapped around her.

Rosevetha shivered, and smiled at Ilona. 'You see your father, don't you? He waits for me.'

'But why, Mother? And why now, when I need you most?' asked Ilona.

'Destiny, my child.'

Rosevetha closed her eyes and withdrew into herself, enjoying once more the sweet caresses of Cloelius Aelius. He was from a family of the old world, like the man who would soon take her daughter – not a Roman, though he was called one. Rosevetha delved into the small bag attached to her rope belt that never left her side. Two clay figures filled her broken hand: gifts from her man, and the reason he went on that last mission despite her warning. Turan, a symbol of her man's love, and Lasa, controller of fate. Why did he believe so strongly in fate despite the alternative she offered? Now he was with Lainth and soon she would join him for all time, returned to the form he knew and loved, no more the wrecked shell that she had become.

'Who was my father?'

Rosevetha's eyes glazed momentarily before she shook her head and turned to face her daughter. 'I was pregnant with you when he marched off to the devil's forest at Teutoburg. I tried to warn him but he wouldn't believe me. It was the only time he didn't.' Rosevetha's head dropped at the memory of their parting.

'He was from one of the lost Legions?' Ilona recoiled.

'He was a Senior Centurion when he first called on me. I knew he was coming, and like your man, he didn't. He was promoted to Camp Prefect of the 17th Legion. We were happy and he planned to retire when he returned from that fateful mission, but I knew he never would.

# ILONA

'I wasn't always crippled like this, you don't remember me as I was before? When the Romans returned for their lost Eagles, villages were razed and their people killed or enslaved. Anyone who fraternised with the Romans became targets of revenge by the local tribes. A lesser Chauci chieftain named Agi beat me because of my relationship with your father, until I cursed him.

# Chapter 1

Artorius raced between each mutatione. To his right, marshland spread from the river, teeming with life, to its heavily wooded edges. To his left there was a wide open plain of tall grass, broken occasionally with cultivated ground and backed with mountains rising away from him. Artorius strained to see even the slightest movement that might mean trouble in the dark interior of the forest. Heavy grey clouds swept up the valley into his face, bringing with them snow and an icy blast. The fall became so heavy that he couldn't even see the river and had to rein his horse in. Was this his fifth or sixth horse? He couldn't remember.

Pulling his paenula tighter against the cold, Artorius smelt smoke and followed his nose till a dark shape appeared to his left. Walking his horse towards it, smoke trailed from a hole in the roof. *The prospect of warmth*, he thought. Underfoot he saw cultivated ground disappearing under a carpet of snow. Hobbling his horse, he knocked on the stout wooden door; sliding bolts announced a response.

A crack of bright light escaped, but no one stood in it, then a faint female voice called out: 'Who is it, what do you want? My husband will return soon.'

'I am a Roman soldier heading for Mogontiacum, but the weather is so bad I cannot see. Do you have a barn I could use?'

'Go behind the house, put your horse there and come to the rear door,' said the voice as the door was bolted shut again.

Artorius found a small thatched building with a single cow, a small pony and an empty stall, where he hobbled his horse. Knocking on the rear door, it was opened almost immediately. The heat and light from within stunned Artorius momentarily.

'Come in quickly, you're letting the heat out,' called the same voice.

Artorius stepped warily inside, hand on his spatha, to find a large fire belching out heat. Perched above it was a large steaming pot with welcoming smells that tantalised his taste buds. His eyes shot around to find an attractive, pale-skinned young woman with long red hair tied at the back and sparkling green eyes, sword in hand. She pointed it at him with her back to the wall.

'I mean you no harm. All I ask is a little shelter till the storm subsides. Will your husband be long?' enquired Artorius.

'Why do you ask?' she snapped.

'I am Centurion Artorius Civilis. I'll remain with my horse until he returns, if you prefer?' He unclipped his spatha scabbard and laid it on the floor, holding out his empty hands.

The female let the blade point fall to the floor as she pointed to a stool by the fire. 'You may sit there and warm yourself while I feed my mother.'

Artorius sat, noticing a bundle of clothing on a small cot in a dark corner, which started to move. A withered toothless face emerged from under the bundle, with eyes like embers looking straight at him.

'What you let him in for? Has he come to see me?' she said in a local dialect which Artorius struggled with.

'What does she mean?' he asked.

The young woman translated her mother's words into perfect Roman. 'You really must be lost. This is Rosevetha, the seer, your people often come to her. I am her daughter, Ilona.'

'Never heard of her, I seek only shelter from the storm,' answered Artorius.

'So, you said. Would you like some food? It's vegetables

with a little rabbit.'

'If you can spare some, I would be very grateful and will pay.' Artorius reached out for the bowl and spoon that was offered to him.

Rosevetha sat up in her cot; her body was small and bent. Artorius felt her eyes piercing deep into his soul as Ilona sat on the cot's edge and fed her. Artorius devoured his offering in the warm surroundings and looked around the building's interior where, except for the sword, there was no obvious evidence of a male.

'I take it you have no husband?' Artorius remarked.

'What makes you think that?' asked Ilona.

'A single sword, no shield or other weaponry, and no men's clothing,' he commented.

'I did, but he had an accident,' replied Ilona.

'Not a great loss,' said Rosevetha. 'Let me have your hand, young man. You have suffered much recently, maybe I can find good news for you.' She now spoke in fluent Roman, to Artorius' surprise.

'I don't believe in that sort of thing,' he said defensively.

'No need to be afraid, she sees many things,' added Ilona.

'You have lost two males you were close to, and now you seek the man who did it.' Rosevetha sucked in her breath and, reverting to her own language, spoke to her daughter. 'Your man has come, as I said he would.'

'What's she seen?' queried Artorius.

'The man you seek was here yesterday,' replied Rosevetha.

'Were others with him?'

'There were, but they travelled on without him,' Rosevetha responded.

The blood drained from Artorius' face in shock. Ilona reached out and took his hand, and initially he pulled away. He considered Ilona's face. She was truly beautiful and he couldn't look away from her eyes.

'You have a beautiful wife and family, but you must return to them as soon as you can,' Ilona stated, tears trickled down her face and she looked away.

'Why? You're the second person who has told me this,' said Artorius.

'I cannot say for now,' said Ilona, passing Artorius' hand back to her mother.

Rosevetha held his hand in a vice-like grip that was unimaginable for one so old. She ran a finger across his palm and, looking to her daughter, she took his other hand.

'Beware the man with a "V" in his name. He wants you dead before you reach Mogontiacum, and only if you survive will you see Rome again,' she related.

'I don't understand, tell me more,' demanded Artorius.

'If you return I may see more then. You will be able to leave in the morning,' responded Rosevetha.

She turned away, whispering to her daughter, and the two women continued to look at a stunned Artorius. Ilona produced a wolf pelt and offered it to him, and he took it gratefully.

Rosevetha scooped a beaker into a pot beside the fire and, slipping a powder into it unnoticed, passed it to Artorius. 'This will aid your sleep.'

He lay in a corner on the floor against the wall, and in the firelight, he watched the two women, who spoke in whispers, lay down together. Sleep finally crept over Artorius as he reflected on the revelations. He kissed the family ring, praying to every Etruscan god to help him. Artorius' dreams were filled with images of Ilona. She crept over to him and, dropping the blanket she wore, stood naked before him, revealing her beautiful body in the partial light of the fire. Her long red hair hung loose and her dark nipples were hard and erect on firm breasts, a thick red triangle of hair covered her pubic mound. She knelt in front of him and removed his braccae and loincloth, revealing his large erection, which she took firmly in her hands.

Straddling it, Ilona took Artorius deep inside her, taking him to incredible highs before slowing, preventing his final explosion till she was ready to share it. Kneeling above him she kissed him, then stood, replacing his braccae, she wrapped the blanket around herself and walked away.

Artorius woke with a start at movement around him. He struggled to remember where he was as a beautiful apparition appeared in front of him.

'The snow has stopped and the day is breaking,' whispered Ilona.

Artorius was offered further hot food and drink, devouring it with as much relish as he had the previous night. Ilona produced a tied bundle of victuals. As he went to leave she kissed him, and he didn't know why, but he returned the kiss. Was it a dream?

Outside, the door shut behind him, Artorius stretched and sucked in a deep cold breath which burnt his throat. The ground was white with a thin layer of snow and footprints travelled between the house and the shed where he found his horse warm and fed. He mentally thanked Ilona. Artorius found he hadn't strayed far from the road and travelled as fast as possible with only about thirty miles to his goal. Pushing onward, the river seemed to drift away as the marshy areas grew with little habitation. Traveling northwards, the valley sides narrowed and the forest appeared to close around him, making Artorius nervous. Thick, light grey clouds brought large flakes of snow, reducing his vision again.

He halted at an uprooted tree that blocked his way. Too high to jump, too low to go under, it forced him to dismount as he scanned the surroundings with no obvious footprints. Taking the only option, he climbed the valley side carefully to find the tree had been cut. Surveying the area again, nothing moved, not even animal tracks pierced the snow as he withdrew his spatha. Artorius slipped with every step he took whilst desperately hanging on to the horse's reins; the beast grew more and more agitated. One slip too many sent Artorius rolling down the slope and, dropping the reins, his horse bolted.

Picking himself up, he followed the hoof marks in the snow. He had no choice or he would have to walk to the next mutatione. A twig snapped behind him, and as he spun around he felt something heavy strike him from behind. Darkness followed.

*

Artorius woke shivering, his armour in a pile beside the tree to which he was tied. A group of tribesmen had their backs to him and were talking to what looked like Roman officers. One stepped away from the rest, limping. Artorius' heart sank. Victus!

'I've waited a long time for this and I'm going to make you suffer, very slowly. These are the same men that helped me kill that fucking son of yours. I will hide for a while till I'm forgotten about, but you will be gone and so will your family, and then I'll return to Rome. These men will tell your family they found you dead and cremated you with honours,' Victus said, laughing.

'They'll catch you and your men and you'll all get your just desserts,' responded Artorius.

Victus punched him in the face, his nose twisting on impact. Blood splashed into Victus' face and, wiping it clean, he laughed again.

'Is that the best you can do?' said Artorius.

'The smell of blood should bring the wolves; they will

never find your body,' said Victus smugly.

Artorius watched the group pack his uniform on to a mule. The tribesmen left, having been paid by Victus, leaving two Centurions. One Artorius recognized and three others he took to be Tribunes.

'You should never have returned, but then I'm glad you did. Time to leave, gentlemen,' Victus said as he punched Artorius in the stomach, causing him to double in pain and gasp for breath.

'We can't just leave him here,' exclaimed the youngest Tribune.

'You will, now get on your horse and do as you were told. Have no fear, Artorius, I'll not kill you, but I'll leave the wilderness to do that for me. Goodbye.' Victus punched Artorius once more, this time in his kidneys, and in excruciating pain Artorius slid to his knees.

With everyone gone, Artorius tested the ropes, but already they cut into his wrists as he tried to raise himself. The temperature was dropping fast and there was nothing he could do. If anyone came looking, it would be too late. In the distance, he could hear the howl of wolves; had they picked up the blood scent already?

Further down the track, the remaining Centurion and the young Tribune watched as Victus and the others disappeared, the fallen tree separating the two groups.

'I need to relieve myself before we travel to Argentoratum,' stated the young tribune as he slipped back into the trees.

'Don't be long, and don't forget there are wolves about,' demanded the Centurion.

Following the hoof marks in the snow, the young Tribune made his way back to Artorius. He watched as Artorius struggled to stand with his ropes tied. Slipping from his horse, the young Tribune took Artorius' spatha from his saddle bag and approached from behind.

At the noise, and feeling the ropes slacken, Artorius stood without turning, waiting for a blow that never came.

'I cannot leave you defenceless. You are a soldier, after all, and a fair man,' said the young Tribune.

Artorius turned to face the young tribune. 'Help me and I'll see you safe,' he offered.

The young Tribune shook his head and, forcing himself upright, he tossed Artorius' spatha into the snow. Mounting his horse, he saluted as he walked across the snow-covered ground, following the hoof marks from earlier.

The grizzled Centurion didn't speak a word when the young Tribune reappeared. Luckily the Centurion hadn't followed him when he'd said he needed to empty his bowels. At least he had given Artorius a chance, a slim one, but he was a good soldier despite all that Victus had said. The young man's own conscience was clear.

Once more Artorius was alone, barely clothed. The temperature was dropping fast and he only had his spatha for protection against wolves and hostile tribes. The moon shone bright above him; footprints in the snow from his adversaries headed north and south. Then Artorius remembered Rosevetha's words:

'When you return.'

In an instance, he knew he had to head south. Looking at the north star, he followed the footprints behind him. Artorius shivered as he started to walk. He had to find shelter or die!

## Chapter 2

Artorius struggled to walk, his bare feet already without feeling as a deathly peace lay around him. His thoughts slipped back to Rome and the last time he had kissed Amoria goodbye. This was Macro's fault – if he hadn't been sent back to the Legion he wouldn't be here.

Artorius couldn't give in, though he could barely feel his hands as he began to freeze and the dried blood in his nose and throat intensified his breathing problems. He shivered at the thought: *it was walk or die!* The moonlight on the snow blinded him as he struggled to focus, but he plodded on blindly. The will to live burned deep in his soul, the picture of his family paramount in his mind. With teeth chattering and skin like chalk, Artorius staggered onward.

He sensed the wolves growing closer, could almost feel their hot breath on his back. As the forest thinned, Artorius heard running water and, staggering into the open, he saw a cleft in the rocks and glanced back. The trees had grown eyes, hundreds of them, all moving towards him. His legs turned to lead as the pack emerged from between the trees, appearing larger than any he had seen before.

Spittle dribbled from the jaws of a black alpha male that led the group. It stopped about a hundred paces away, growling, its yellow teeth glowing brightly in the moonlight. Two wolves approached it in flanking positions as it flicked its head in Artorius' direction. The two moved stealthily towards Artorius, who plunged his spatha into the snow and knelt, shouting at the top of his voice.

'Lainth, goddess of death, accept my poor soul this night!'

Artorius rose, adopting a low defence as the two wolves

sped towards him. The lead wolf leapt for Artorius, who rammed cold metal deep into its stomach as it flew over his head. The impact knocked him from his feet, his spatha lodged in the creature's spine.

Pain ripped through Artorius' brain as he realised the second wolf had his arm in its jaws. As it tried to drag him away, the spatha was pulled free from the other creature. Swinging the spatha with his good arm and rolling towards the other wolf, Artorius smashed the pommel into its head, rendering it unconscious. Its jaw slackened and Artorius extracted his arm, blood oozing from the puncture marks.

Struggling to stand, he faced the alpha male, who walked slowly towards him, growling. Artorius stabbed his spatha down into the unconscious creature before him in defiance of the alpha, who howled in anger, venom filling his eyes.

*

As Ilona extinguished the oil lamp beside her cot, she wrapped a deer hide tighter around her. The image of Artorius' naked body, which she had shared only hours ago, filled her mind with delicious thoughts. He was the only other man she had had – or would have; so, her mother had prophesied. As she felt her body tingle, her blood suddenly went cold at the howl of her wolves. She knew better than anyone that they only came close when there was trouble.

She looked to her mother, who knelt in front of the fire and threw a powder into it. The flames exploded into shades of blue. Rosevetha started to hum and gesture with her hands. More powder created red flames, and slowly she turned and looked straight through Ilona, pointing to the door.

'Your man was captured, but is free and lost in the white

wilderness. Wolves are tracking him. Find him before they do. Go!'

Without question, Ilona dressed in her warmest furs and gathered spare pelts. As she was about to leave, Rosevetha slipped a small pouch into her hand.

'It contains the Roman's loincloth. Your pets will follow the scent, but be quick, he already grows weak.'

The icy blast struck Ilona in the face as she opened the door, the snow stacked halfway up the frame falling inward. Stepping out into the surrounding whiteness, she collected her bow and arrows as she went. Once her mountain pony was saddled she looked to the forest where yellow eyes sparkled in the moonlight: her pack was waiting. She lifted her head and howled for all the night to hear. Donor stepped stealthily from the trees and her hands ran down the soft fur of her alpha male as he rubbed his head against her and howled. Suddenly she was surrounded by wolves.

Ilona offered them the pouch to smell.

'Find him, Donor,' she commanded.

The pack turned and slowly melted back into the forest, Donor pacing Ilona on her pony. In the distance, another pack called. The night was bitterly cold and she struggled in the deep snow as the night slipped away. Ilona found the fallen tree, footprints led to another with a discarded rope at its base, as the howls from the other wolf pack rent the air. Donor growled and the hairs on his back stood up.

'Not yet. Spread out and find him,' commanded Ilona.

She followed the single human footprints amidst a mass of wolf spoor, her own wolves responding instantly, racing away from her. She followed quickly behind her pack as her pony grew skittish at the sound of other beasts. The whiteness before her was only broken by the forest sentinels that towered above her, their limbs heavy with snow. Donor howled as he spied the second pack, calling his own close and waiting for Ilona.

The rogue alpha howled back at Donor, his pack members edging backwards into the open ground. Artorius saw this as his last chance, and though his injured arm was numb with cold, he spun in the direction of the cleft and attempted to run. He was moving, but he couldn't feel his feet or legs. His life became one of slow motion, his lungs almost at bursting point as he propelled himself forward. Heavy footfalls sounded behind him and he tripped over a hidden tree root, spilling forward into the snow, clutching his spatha. Rolling on to his back, Artorius found the alpha circling him. Its yellow eyes pierced deep into his soul, but he stared back in defiance, screaming as he did.

Ilona heard the scream. Donor looked up at her.

'Take them now,' she cried.

Ilona's pack answered immediately, sweeping from the forest into the open. The two packs faced each other, snarling. The alpha looked at Artorius, then his pack, and turned, loping back to them.

Artorius tried to stand. His body was weak, but his will was stronger as he crawled towards the cleft. Behind him the world exploded. Two wolf packs charged each other and the sounds of pain and terror filled the air.

Ilona stepped out of the forest trailing her pony. She could see a figure crawling towards the rocks, and at first, she wasn't sure if it was man or beast.

Donor tore into the renegade alpha; no quarter was given between them as they rolled in the snow. Donor, the larger of the two, commanded the upper hand and sensing victory, bit deep into his adversary's spine. The animal screamed in pain and collapsed in the snow in its final death throes, blood dribbling from Donor's jaws. The smell of blood hung in the air and the ground was littered with bodies fed upon by Donor's pack. Ilona made her way towards the cleft.

Artorius was delirious; heavy footfalls crushed the snow behind him and he dared not look back. The snow blinded him as he crawled ever slower, feeling rather than seeing his way. The cleft was just a dark hole, but a welcoming one as he collapsed into it and propped himself up. He tried to survey the fading night. The silence was deafening. He rubbed at his eyes, but they failed to focus. A shadow blocked the moonlight – the biggest wolf he had ever seen, but it appeared to stand on two legs. With his spatha in front of him, Artorius awaited death as darkness surrounded him, and he thought he could hear a woman's voice. *But how could that be?* he thought, as unconsciousness claimed him.

Artorius' skin was as white as snow, and blood caked his injured arm. Donor, beside Ilona, stepped forward and licked at the teeth marks on his arm. Ilona knelt beside him, praying she wasn't too late. A weak pulse pumped in his neck. Rosevetha had been right: Artorius was a fighter and he would make a strong father for the son she carried.

Ilona knew she had to get him out of the cold and warm him slowly or he could still die. Fetching her pony and some stout branches, she lashed them together and tried to lift Artorius, but he was a dead weight. She knew she had to move him, and now, so grabbing Artorius under his armpits, she dragged him on to the makeshift sleigh and wrapped him in the pelts she had brought.

It had been a good night. Artorius was alive and she had new additions to her pack. Slipping a rope around the renegade alpha male's body, Ilona attached it to the sleigh, a fine trophy and a welcome addition to their fur

16

supply. The snow was stained red with a dozen dead wolves, all of which were being devoured by her pack. Donor lifted his head and howled, the pack responding, and Artorius twitched at the sound subconsciously.

Ilona retraced her steps as the early morning sun's warmth bathed her back. Smoke curled skyward from her home as she drew closer. Bidding Donor and the pack farewell at the door, she ruffled his fur as he howled at the new sun. In an instant, the wolves had melted into the trees.

The door opened and the bent form of Rosevetha emerged into the snow. 'Don't dawdle, get him inside and warmed or he will surely die. Get his clothes off, and yours too – your body will warm him. I'll prepare a potion to warm his insides.'

Ilona stripped Artorius of what little clothing he had and covered him with furs. Slipping out of her own coverings, she climbed underneath the furs, his body so cold against her, but she wasn't going to lose him now. Wrapping herself around him, her skin tingled at the expectation of their future. A real man at last, but how would he cope with his family's destiny?

Rosevetha bent over the couple, and with Ilona's help, poured her potion into Artorius' mouth.

'This will help the fever, but with your warmth he should survive. Donor's tongue will have cleaned the wound; this herb will do the rest. This man's friends will eventually come for him, and by then you must be everything his wife was if you are to remain together,' croaked Rosevetha, taking Artorius' damaged arm and wrapping an herbal poultice around it.

'Will he stay willingly, Mother?' enquired Ilona.

'That is up to you. Life is a succession of two roads.'

The potion warmed Artorius's inside. He thought he was

awake, but his eyes wouldn't open. As he floated between life and death, his parents appeared to him but never spoke. Sometimes they even brought Cassius and Porcia with their little boy. He stood looking down at himself, white as snow, next to a strange woman and a bent and twisted hag who filled him with potions. The women looked familiar, but he didn't know why. Day and night no longer had meaning.

Ilona barely left Artorius' side over the following days. He had suffered severe exposure and there were days she thought she had lost him. She saw the couple he called his parents and a younger couple with a child. She cried for the pain he had suffered and feared he would reject the child growing inside her. Rosevetha had foretold that visit, and their coupling, and she knew the child would be a son, but his future depended on his father.

There were nights when Artorius called out for Amoria. Regrettably, Ilona pretended to be her as he clung tightly to her body. She envied his love for this woman and dreaded the day he would find she was gone. Somewhere in Rome his wife was oblivious to his predicament and the knowledge that the future would be cruel to them both. *From that ruin, I must give Artorius hope*, thought Ilona.

The wolf bite festered and Rosevetha was stretched to stay the putrefaction. Artorius lived in a euphoric world, not comprehending reality, his spiritual visitations becoming more frequent as he slipped deeper into the fever. His whole body suffered from lack of movement, and sores covered every part, despite Rosevetha and Ilona's efforts to create frequent movement in his limbs. They had struggled at first, but Artorius' weight loss aided the situation as a new moon came and went.

'I cannot give him much more of my potion or he will die

anyway. The time has come to let his gods save or take him,' remarked Rosevetha.

'But you said he was strong and would fight!' responded Ilona.

'Most would have passed to the shades long ago. It is time to find out how strong he is. I have taken the dead skin from his wounds, but I can't do any more – his body must do the rest,' insisted Rosevetha.

'Then I shall pray to his gods that he will live, because my son's life depends on his survival.'

Ilona was pale, each morning waking to be violently sick. Rosevetha smiled at the daily eruptions, stating they were normal. Artorius, meanwhile, had lost half his weight and his body looked as if it had been starved, such was the battle he was fighting. Delirium walked hand in hand with fever over the next few days, Ilona crying herself to sleep as she lived his horrors with him.

## Chapter 3

Fresh snow fell and visibility declined, reducing the Centurion and Tribune's progress to a bare walk, the cold biting deep into every exposed piece of skin as the pair reached Argentoratum. The Centurion suggested that the Tribune bag their armour to avoid recognition and unwanted questions. They were to pose as father-and-son wine traders making for Rome who were caught up in bad weather. Avoiding the garrison, they slipped through the muddied side streets, avoiding any busy taverns and arriving at a riverside inn where the food was good, but the cots had seen better days.

To the north, Victus led the mule carrying Artorius' armour and the remaining conspirators trotted behind as Mogontiacum came into view. The hour was late and the guard were preparing to seal the gates for the night as the group slipped in, Victus with head covered lead the party to a smithy in the back streets. Having had a private conversation with the owner, the group's horses were whisked away.

'Your uncle Gaius lives here, Tribune Publius, but what you didn't know is that your uncle is a Sejanus supporter like yourself. We'll meet you at the Grapes Tavern when you have arranged a meeting. Just ask for the landlord,' Victus said, waving Publius away.

Victus entered the rear of the Grapes Tavern and after speaking to the landlord they were led to an upstairs room out of view.

'Would you like company, gentlemen, with my special wine, or just privacy?' the landlord enquired.

'For now, just your good wine and privacy. We are expecting company later, if you can direct him this way. Perhaps your ladies could entertain us later, we'll see.

No one must know we are here, understood?' Victus slipped a coin into the landlord's hand.

'As always, your wish is my command, Praetorian,' replied the landlord, slipping from the room and returning with a flagon and beakers.

'We need to lie low for a while and hopefully the tribune's uncle will arrange that. Drink up, the wine here is particularly good,' stated Victus, pouring wine into a beaker.

He watched his fellow conspirators as the night passed slowly. The Centurion repeatedly cracked his knuckles to the point of annoyance, whilst the smell of sweat dripped from the remaining Tribune. Stress was etched deep into the faces of both; Victus knew that he couldn't trust either and planned their demise.

It was a late hour of night when Publius returned, his face indicating his uncle's reply.

'After hearing the news from Rome, my uncle Gaius has refused to shelter us at his house. With Sejanus dead, he will deny any knowledge or involvement, however, he does offer us a Senator's estate that he oversees and thereafter refuses any further contact. He has provided some funds, but cannot and will not offer any further financial support and when the great pass clears in the spring, we are to leave. My uncle stated that he will find an excuse to travel to Argentoratum and will sort out the mess there. He finally warns us that if we try to contact him again, he will have us arrested for treason,' stated Publius.

Victus erupted, smashing his fist into the small table, scattering the flagon and beakers alike before grabbing Publius by the throat.

'You will go back and arrange a meeting. If he won't meet me, then you can warn him to watch his back and especially that pretty daughter of his. She must be, what – fourteen years old now?'

'He expected your reply and orders us to take up residence at the estate by morning or suffer the consequences,' responded Publius.

'Is this what we can face for the rest of our lives?' asked the Centurion.

'Shut up. Gaius has made a fatal mistake; he will regret this day. Now get your things together, everybody,' ordered Victus.

As the day dawned, Victus' group made their way to the smithy and they watched as Victus whispered with the man before placing a bag of coins in his hand. The day broke with a fresh fall of snow as the group followed the supplied directions; the smithy also departed to carry out his assignment. Victus' group settled into the seclusion of the estate, having woken the staff, as miles away screams woke Gaius. His daughter was missing and her maid's throat had been cut. He shouted profanities in the name of Victus. Gaius knew he would never be able to prove anything, but vowed he would find his daughter and take revenge on all those involved.

Later that day the smithy arrived at the estate with a young, drugged female tied over his horse and was met by Victus, unnoticed by the others. The female was secreted in a room he locked with the only key. Victus took control immediately of the estate, killing all the males, and in his unstable state thought nothing of abusing the female staff, much to the disgust of his fellow conspirators. Fractures developed in the group. Publius and his fellow Tribune refused any involvement in Victus' debauchery, while the Centurion took the easy way out, sinking into alcoholic oblivion. Publius challenged Victus' leadership with the support of his fellow Tribune, both threatening to leave.

'If you think you are good enough to challenge me, try it, because the only way you'll leave is over my dead body. We are all in this together. Like it or not, you are all wanted men, like me.

All we must do is sit back and enjoy ourselves till the dust settles. Then we reappear and rebuild our lives. Tiberius won't live forever,' snapped Victus, face-to-face with Publius, as his hand slipped to his sword.

'You are mad! The way you treat the women is sick, we want nothing more to do with you. I will go to my uncle and ask for his help. We are leaving, whatever you say.' Publius looked to his fellow Tribune for support.

Publius was too preoccupied to see the swift stabbing movement as Victus plunged his sword upwards through his stomach and into his heart. Publius, in shock, stared at Victus. Blood poured from his mouth and he collapsed onto his attacker. Victus pushed him away, watching him fall to the floor, his sword slipping easily from the wound.

He turned towards the remaining Tribune, who shook his head and vomited. The Centurion was unable to comprehend the scene before him and didn't care anyway. The remaining Tribune disappeared the same night, slipping away while the rest slept.

*

Meanwhile the young Tribune and Centurion headed south from Argentoratum, spending nights in abandoned hovels and any non-military accommodation they could find. The Tribune took to drinking heavily, and the Centurion watched him like a hawk in case he betrayed them. The task became more strained as the Tribune drank himself into oblivion nightly, before falling into his cot. His depression worsened as they travelled further south; leaving Artorius as they had, played heavily on the young mind.

The Centurion saw his travelling partner as a threat to his life and started to plan. Reaching Aventicum with the great pass in front of them and the weather still bitterly cold, they set about finding good quality furs. Saturnalia was fast approaching and the Centurion had hoped to reach at least a large Roman town and its facilities by then. He always enjoyed Saturnalia, especially the well-to-do women who became quite wanton. He liked to indulge in any that came looking for a bit of rough.

With that in mind, the day had barely started and the wind had dropped, and the skies were clear as they set out towards Octodurus. The young Tribune had been dragged from his cot in a drunken stupor, the Centurion strapping him to his horse. It was only as he packed the Tribune's horse that he realized Artorius' spatha was missing. Presumably the stupid child had lost it, and with the state he was in, there wasn't any point questioning him till later.

The road was a quagmire of snow and mud, clinging to the horse's hooves; they were barely able to trot. The pair passed the mutationes without stopping as they plodded south, theirs being the only footprints in the unbroken snow. The winter sun cast eerie shadows through the encompassing forest as the road climbed to its peak above the great pass. The thinning air bit deep into their lungs as they reached the head of the pass and the descent started. In the distance, the Centurion could just make out what he believed to be Octodurus. The Tribune struggled to remain atop his horse, the previous night's drink erupting into the snow.

'About time you got a grip of yourself. Carry on drinking like this and you'll be dead before you reach Rome,' warned the Centurion.

The Tribune wiped the vile taste from his mouth and mumbled an acknowledgement, trying to focus through his bloodshot eyes. The horses continued their slow downward course towards Octodurus as the sun followed them. The last hour of day had passed as the snows started to fall again, and the smell of wood fires heralded the nearness of habitation. Lights like stars pierced the darkness as they grew closer, looking for board and lodging for the night. The smell of burning metal caught the Centurion's nose: a smithy and a place for the horses. Turning into a side street, the furnace illuminated the night and highlighted the smithy working in it. Lodging the horses, they were directed to the Boar Inn, which was brightly lit and busy with as many tribesmen as Romans.

The Centurion forced a seat by the fire for himself and the Tribune, who was as white as a sheet. The owner's wife Brunhilda attended to them as they requested food and wine. The Tribune gobbled the offered stew, asking for more, and then started on the wine.

'Go easy on the drink. While I remember, what have you done with Artorius' spatha?'

Brunhilda's ears twitched at the sound of Artorius' name being mentioned.

'It's in my pack, why?' asked the Tribune.

'No, it's not. What have you done with it? I know you wouldn't have lost it,' responded the Centurion.

The Tribune gulped a second beaker and, looking at the Centurion, laughed.

'What have you done? It was when you needed a shit, wasn't it? You, stupid fool, you let Artorius go and gave him his sword!' The Centurion punched the Tribune so hard he was propelled backwards and landed on a table, scattering plates and mugs alike.

Brunhilda screamed for Paulinus and as he made his way from the kitchen he heard breaking furniture. Taking his long knife, he threw the door open to find an older male with his hands around the throat of a younger male, spread-eagled across a table. Two tribesmen tried to drag the Centurion off, one recoiling with a broken nose from the Centurion's elbow. The remaining clientele scattered out of range. The second tribesman drew his sword and swung at the Centurion who, with lightning reaction, drew his gladius and blocked the strike. The Tribune rolled off the table, breaking the moment, and the Centurion slashed his gladius down into the tribesman's leg.

Paulinus, seeing his chance, smashed the knife pommel into the Centurion's neck to a sound of breaking bone. Involuntarily the Centurion collapsed to the floor alongside the injured tribesman. Brunhilda quickly went to help the tribesman – he had a deep wound, blood poured from it. The Tribune fell to his knees, vomiting amidst the chaos as the Centurion lay motionless and the tribesman screamed. Paulinus checked the Centurion and, looking at Brunhilda, shook his head.

The injured tribesmen were aided into the kitchen by Brunhilda.

'They were fighting over someone called Artorius,' she said in passing.

Paulinus grabbed the Tribune by his collar, lifting him off the floor, and pinned him to the wall. He was crying and a damp stain spread around his groin.

'Who is this Artorius you are fighting over?' Paulinus demanded.

'They left him for dead, he didn't deserve that – the wolves!' mumbled the Tribune.

'Who left him for dead?' asked Paulinus, shaking the

man.

'They all did; they wouldn't listen to me.'

'For Mithras' sake, who?' demanded Paulinus in frustration.

'Victus! They stripped Artorius of his uniform, which they're taking back to his family in Rome, and then they tied him to a post. Victus broke his nose and there was blood everywhere, then we heard the wolves and we left. I cut him free and left his spatha, but that was four or five days ago, in the forest between Argentoratum and Mogontiacum.' The Tribune was now sobbing into his hands.

'You will show me where you left him or I'll kill you,' demanded Paulinus as he tied the young Tribune's hands.

Paulinus dragged the dead Centurion into the snow, where he stripped the body and rolled it into a partially frozen stream, watching it sink.

The clientele stared in shock as they watched Paulinus clean the blood away from the floor and tables. He called forward two locals who were known for their horsemanship.

'Wald, go to my brother Augustinian in Augusta Praetoria with an urgent message. Stein, I need you to go to the village and give the same message to Herax. I know the weather is bad, but you will be well paid, I'll see to that.' The two looked at each other and nodded before trooping outside. Paulinus scribbled two notes and stepped into the bitterly cold night, where Wald and Stein were already mounted and waiting.

'Travel fast and stay safe.' The two raced away in opposite directions, while Paulinus prayed for a speedy reply.

Wald returned with Augustinian two days later and,

deciding not to wait for the others, they set out for Argentoratum with the Tribune, despite his objections. As day broke, the three men headed north towards Herax's village and as they did so, a message was travelling more slowly south to Drusus via Tresus.

## Chapter 4

In Rome, Marcus, Tia and the family tried to be inconsequential in their surroundings, oblivious to events in Germania. Hades had lost his spirit and pined for his master; even when Tia took him for a ride he seemed to struggle.

Amoria was convinced by the couple that the estate visits should be longer, allowing them time to themselves which the presence of Marcus' sisters interrupted. They continued to refine their combat techniques with the staff, as a precaution, before racing to the river, divesting themselves of their clothes and plunging into the cooling waters. They shared their meals with the staff, who in turn shared their memories of Marcus' grandparents.

Their nights together meant Marcus' grandparents' beautifully decorated bedroom, where their increased fitness led to heightened sexual passion. They exhausted themselves, rising late, staff joking that they were joined at the hip. It was always with regret that they returned to Rome and a less active lifestyle.

So, engrossed in each other were they that they failed to keep in touch with Aaron and Rachel until Amoria asked about the progress of the manumission papers. The year was progressing to its end, and the Ides of November had come and gone with no word from Artorius. The first snows came, but they hadn't been heavy. Amoria resigned herself to a spring return for Artorius.

Aaron appeared at their tenement one morning wrapped tight against the icy cold winds that forced their way through the narrow streets. The cold made no difference to the smells that hung on the air and the filth that filled the streets in the Aventine.

'Welcome, Aaron. With Father, away, Tia and I have been busy managing the estate. Have you any news about the manumissions?' said Marcus by way of an apology.

'The manumission papers are ready and I have several errands for you and, of course, Rachel would love to see you both. Aristoteles will travel to the estate to serve the papers on the staff on your father's behalf and settle any bequeaths. He would like to do it before Saturnalia?'

Marcus nodded. 'Warm yourself, Aaron, have some wine. Tia and I will walk back with you to Aristoteles and Rachel.'

Marcus offered his father's best wine and Amoria gestured to a stool close to the fire, which Aaron welcomed.

'Any news from Artorius?' their guest enquired.

'With the first snows, it is unlikely I will see my husband before the spring now,' Amoria replied, holding back her tears.

'He will return as quick as he can, and safe,' said Aaron assuredly.

Amoria sat thoughtfully in a corner, while Tia watched the girls from Marcus' knee. After a little more talk and some wine, Aaron bid farewell to Amoria and Marcus led the way out on to the street.

The human tide dodged each other, who in turn dodged the street effluent. Marcus and Tia, hand in hand, followed Aaron through the streets to Aristoteles' office in the Forum, where arrangements were made to meet at the estate. Thereafter, the three continued to Aaron's house where Rachel awaited his return. Marcus and Tia were like adults, she thought, not the children they were; their love was obvious to any who gazed on them. Daylight was slipping away when Aaron suggested they should make their way home.

Alia was already asleep, Verina and Amoria were deep in conversation about marriage when Marcus and Tia arrived back at the tenement.

'What's all the talk of marriage?' asked Marcus.

'Your father's cousin who lives in the Alpes Graiae has sent a request enquiring about your sister's age. A Senatorial family are looking for a bride for their eighteen-year-old son.'

'Verina is too young,' stated Marcus.

'I am almost thirteen,' snapped Verina.

'It would only be a promise of marriage at this stage, and besides, your father has the last word and he won't be home now till spring, by which time Verina will be thirteen.'

'Back in my village I would have been married and probably have a child by now,' added Tia.

'We are as good as married,' whispered Marcus.

'I heard that, and you have your grandfather to thank for that. I counselled against allowing your relationship, with you being so young, but I was reminded about your father and me. We were sixteen and twenty-one and grew up together.' Amoria's thoughts drifted back to Artorius.

*

Marcus woke early the following morning, wrapped around Tia. His hands sought her small breasts and played with her nipples. Tia, pretending to be asleep, burrowed closer, feeling Marcus' growing member against her back. Marcus' hand slipped to the wetness between her legs, causing Tia to moan gently. Opening her legs, she touched herself to increase the pleasure. She turned towards him, and their two bodies slid together with the ease of frequency. Sweat glistened on

31

their bodies as they collapsed together, Tia exhausted on Marcus' chest.

Amoria called them, causing an involuntary reaction. Marcus leapt from the cot, almost tipping Tia on to the floor. She lay on her back with a shocked expression on her face, admiring Marcus' naked body.

'We need to be at the estate for Aristoteles,' he acknowledged.

Tia slipped from under the remaining covers and leapt into Marcus' arms, and their lips touched, causing Marcus' body to react the way Tia knew it would. Still held in his arms, she slid down his body and took hold of his member.

'Better save this for later if we're in a hurry,' Tia teased, walking away to dress.

Marcus stood, bemused, and then ran his hands down Tia's back as she bent to dress. Slipping his erect member into the warm and wet that lay between her legs, he then withdrew, spinning Tia around. She wore the wicked smile he loved.

'Till later then,' he said, kissing her passionately.

The couple, hand in hand, slipped into the kitchen blushing as Amoria looked at them in her knowing way.

'I presume you have worked up an appetite?'

Marcus looked to Tia and nodded, and they helped themselves from the plates on the table.

A short while later, having collected their horses, Marcus and Tia walked them through the teeming streets, where rotting vegetation and emptied night buckets littered the runnels at the edges, the smells repugnant. They hurried as best they could to leave the Aventine and, crossing the river, they cantered towards the estate. Entering the gate when it was opened for them, they found Georgiakis and Aristoteles deep in conversation in a foreign language, which Marcus presumed to be Greek. He offered his hand to Aristoteles, apologizing for their tardy arrival. 'Georgiakis and I have been talking about the estate; you have done exceptionally well under your combined supervision. Lead the way, young man. It's a great day for the staff and we can't leave them waiting,' explained Aristoteles.

The collective staff waited in the kitchen. 'This day has been a long time coming and a promise made by my late grandfather to you all. You are all now free and shortly you will be issued with a manumission document. There is employment for everyone who wishes to stay, and with pay,' Marcus announced, before inviting Aristoteles to take over.

Aristoteles called each member of staff by their old name and handed them their manumission papers in their new Roman one. Aristoteles read from Lictus' will, handing each person various amounts of coinage from a box Georgiakis had carried in.

'In celebration of Lictus, the table is laid for all to enjoy and may we all toast the great man that Lictus Civilis was. To Lictus, thank you for being who you were to each of us,' toasted Marcus.

'Lictus,' came the united response, tears evident in many eyes.

Marcus woke the following morning and, gently rolling Tia away, slipped out of the bed and into the kitchen. Last night's debris had been cleared. Aristoteles was sobering himself with a warmed juice created by Dorina.

'How's your head?' joked Marcus.

'Not bad – till I get home that is, then I'll get a headache, but thank you. He was a great man and a very good friend. I must return home, if you will allow?' requested Aristoteles.

'Will you be continuing to act for my father's estate?'

'I need to speak to your father about that. If anything happens in the meantime, the estate is yours as your grandfather directed,' stated Aristoteles.

Marcus stepped back in shock. 'Father should be back in early spring once the great pass is clear,' he replied.

Collecting breakfast, Marcus made his excuses and returned to his room, Dorina winking at him as he left. Tia was already awake when he offered her the tray.

'I think you owe me something from yesterday morning.' Tia pulled the cover aside, revealing her stunning nakedness.

*No choice*, thought Marcus, placing the tray down and dropping his tunic to the floor.

'You don't need any encouragement, do you?' laughed Tia, looking at him standing proud in front of her.'

'You or food? No choice, you any day,' he said as he ran his hands softly up her legs, making her squirm at his touch.

The atmosphere around the estate changed that day. Marcus became inundated with requests from the staff asking to bring their secretive partners to the estate, both male and female. Initially he had run all the details past his mother, but her interest had waned, leaving all decisions to the couple. The estate became a small village and the new occupants brought lucrative trades with them and everyone enjoyed the financial benefits.

Hades never recovered from his master's death, losing weight and refusing his food despite the care Tia lavished on him. One of the new partners, Lucretia, spoke of a leaderless herd of wild horses which roamed north of Rome in the old Etruscan lands. It was a hard decision, but it was considered the last resort by Tia that Hades should be released to the wild. She and Marcus tried to broach the subject with Amoria, but any mention of Lictus reduced her to tears. Marcus had never known his mother so sad.

One day, after visiting the estate as usual, Marcus, Tia and Lucretia set off north to Lucretia's village on the road to Volsinii. The village was not as Marcus had expected. The houses were of stone and their roofs were thatched, but they looked very poor. Lucretia was welcomed with open arms and having explained the reason for the visit, the villagers begged involvement. On a bright cold winter's day, the grass beneath their feet crisp with frost, the whole village took a very thin and morose Hades on an early morning walk. Entering a lush meadow to a beautiful lakeside with wooded surroundings, Marcus thought he was in a dream. The lake was crystal clear, its edges covered with early morning mist, and through it Marcus could see a herd of wild horses watering. He looked to Tia, who had tears rolling down her cheeks. She looked at Marcus and mouthed a single word: 'Yes.'

Hades' ears pricked up as one of the horses called out. Staring across the lake, he answered back as Tia slipped the rope from his neck. Hades nudged her and she kissed his forehead.

'Go and be free.' She pointed across the lake.

Hades slowly walked forward, looking back occasionally as other horses called out across the lake. Rearing on to his rear legs, he let out a bellow, then raced away. In response, the herd on the opposite side of the lake ran towards him.

'He will lead them and there will be many fine horses sired from him,' said Lucretia, resting her hand on Tia's shoulder.

'We will return and watch his herd grow,' responded

Marcus, taking a tearful Tia in his arms.

'Thank you, I'd like that. This place reminds me of home, with pasture, lake and wild horses. I wish we were there now,' Tia said, her shoulders dropping.

'My village monitor the herd; the men use them when they scout for the legions. My people follow the old ways, we are Etruscans like your grandfather,' said Lucretia.

'Thank you for sharing this place with us.' A tearful Tia hugged Lucretia.

Hades was already surrounded by the herd, a white mare taking instant interest in him. Tia looked on, wishing him a long and happy life where he belonged, with his own. She clung tightly to Marcus as the villagers trickled away, leaving the couple with the view and their thoughts.

'I am sorry I cried, but this place reminds me of my home. Maybe one day it could be ours?' Sitting on a rock on the lake's edge, the couple watched the herd. Hades glanced back across the lake and Tia tried hard to compose herself, but struggled.

'I can't give you back what you lost, I'm sorry,' Marcus said, not knowing what else to say or do to help.

'You have given me back my life and something I never thought I would have. Freedom, and love for someone who loves me. Thank you,' answered Tia.

The sun sank into the forest as the herd walked out of sight, Hades calling to Tia one last time. Lucretia was waiting when the couple finally returned to the village and offered comfort for the night. Marcus and Tia enjoyed the hospitality and their thoughts turned to their own growing village, the family estate.

Marcus had decided to celebrate Saturnalia by gathering everyone's family and friends to the estate, after Amoria had collapsed under pressure from the children and agreed. As the family entered the track late the following day, the estate looked to be on fire, the walls aglow with beacons. Marcus' sisters and even his mother was awed by the sight. The whole estate came out to greet them and introduced themselves to Amoria, who looked in shock at Marcus.

'Where have all these people come from and where do they sleep?' she enquired.

'The staff quarters,' Marcus said, pointing to a new thatched building alongside the barn, where smoke curled skyward.

'Your father will be so proud of what the two of you have achieved. I look forward to showing him in the spring,' Amoria said to Marcus and Tia.

'Where's Hades?' enquired Verina.

'Hades pined after your grandfather died, and we set him free in a beautiful place with his own herd,' replied Tia.

'Can we go and see?' Alia and Verina asked excitedly.

'Of course, the whole family can visit him, but we need to let him settle. Lucretia's people will look out for him till then,' replied Marcus.

The estate was a hive of activity as relatives came and went, bringing small gifts and enjoying the festivities. Aaron and Rachel joined the family, adding their own twist to the time of year. Artorius was always in their thoughts and often the subject of their toasts. The time flew by, but as the excitement waned, Amoria rallied everyone to return to Rome.

It was not the happy return all had hoped for. The story on every tongue was of the horrors inflicted on Sejanus' family. Rumours ran rife like the Tiberis, full of filth and degradation, especially those of the horrors exacted on Sejanus' daughter, who was little older than Alia. Shock was etched deep on the faces of Rome and the reputation of the Praetorian Guard was one of depravity. Amoria feared Artorius' return and his reaction. Would she lose him once again to the Legion?

## Chapter 5

It was the Nomes of Ianuarius before Drusus received Paulinus' message, punching the inn wall in frustration at the delay. He was torn between warning the family of false friends or confirming Artorius' death. Taking his lucky Sestertius from a pouch on his belt, he tossed it high in the air as he looked out on the snowy landscape.

'Why do you need to try your luck, when you know what you need to do? Take me with you,' demanded Magda, snatching the coin out of the air.

'If I go north. No, when I go north, I need you to remain with your sister. One day I promise I will take you with me, but for now, please!' Drusus reached out as Magda returned the coin, shrugging her shoulders in resignation.

Plans made and provisions loaded, including his old uniform, Drusus donned his thickest fur clothing, boots and gloves. He stood in fresh snow, and steam rose from his breath as he looked first at the sky then the mountains he faced. It was a matter of family honour and a promise.

'Come back safely, you are like an older brother to me,' said Magda, taking Drusus' hand firmly.

'You'd better get back safely and soon, there are things I need doing in the spring,' Helga said, hugging her husband close. The three laughed at the comment.

'I will find a man worthy of you one day, Magda. As for you, my love, I will miss you and my son every moment till I return. My spatha, please,' requested Drusus as he mounted his horse.

He walked his horse away from the inn, through slush and muddy streets, till he reached the military road which showed signs of use despite the snow.

\*

On the estate outside Mogontiacum, Victus had tired of the Centurion who spent his life in a drunken stupor, but he needed him to deliver Artorius' armour. After that, he was expendable. The smithy continued to supply the estate with young girls and it didn't matter to Victus whether they came willingly or not. It was on one such visit that he disclosed that a member of estate staff had alerted Publius' uncle of his nephew's death. Victus decided it was time to move, and in tracing the informant, he started the systematic torture and death of the female staff. Having found the culprit, the remaining females were left to the smithy to dispose of as he saw fit. The Centurion, in his alcoholic oblivion, didn't comprehend what was happening as Victus torched the empty estate, hiding the carnage therein. Victus and the Centurion headed towards Genua, Victus opting for a sea return to Ostia Antica and a score to finally settle.

Publius' uncle arrived to find the estate in flames, with no sign of his daughter and Victus escaped. As he had promised his nephew, Gaius travelled towards Argentoratum and the 2nd Augusta to attempt to repair the damage.

Drusus reached Vercelum, where Tresus awaited him and they rode on to Herax's village. As the two pair of ex-soldiers travelled independently north through the mountains and passes, the weather grew increasingly cold and the snow deep, but no fresh snow fell. It was five days later that the four soldiers finally shared hot wine together in Herax's village.

'This little piece of shit was the last one to see Artorius alive,' said Paulinus, dragging the young Tribune with his hands tied in front of Drusus.

'I want to know exactly what happened and where you last saw Artorius,' demanded Drusus, grabbing the

Tribune by the throat.

The Tribune squirmed in Drusus' hands as he related his part, especially his release of Artorius as the wolves gathered.

'Your release of Artorius may be the only thing that will save your life. We need to ride to Argentoratum to see what the situation is there and if they have any new information,' stated Drusus.

'I have made enquiries in the neighbouring villages, yet we have heard nothing. Gigantrex and I offer our swords, if you will have us?' stated Herax, as six hands reached out as one, and collectively shouted Artorius' name.

## Chapter 6

The winter's sun shone as the snow withdrew and Artorius opened his eyes for the first time since the attack. He stared around, not comprehending where he was. Lying beside him was a beautiful red-haired woman, her face familiar. *Why did he share her bed?* He had never betrayed Amoria before, yet here he was.

A crackling fire caught his ear and he looked towards it. He saw a wizened old woman with her back to him. She turned, staring straight at him, her eyes boring deep.

'So, you have finally woken. You walk well with your gods? You are from an old-world family, aren't you?' she asked.

'Where am I?' Artorius tried to sit up, clutching the black fur around him.

'It has been a while, and you have walked the fine line between life and death. Don't you remember? I am Rosevetha, and you share my daughter Ilona's bed. Without her you would have died over a moon's cycle ago.'

'How long?' demanded Artorius.

'Saturnalia, past a moon cycle ago.'

'The last thing I remember was crawling into a cave and seeing a two-legged wolf.'

Rosevetha cackled. 'That was Ilona, I sent her after you when you were lost in the snow.'

'What about the wolves?'

'My daughter controls her own pack – she nursed the alpha male, Donor, when he was a pup,' replied Rosevetha.

'A wolf pack?' Artorius was astonished.

'Yes,' came the answer, as Ilona looked up at him.

The memory of the beautiful eyes in front of him flooded back.

'I should be on my way back to Argentoratum and Rome. What have I done?'

'You could try. The snow is deep, your friends think you're dead and your family presume the winter has trapped you,' said Ilona.

'I must at least attempt to return to my camp.' Artorius attempted to stand, but his arms were too weak to support him. He looked at his shrivelled left arm, the skin red and puckered.

'I didn't imagine the wolf attack?' he asked.

'My pack saved you. Now the fever has passed, it's time to rebuild your strength. You will need to be physically and mentally strong for the future,' added Ilona.

Rosevetha cut Artorius short before he could ask what was on his mind 'All will be revealed in due course, but for now, eat this.'

Artorius kept a careful eye on his skeletal body as he started his daily exercises, watched closely by Ilona. He slept alone, still in shock at the revelation of his survival. Ilona informed him that the fresh kills found daily outside the door were thanks to her pack. His respect for her grew daily, and he couldn't help thinking what a wonderful wife she would make someone.

As his strength grew, he repaid their kindness in any way he could, but time dragged until he was strong enough to practice with his spatha once more. Ilona clothed him from furs, laughing when she told him that it was the renegade alpha male's fur, that kept him warm at night. With his increased exercise in and out of the hut, his body began to resume some of its previous form, though he remained thinner and weaker than he had ever been, his hair snowy white, as was the beard he grew.

The closeness between Ilona and Artorius bloomed, and they laughed together as they talked of their different lives. He noticed more and more that she went out of her way to touch him, and the effect was electrifying. He felt ashamed that he should feel this way for another woman, with Amoria waiting for him.

The snows came less often and they ventured out more together, Ilona introducing Artorius to Donor and her wolf pack. She was an expert archer and his prowess with a spear drew her admiration. Donor initially eyed him with suspicion, but as they began to hunt together they achieved an understanding.

As the days went on, Artorius noticed Ilona trying to hide the swelling of her stomach. 'Who's the lucky father, Ilona? Some young buck, I presume?'

Ilona struggled to close the fur around her, looked to her mother and burst into tears.

Rosevetha looked back from the hearthside and shrugged her shoulders. Artorius looked suspiciously from one to the other.

'How do you feel about me, Artorius?' Ilona enquired.

'You are a beautiful woman and would make any man proud to share their life with. Why?'

'Do you remember the first time you stayed here?' she asked.

'Vaguely. I had some strange dreams that night.'

'Dreams about you and me?'

He looked at her. 'It wasn't a dream, was it?'

'It wasn't. I lay with you and I am now carrying your son. Mother foretold of your visit, our coupling and my pregnancy.'

'But I'm married and I love my wife deeply. How could

this happen? I'm sorry,' Artorius pleaded, holding his head in his hands in shame. He realised that sometimes when he woke, having slept for days at a time, Ilona, who had craved these times, had lain with him. Artorius had dreamt of sexually fueled nights with Amoria, who appeared to be pregnant, but that was just his imagining – or was it?

'It was meant to be. Turan weaved her magic,' remarked Rosevetha.

Artorius threw on his fur coat and, snatching up his spatha, stepped outside. He slammed the door behind him; snow falling from the roof showered him, increasing his anger. His mood deepened and he could hear the raised voices of Rosevetha and Ilona inside. He swung his spatha with a venom he used only in battle, hacking chunks of wood from stored logs.

It wasn't all Ilona's fault. He must have taken advantage and his body was more than willing, as he remembered. Another son... He didn't question how they knew, because they knew everything. He suddenly remembered the warning, from two different sources, to return home as quickly as he could. What did it mean? With this thought in mind, he re-entered the home to find Ilona again in tears.

She looked up at him through reddened eyes.

'Why did you tell me I needed to hurry back to Rome? What had you seen?' demanded Artorius.

Ilona went to answer, but was stayed by Rosevetha. 'The future is only what might be. I see much, but some things are best left unsaid until their fruition. Your fight with one called Victus will be a long and bitter one, and your son will be the resolution.'

'Which son, and what of Ilona?' enquired Artorius.

'That is for you and Lasa, the goddess of fate, to decide. I can say no more.' Rosevetha turned back to the fire.

Ilona felt hurt for the first time in her life – she looked through Artorius and he could feel it. There was a hidden agenda and he could do nothing but ride out the fates.

As the days passed, Artorius spent many hours deep in thought, but he continued his forays with Ilona and the wolves. He couldn't help the fondness that had grown between them. She was carrying his son, after all, so he vented his anger towards Rosevetha, needing someone to blame.

A new moon came and went. The snows continued to recede, but the occasional fresh falls didn't help the angst Artorius was feeling. Donor, sensing the situation, never left Ilona's side when they hunted, which was becoming less frequent with her condition.

Artorius felt a deep compassion and friendship for Ilona, such as he had only ever shared with one other person: Amoria. He slept poorly, often awakening to find Ilona in her own furs beside him. His foreboding grew deeper every time he found the two women whispering together and looking at him. Sometimes he would return from hunting alone to find Ilona in tears. He couldn't help himself, hugging her close. Whenever he asked why, she blamed the pregnancy and looked to her mother, who shrugged her shoulders.

## Chapter 7

Artorius hadn't returned, nor was there any sign of replacements, and the fact that Scorus was enjoying control of the Legion worried him. He was lounging in the Legate's office, enjoying the wine collection, when his enjoyment was interrupted by a loud rap on the office door.

'Sir, begging your pardon, but there is a senior Tribune from Mogontiacum outside demanding to see the Legate,' said the clerk.

'You'd better show him in.' Scorus stood, adjusting his uniform.

Gaius stormed into the office. 'Camp Prefect, where is your Legate?'

Scorus saluted crisply, which was ignored. 'He's in an urn waiting to be repatriated to his family, sir,' he replied.

'What on earth do you mean, in an urn?' demanded Gaius.

'He took his life instead of facing the senate on charges of conspiracy with Sejanus. He left a list of fellow conspirators, but some escaped before they could be arrested. I have taken charge of the Legion until a Legate is sent from Mogontiacum. I sent Senior Centurion Civilis to explain what has happened here and yet have had no reply,' explained Scorus.

'How dare you take control! Where are the other Tribunes, my nephew, Publius?'

'The remaining Tribunes are little more than children. Publius was your nephew, really? He went missing with the others and was one of the named conspirators. A thought comes to my head, bearing that in mind – can I trust you?' enquired Scorus.

'How dare you accuse me!' Gaius' face adopted a puce colour.

'Why have you come to Argentoratum, Tribune, if you aren't here in response to my message?' asked Scorus.

'I came to pay my respects to my nephew, and what business is it of yours anyway?' demanded Gaius.

'Since I oversee the 2nd Augusta till someone is appointed, and your nephew was a conspirator against the Emperor, I have every right. Clerk, get in here now.' The clerk shuffled in again.

'Fetch acting Camp Prefect Scipio immediately,' ordered Scorus, inviting the Tribune to sit, which he refused to do.

Camp Prefect Scipio marched into the Legate's office, saluting crisply, and was introduced to the Tribune by Scorus.

'What I am about to suggest I am sure will offend your high upbringing, but due to the circumstances I have no choice. Scipio, please arrange an escort for the Tribune back to Mogontiacum and go with them. I want you to take copies of the orders from Praetorian Prefect Macro to the Legates of the 14th and 16th Legions. I will also send a copy of Longinus' named conspirators and the justification for sending the Tribune back under guard.'

'How dare you, you are acting above your rank,' responded Gaius indignantly.

'I am the temporary Legate and as such could arrest you on Tiberius' authority, but I will leave you in the care of your Legate. Please surrender your sword or I will have it taken from you.' With his outstretched hand, Scorus accepted the offered weapon.

'Please remain here while I have the documents copied,' Scorus said, leaving the room.

\*

At the same time, four battle-ready ex-soldiers and two local tribesmen, approached the barrack gates at Argentoratum abreast in a line, causing a reaction they hadn't expected. The guard commander was called and responded. He stood in awe as he welcomed them in.

'May the gods be praised, some of the meanest sons of bitches it was ever my honour to meet! Ex-Centurion Drusus, what brings you back to these hallowed grounds, and in such mixed company?'

'Marcus Africanus, I can't believe you're still in the land of the living and looking so well. How is Marianne? Still playing hide the rod you, lecherous bastard?'

'Why of course, and what brings you here and in uniform?' responded Africanus as the two clasped hands.

'The whole story deserves to be told in the best inn in town, but I have to see the Legate first,' replied Drusus.

'Sorry, he fell on his sword a while ago. Camp Prefect Scorus has taken charge.'

'Have you seen my cousin, Artorius Civilis?'

'He headed north some time ago and should have returned by now. There's a senior Tribune from Mogontiacum in with Scorus now. What are you doing with that young Tribune? He went missing and is wanted for treason.'

'He was the last one to see Artorius alive somewhere on the road to Mogontiacum. Will Scorus see us?' asked Drusus, dragging the Tribune from his horse.

Africanus strode over to the Legate's office, where he found Scorus overseeing the preparation of some documents. He related the request.

'Bring them all over, I want to try something,' said Scorus with a smirk across his face.

Africanus returned with Drusus' party and they were introduced to Scorus. Scorus glowered at the young

Tribune, punching him hard in the stomach, dropping him to the floor, gasping for breath. Scorus addressed the young tribune. 'Let us hope we find Artorius, and alive, or I will personally cut you into little pieces for the wolves. Look in the Legate's office and tell me if you know the gentleman with acting Camp Prefect Scipio.'

The young tribune was raised to his feet and, as the door to the other room opened, the blood drained from his face.

'You know him, I take it. Now tell me what you know?' ordered Scorus with a wicked smile.

'That is Publius' uncle. Victus and the others were supposed to hide on his estate till the spring, he's part of the conspiracy.'

'Scipio, bring the Tribune out here, we have someone to meet him,' Scorus requested.

The Tribune emerged from the inner office feeling very full of himself until he saw the young Tribune.

'How have you survived when my nephew hasn't?' Gaius demanded.

'He has implicated you in the conspiracy, what have you to say?' asked Scorus smugly.

'It was all Victus' doing. I was heavily in debt and I was promised promotion and wealth. When my nephew arrived at my door I refused to let them stay, but gave them access to a friend's estate. My daughter went missing and still is, Victus must be involved. I was informed that he had killed my nephew and so I went to arrest him, but he had slaughtered all the staff on the estate and set fire to it. My Legate knows nothing of this. Allow me my sword to do the honourable thing,' pleaded Gaius.

'You're not getting the easy way out, you bastard. Your class are all the same,' snapped Scorus, spitting into the

Tribune's face.

'You will go back to your legion under guard, where your Legate can decide what to do with you. As for you, young lad, you will lead this party to where you last saw Senior Centurion Civilis, and you'd better hope he's alive. Scipio, I want your best local trackers and I want them out there checking every village and hovel between here and Mogontiacum,' ordered Scorus.

Drusus' group retired to a local inn with Africanus, where the night was alcohol-fuelled. Six with thick heads sucked deep on the cold air as they strode across the parade ground to the Legate's office in the last hours of night.

'I've asked for Camp Prefect Brachus' help from the 14th; he knows Artorius and I have no doubt he will do all he can. Good luck, I expect to have been relieved of my command by the time you return,' explained Scorus. The Romans saluted, followed by crushing handshakes.

A short while later, Drusus took the point with Herax and Gigantrex, Gaius' escort followed and the remaining three covered the rear as they exited the camp. The group cantered past six mutationes, the distance the young Tribune had mentioned. As they left the river plain behind them, they were surrounded by thick forest on each side of the narrow military road, travelling at a slower pace. The young Tribune called out to stop, and Drusus reined in his horse.

'It's here, I'm sure it is. We chopped the tree down around the next corner,' stated the young Tribune.

Herax nodded to Gigantrex to follow and rode out of sight. The escort spread out around the captives, interspersed with Drusus' group. Gigantrex returned moments later confirming the presence of a fallen tree. Drusus took the reins of the young Tribune's horse and led it around the corner to where Herax was waiting.

'This is the place. We watched from up there and followed him as he lost his footing and his horse ran off. It was Tribune Publius who felled Artorius from behind, and while he was unconscious Victus ordered him stripped of his uniform. Then we tied him to a tree over there.' The young Tribune pointed to his right.

The moment was shattered by the howl of a wolf and all heads turned in its direction.

'Scipio, we have our marker. We'll travel with you to Mogontiacum where we can pool any information that is there before we start our search,' said Drusus.

A whistling sound followed by a thud made Drusus turn his head to see the young Tribune fall dead from his horse.

'Protected dismount!' Drusus screamed as other arrows bore death to the group.

The horses were grounded with cavalry shields facing outwards, covering both sides of the track. A scream came from the right of the track and three tribesmen with sword and shield appeared out of the ground, running at the grounded group. Gigantrex braced himself for impact, and one adversary faster than the rest rushed in as Gigantrex sliced at the man's stomach. Blade and flesh met in an explosion of blood and entrails. The following two barely had a chance to stop as Gigantrex, stepping forward, swept one man aside with his shield, Herax dispatching him as he rolled in the snow. Sparks showered the air from multiple blades clashing as more tribesmen broke cover from the trees above.

'Form line! Let's meet them head on,' Drusus shouted, racing towards the frontal assault. The four veterans collided with the tribesmen, their rear covered by the escort. Swords and axes cleft the air from both sides. Herax, leaving Gigantrex to finish his fight, hit the tribesmen from the rear, his blade hacking into the back of the nearest man and exposing shattered bone. An axe split Drusus' shield, twisting it away as a tribesman towered over him. A second, seeing a gap, drove his sword towards Drusus' stomach which was barely parried as the freed axe was again aimed at his head.

Augustinian's spatha slid between Drusus and Paulinus, burying itself deep into the groin of the giant. The axe dropped to the floor as shock filled the man's face and, clutching vainly at the spatha being withdrawn, collapsed on to Paulinus. The line moved forward, the gap filled by Scipio. Herax found himself surrounded. Deflecting one blade and slicing down into the leg of an adversary, he carved flesh and bone. A small male, seeing the gap, ran his blade into Herax's stomach. Herax spun at his attacker, missing him, but separated the next man's head from its shoulders. Blood sprayed high into the faces of their attackers as the head bounced away. As the blade was ripped free from Herax's stomach, he slumped back against a tree and the small male stepped too close, for in his dying moment Herax rammed his blade into him.

Elsewhere, blades slashed, blood sprayed and bodies fell, staining the snow. Drusus' group stood soaked in blood, everyone displaying degrees of injury, but none serious except for Herax. Gigantrex stood over the torn bodies of two, wrapping a cut to his own leg. Herax sat with his back to a tree, ghostly white, holding his stomach as dark blood oozed from a fatal wound. Three lay dead around him as Gigantrex hurried to his side.

'The time has come for you to take my place; I am proud of you, son.' Herax removed the torc from his neck, handing it to Gigantrex.

'I thought to die in my bed, but instead I die in battle the way every warrior deserves.' Herax's head fell forward as he exhaled, his hands limp.

'He died in the way of all warriors and we will honour his death,' said Drusus, gripping Gigantrex's shoulder.

Drusus surveyed the gory scene of blood and guts that covered the ground, where seven tribesmen and two escorts lay dead. Paulinus was still trying to drag himself clear of the man mountain that had collapsed on him, much to the hilarity of the others. The elder Tribune lay still on the floor, an arrow piercing his throat, and the scent of death lay heavy on the air as the howls of wolves filled it.

'Time to gather our dead and move before the wolves join the fight. Gigantrex, take your father home?' offered Drusus, helping Paulinus to his feet.

'My father died the way he lived, sword in hand, killing to protect his family and friends. We will offer up his spirit at Mogontiacum and take his ashes home when we have found what we search for. Thank you for his chance to die with honour,' Gigantrex said, taking Drusus' hand in a strong handshake.

The group left the dead tribesmen, their own dead carried across their respective horses, Herax's horse led by his son. It was the time of shadows as the troop rode through Mogontiacum's gates and Drusus requested a meeting with the guard commander and the Camp Prefect. The latter appeared first, a short stocky man with greying hair and a white drooping moustache, his armour immaculate as Drusus remembered him.

'What's this? Aren't you past these stupid games, I thought you'd been domesticated?' responded Brachus.

'Vicious rumour, and before you ask, I domesticated Helga and we have a son,' Drusus replied, smiling.

'That's two drinks you owe me, but what brings you this way? Have I missed a war?' Brachus looked at the group, covered in blood.

Drusus slipped from his horse and, taking Brachus to one side, explained his mission. Scipio produced the documents he had been entrusted with and offered them to Brachus.

'The Legate would be the best one to give these to. As for the senior Tribune, he was one of mine. A shame, he was a good soldier. Sort your horses and wrap the senior Tribune in a blanket.

We'll wait on the Legate's decision on how to tell his family – it's his wife's brother.'

The group assembled in the outer office of the Legate. Brachus knocked and entered on his own. It seemed a lifetime before he re-emerged and invited the group into the office. The Legate was a weasel of a man, his most prominent feature being a hooked nose that had been broken at some time in the past, probably at the same time as the scar that tore across it.

'Apologies, gentlemen, I needed to read all the dispatches before I spoke to you. The 2nd Augusta is in a mess. I would have sent my sister's husband, but unfortunately, he was involved in the conspiracy, as you know. That without saying, he was a good and honoured soldier who leaves a wife and two children. With your agreement, I would like your silence on the matter to protect his family any further heartache?'

Drusus looked around at his gathered group, each nodding in turn. 'Sir, I think you have your answer.'

'I cannot thank you all enough. I will personally do everything I can to find your missing friend. Camp Prefect Brachus, could you arrange for my brother-in-law's body to be reunited with his family with your usual tact? As far as a replacement Legate for the 2nd Augusta, I must talk to my sister Legion's Legate. I will also make urgent enquiries into where this Victus Claudian has gone. My own local scouts will check all the nearby villages and farms, but that will take a while in this weather, so you must enjoy our hospitality. Gentlemen, once again from my family, thank you. I am sure at some point there will be a reward from the Emperor for delivering these dispatches. Any questions?' asked the Legate.

'Sir, do you need the escort any further?' asked Scipio.

'I think it only fitting that the temporary acting Legate for your Legion should be escorted back, especially after the attack. The escort can also enjoy a couple of days' rest and recuperation at my expense. If you have nothing further, I am sure you will want to be fed and watered.

Dismissed.' The group collectively saluted and withdrew.

*

Februarius was fast approaching, but the days dragged by. Sightings were reported, but never came to anything. Drusus' group rode with the scouts rather than vegetate, but each day a little hope died, though no one spoke of it.

## Chapter 8

There was a tang of salt in the air and overhead the seagulls screeched as Victus and the Centurion, trailing a mule, exited the military road. The climate had warmed as they travelled closer to the coast, ground was crisp with late frosts. The Centurion had suffered badly: some of his fingertips had turned black and the pain was excruciating. Making enquiries, Victus headed for the Villa Aphrodite, and his mind filled with delicious thoughts of Naomi.

The villa was located on a coastal aspect just outside of Genua. It was walled above the height of the average male and the gates were guarded by two of the biggest Nubians Victus had ever seen. Once inside the gate, the villa lay in front of them surrounded by grassed areas, with large-tailed exotic birds strutting on them. Small paths scattered from the main one to smaller out-buildings. A fountain with sea monsters stood outside the main door, which was opened by one of Naomi's girls from Ostia.

Having arranged medical help for the Centurion with a little sexual diversion, Victus was shown to the observation room. Naomi, in a transparent covering, stood with her back to the spy holes, flicking a whip across the chest of an elderly pot-bellied Senator who was manacled and gagged naked to the opposite wall. She flicked the whip slowly down the male's torso, increasing the tempo, and his eyes said it all as he desperately tried to avoid the whip strands. As if sensing an audience, Naomi turned to face the spy holes and walked towards them. She stood in all her glory, legs spread wide, and bent to blow a kiss directly at the voyeur.

Victus' mouth dropped open. Naomi was plumper –

*obviously living too well*, Victus thought. It was almost too much for him, and he pondered forcing his way in and throwing her on to her back and pleasuring her till they both collapsed, but instead he watched and masturbated until she had finished.

Naomi left the retired Senator semi-conscious and hanging from the wall, and walked into the observation room where Victus was rearranging himself.

'Now that was a waste, I didn't expect you for a few months,' said Naomi, taking his member in her hand and lowering her mouth on to it.

'You know best how to resolve that,' mumbled Victus, already enjoying the motion.

It didn't take long before blood pounded through his member. Pushing Victus on to his back and spreading herself wide, Naomi slid down his erection. From there the sex was rough and forceful, the way they both enjoyed, until both were sore from the encounter. Over the next five days Victus and Naomi only emerged from the bedroom to relieve themselves. Victus finally went in search of the Centurion and found him slipping between drug-induced euphoria and sexual pleasure. Naomi joined Victus, laughing at the state of the Centurion.

'Your ladies certainly know their business, Naomi.' Victus groped her through her flimsy clothing.

'I kept him occupied so we could indulge each other. What's he with you for, anyway?'

Victus slipped his hand under her wrap, the touch of her skin stirring his loins as they entered her private quarters, a room far removed from the sexual den they had just left. Victus explained the reason for his and the Centurion's presence in Genua.

'I need to return to Rome to finish the Civilis family then find somewhere to hide for a while, and I thought you might enjoy my company.'

'I think we both know the answer to that. Our business is doing well and I intend to expand and offer more of what we enjoy. There is a big market for sexual fantasy shows with animals and mixed groups, the more exotic the better. It isn't the safest time of year to travel by sea,' Naomi remarked.

'Don't worry, but if anything does go wrong the business would be yours. We need to wean the Centurion off the poppy juice before we travel. In fact, you would probably be the best-placed person for finding us transport.'

'I think I could manage that, though it'll cost and you know how I like my payment,' Naomi said, grinning suggestively.

The pair retired early, but were too preoccupied with their own thoughts to indulge in each other initially. Naomi was surprised that Victus hadn't noticed or commented on her swelling stomach or the more cautious sexual antics. She thought to broach the subject of a family, but stayed the discussion until his vengeful madness had subsided. Victus had noticed the change in her, and presumed it was from the opulent lifestyle of the villa. Fatherhood wasn't even a grain of thought in his tortured brain; vengeance dominated.

Victus straddled Naomi. She looked expectantly at him while he secured her wrists and ankles with the much-used ribbons attached to her bed. He groped for and found her favourite soft leather whip, raising pink welts on her flawless soft skin. Tears of pain and pleasure caused rivulets of charcoal to run from Naomi's eyes to her cheeks. Finger marks covered her throat where Victus had held her as they attained a mutual orgasm, before collapsing on to her, still secured. His final act was to release her before both collapsed into exhaustive sleep.

*

A thick wintry mist hung over the harbour and fading lanterns swung in the light morning breeze as Victus, the Centurion and his prostitute boarded the cargo ship for Ostia Antica. The rigging was coated in ice, the deck wet and slippery and the sound and stench of terrified livestock erupted from below. The crew grumbled at a voyage now, but Victus didn't care. His thoughts were of vengeance.

He watched the Centurion and his prostitute sat huddled under furs, guarding Artorius' armour.

By the time the three had boarded the ship, Naomi had roused and sat drinking warm milk. She caressed her stomach and smiled.

## Chapter 9

In Mogontiacum Drusus was racked with guilt at his failure to find his cousin, as the Ides of Martius had arrived with still no reports of Artorius. The snows had melted and movement into the countryside was increasing. The group gathered each evening in the local inn, having joined scouting groups and patrols but always with the same result – nothing. The group seemed particularly sombre on this occasion, and it was obvious to the collective that they had reached the point when enough was enough.

'Brothers at arms, we have done all we can, we can't search forever,' said Drusus. 'Artorius has been missing for four months and the scouts and ourselves have visited every village within a fifty-mile radius. As the snows are melting, now would be a good time to return to our homes. Thank you, everyone, for what you have done.'

Heads dropped around the table, but they were thankful they hadn't been the one to suggest a return home.

'One of the locals has mentioned a seer by the name of Rosevetha. She lives with her daughter, the "Wolf Queen", on the forest edge between Mogontiacum and Argentoratum. She has found missing people before,' offered Gigantrex.

'Why haven't you mentioned this before?' demanded Drusus.

'Do you really believe in these fairy tales? A seer and a wolf queen, whatever that is? We have lots of people who claim to see things, but they never amount to much,' added Paulinus.

'I was talking of our plight to a trader from Argentoratum and he claimed Rosevetha told him where to find his son. He had been kidnapped, but he found him where she said he would,' explained Gigantrex.

'Do you know how to find her?' enquired Drusus.

'We really are clutching at straws now, but anything is worth a final try,' added Tresus.

'The trader is returning to Argentoratum tomorrow and said he would happily show me. He is going there anyway; he takes the seer a present on the anniversary of his son being found.'

'Right, gentlemen, I'm game for one last sortie. Is anyone else coming?' enquired Drusus.

'Count me in, I want to see a wolf queen,' joked Paulinus.

'Be careful what you mock, I have seen many strange things in the woods,' said Gigantrex sternly.

'I didn't mean to offend you, Gigantrex, but you must admit it's intriguing?'

'Tresus, Augustinian – are you coming?'

The brothers looked at each other and without hesitation answered a resounding, 'Yes.'

The five of them stood and downed their drinks, slamming their beakers on the table. The clientele jumped and the landlord felt for a club under his tunic.

Augustinian saw the movement. 'Just a pledge, landlord, to a lost friend. Fill them up, we visit the seer and the wolf queen tomorrow for help.' The landlord firmly clasped a talisman that hung around his neck.

'Is there a problem with that, landlord?' enquired Augustinian.

'No, but they say she sees all, and the daughter controls the wolves in the forest around them.'

'We are in for a treat, Paulinus,' suggested Drusus.

The night passed easily with fresh and final hopes of finding Artorius. Returning to the barracks, their mood had noticeably changed.

*

The day had barely begun, and a thick mist covered the ground as the five men funnelled from the barracks, trailing their horses. A small cart waited outside, powered by a single horse whose owner stood warming himself by the blacksmith's fire.

'Big Man, you didn't say there was five of you,' said the trader.

'Is there a problem with that?' enquired Gigantrex.

'It's a large number and it might seem intimidating.'

'When we arrive, Paulinus and I will accompany you to the door. You can explain our presence to the seer and then we will step forward,' responded Drusus.

'That should be okay. If there are any wolves, stand your ground. They only attack on command and they are big buggers, so don't spook them.'

With the trader's cart in front, the five trotted behind it on the metalled road, which was awash with mud and melted snow. Mist hung in the air as the sun struggled to force its way into the day.

*

Artorius woke where he slept on the floor, to find Ilona beside him in her own furs. Rosevetha sat by the fire, her eyes locked on him. She half turned, casting a powder into the hearth, which exploded in blue flames. Her eyes moved back towards him.

'Are you hunting this morning?' she enquired. 'I would tell you that your friends who seek you have survived an ambush and will come for you,' suggested Rosevetha.

'Time for me to re-appear,' responded Artorius confidently.

'Your friends will find you when the time is right, and till then you must grow stronger to face the future. This child is your destiny.' Rosevetha pointed to Ilona.

Artorius knelt beside the sleeping mother-to-be. 'If I were not married then I wouldn't hesitate to do what any man should. I will return to Argentoratum and then back to Rome for good. Though I won't be returning, I will provide for her,' he snapped unintentionally.

'Only the fates will decide that,' croaked Rosevetha.

'Please tell me. You know something, don't you?' pleaded Artorius. He looked back at Ilona. 'Why did this have to happen? If I were free I would be honoured to share my life with her.'

'Remember those words in the months to come. Your son will be born on the Kalends of Augustus,' Rosevetha said, pointing at Artorius before passing him a steaming bowl. 'Here, you'll need something to warm you if you are to hunt. Donor is already waiting.'

Donor stepped out of the barn to greet Artorius, who stared at the magnificent beast, still marvelling about how Ilona controlled him. Artorius ran his hand through Donor's fur, and the beast lifted his head at the touch, eyeing Artorius closely. Thick fog surrounded them, the occasional thud of melting snow falling from above as the pair headed into the forest.

Ilona roused and reached out to find Artorius gone. Her eyes searched every crevice of the room to find only her mother, hunched over the fire and staring deeply into the flames.

'Artorius' friends are coming.'

'Mother, what do you mean? Couldn't we lie? Where is he?'

'Donor has taken him into the deep forest, but he will be back when his friends arrive. You have seen it for yourself – I know you see as well as I. His family is not

64

as he expects, he will return to Rome a broken man and then... well! Then we will know if his words mean anything. Now, prepare yourself for the visitors,' ordered Rosevetha.

\*

Donor approached a stream that ran with snow melt. Sitting back on his haunches, he howled into the fading mist. Responses came from all around, wolves trickling out from the forest. Artorius stood in awe as the pack gathered around Donor, eyeing their master's companion suspiciously, the younger ones growling. The pack spread down the bank around a plunge pool, entering the waters as one, and Artorius saw fish for the first time. The fish were herded together and then the pack set about catching them in their great jaws.

*Fishing was never this easy in the Tiberis*, Artorius thought as he watched nature's interaction, but most of all the cunning cleverness of the pack. The wolves gorged themselves as he bathed in the sun that carved its path through the clouds and trees. Sated, the pack lay in the warmth, preening themselves. Spare fish lay gasping for breath on the banks. Donor looked to Artorius and then at the fish; Artorius couldn't believe that a wild animal was offering his spares. He felt like a pupil under instruction, but his teacher was a wolf. Dispatching the fish quickly, Artorius gathered them up and prepared for the return journey. Donor scanned the forest and sniffed at the air, howling, the sound echoing through the trees. A pure white pregnant female approached and nuzzled Donor before they melted back into the forest.

\*

Fresh hope grew with Drusus and his companions as the merchant led the group off the road close to where they had fought the war party. Poking through the snow were bleached and scattered animal bones – the scene of a wild battle. A cave in a cleft of rock stood out in the bleak surroundings. Drusus walked his horse towards it. The cave mouth was wet with melting snow, but inside, the floor was covered with rotting leaves. The winter's sun glinted off something laying on the greenery. Slipping from his horse, Drusus bent almost double and peered in at a partly hidden golden ring – an eagle with emerald eyes. He knew who last wore it and his mind was rocked at the revelation. Artorius! Drusus' face lit up with expectation as he slipped the ring into a pouch as the others tried to see what he had.

'It's nothing. Let's go,' he snapped.

The ground under the horses was heavy with snow-covered mud. The merchant relinquished his cart, having collected a bag from it, and mounted his horse. He seemed to follow an unseen path as he twisted his way through the dense forest. Smoke invaded their nostrils, and the five companions looked around in anticipation and expectancy.

'We are close, as you can smell,' said the merchant, pointing vaguely through the trees.

A wolf howled in the distance. Hands shot to their weapons, ten eyes looking about them.

'Fear not – they belong to the wolf queen, as I said. Don't provoke them if they appear,' the merchant reminded them.

Light invaded the forest, illuminating a cleared area with a wooden building in front of them. The merchant, calling a halt, dismounted. Drusus surveyed the clearing. There were two buildings, one of which belched smoke.

'Stay here till I call you,' said the merchant. Rosevetha will have seen us coming.'

'I hope so, if she's a seer,' joked Tresus, though he wished he could eat his words when Gigantrex scowled at him.

The group dismounted, Drusus and Paulinus accompanied the merchant, stepping across well-trodden snow that was dotted with wolf spoor. A door opened in front of them, and there stood a beautiful and obviously pregnant young woman.

'Welcome, you are expected. Rosevetha will see you,' invited Ilona.

'These men seek a lost friend. I told them the story of my son.' The merchant offered his bag to Ilona, who thanked him.

Drusus, followed by Paulinus, stepped inside. A large fire burned in the hearth and crouched in front of it was a shrivelled old woman.

'Which one of you is Drusus?' Rosevetha asked.

Drusus staggered into Paulinus in shock. 'I am, but how do you know me?'

'You and your friends are looking for your cousin Artorius,' she responded.

'Then you know of his whereabouts?' Drusus' spirit lifted.

'He was left for dead four months ago, but he is alive,' she replied.

'Where? I will pay well for any information,' responded Drusus.

'So you shall. Sit. Ilona, give our guests a drink.'

Ilona offered the hot brew from the pot over the fire.

'Thank you for your hospitality, but if you could just tell us where to find him we'll be on our way,' Drusus responded.

'It is not quite that easy, there are many things to consider,' Rosevetha said, glancing at Ilona.

Drusus looked at Paulinus, who shrugged his shoulders.

*

Donor approached Ilona's home from the rear, out of

sight of the humans he sensed. Artorius looked about him.

'What's wrong, Donor? Is your mistress in trouble?' Artorius approached the hut hearing voices inside.

Discarding the fish outside, Artorius pushed the door open sharply, spatha in one hand and spear in the other, crouching low with Donor beside him. He stared in total disbelief at the two swords aimed at him.

'Donor, stay,' ordered Ilona.

'Drusus! You came for me?' Surprise was written across Artorius' face.

Drusus saw before him a thin wiry male he didn't recognise. The man's skin was tanned, his white hair was tied at the rear and he was sporting a full beard. It was the voice that gave Artorius away. Drusus looked at Paulinus in disbelief as Artorius strode forward and hugged his dumbstruck cousin.

'You look like you've seen a ghost, and if it hadn't have been for these two I would have been. This is Rosevetha, Ilona and this great beast is her pet, Donor.'

Donor lay prone on the floor, eyeing both Drusus and Paulinus.

'Can we speak outside, Artorius?' requested Drusus.

'There's no need, Rosevetha already knows what you'll say,' countered Artorius.

'There are three others waiting in the cold. May I bring them into the warmth?' enquired Drusus, Rosevetha nodded.

Paulinus exited the hut. In a trance, he walked back to where the other three waited, freezing on their horses. Gigantrex reacted first at the look on Paulinus' face.

'What's wrong, where's Drusus?'

'He's inside with Artorius,' responded Paulinus.

'I told you she would solve our problem,' said Gigantrex, full of himself.

'He's living with two women and has a wolf for a pet,' muttered Paulinus.

The three dismounted and followed him. Not a word passed between them, but the looks said it all.

Inside the hut, Artorius addressed Drusus. 'I must discuss a few things before the others get here. As you can see, Ilona is pregnant and before you ask, it is mine. I owe my life and recovery to them both.'

'I found this in a cave. It's yours, I presume,' said Drusus, reaching into his pouch. 'So, this is how you repay them, leaving the daughter pregnant? What about Amoria?' he snapped.

'I didn't intend this to happen – in fact, I don't clearly remember it happening,' his cousin responded.

Drusus looked at Rosevetha, and her look froze him to the spot as she replied, 'Their meeting was fate and the pregnancy preordained. He was not drugged, he thought it was a dream.'

'Some dream! What, are you going to do?' Drusus asked Artorius, his voice softening.

'I need to make provision for them. I can't take them with me, can I?'

'Seer, what of your daughter and her child's future?' demanded Drusus.

'My son's future depends on his father,' answered Ilona.

'And what exactly does that mean?' enquired Drusus, looking at Rosevetha.

'The fates have decided, but it is not for me to tell you. Your son Marcus will do that, Artorius,' responded Rosevetha.

'By the gods, how do you see so much?' Artorius asked.

Rosevetha turned away as Paulinus entered the hut. Gigantrex picked Artorius off his feet, but returned him to the floor as the huge wolf rose and stood, growling, behind him.

'You have lost half of your weight and you look like a wild man. What have they done to you?'

'Welcome, once son of a great chief and now chief in your own right,' said Rosevetha. Gigantrex bowed to her, clutching an amulet around his neck as she stared straight at him.

'You must prepare to return to your Legion, Artorius, and leave us for now,' continued Rosevetha, taking her daughter's hand.

Ilona's head dropped and tears welled in her eyes, seen by Gigantrex.

'Where is the father of your child, maiden?'

'You came looking for him and now you take him away,' Ilona answered.

'You cannot stay here anymore,' said Artorius. 'Come to Argentoratum and I will arrange for you to be looked after.'

'A seer has no place in a Roman camp. Travel with us to my village, you would be safe there under my protection,' offered Gigantrex.

'You only want my powers, but you are right, it would be a good place for my grandson until the time comes. We will await your return,' stated Rosevetha, looking at Ilona.

'What about Donor and his pack?' enquired Artorius.

'They will travel with us; the forest around Gigantrex's village will suit them well,' Rosevetha replied.

Ilona stroked Donor's head and whispered in his ear, Donor turned towards the door as Ilona released him.

'That is settled then. He has gone to prepare the pack,' stated Ilona

'I must return from the dead,' remarked Artorius. 'Then it's back to Argentoratum before heading home. I will return with a wagon and horses to carry you both in a bit more comfort. Time to go, as it will be dark soon. I will lead the way.' The group turned to follow him.

Artorius made to leave, but he couldn't stop himself looking back. Ilona was in tears. She reached out to him, and he surrendered to the request. Taking her in his arms, he held her tight as she lay her head on his shoulder. He owed them his life, and somehow, he would repay them.

Ilona took his head in her hands and kissed him hard on the lips, her eyes burning deep into his soul, and in that moment he saw the two of them with a boy between them. He shook his head as Ilona smiled and turned away.

'He has glimpsed what the future offers. I know what you said, but I had to,' pleaded Ilona as she turned to her mother.

Collecting their horses, and with Artorius using Ilona's pony, he led the way back to the road. The last hour of day had passed before they came in sight of Mogontiacum. Artorius was deep in thought as the guard challenged the group riding into the barracks.

'He'll have to stay in the town, we can't have any old beggar in here,' said the guard, pointing to Artorius.

His appearance hadn't meant anything till now. 'I am the missing Centurion, Artorius Civilis, Primus Pila of the Praetorian Guard! Show respect, soldier,' he snapped.

The guard hesitated before crashing his fist into his breastplate, welcoming Artorius back. The group struggled to restrain their laughter. Artorius returned the salute with a renewed crispness. *Yes, Artorius Civilis is back from the dead*, he thought.

'I think we need to get you cleaned up and back in uniform before someone throws you out of the camp,' joked Drusus, laughter erupting freely from the others.

'Then to the nearest inn. We're dying to hear your story, cousin. While you're sorting yourself out, I'll update Camp Prefect Brachus.'

It was the third hour of night when the six finally assembled again under the sign of the Eagle Inn. Artorius looked even thinner in uniform, his features sharper and his skin the colour of leather, highlighting his white hair. He had certainly aged. All had seen his arm and were desperate to hear his explanation. Finding a table close to the door, Drusus called for a jug of beer. The first mouthful exploded in Artorius' mouth and the rest was guzzled as his friends watched expectantly.

An icy blast followed Brachus through the door, seeking the group. Artorius rose to greet him.

'Am I in time to hear how this hairy-arsed bastard is still alive?' Brachus enquired.

Beakers filled, Gigantrex raised a toast to a friend, back from the dead. One jug became four or five as Artorius related his story, starting from his first visit to Rosevetha and Ilona. Only Gigantrex accepted his story of making love to Ilona in a dream, the rest made ribald comments. The wolf attack had them all transfixed, especially with the intervention of Ilona and her pack. They poked fun at him when he said Ilona had been the two-legged wolf. Gigantrex congratulated himself on having invited the two women to his village – with Ilona's wolf pack, he and his village would be revered by the other local tribes. He wanted – no, needed – Artorius' closeness with Donor.

'So, we are to lose the old witch and her daughter? I didn't realise she controlled the wolves. You certainly know how to pick them,' joked Brachus, slapping Artorius hard on the back. 'When do you leave for Rome?'

'In two days. I have to arrange a wagon and horses till we get to Gigantrex's village. I must stop at Argentoratum to see Scorus, or his replacement, and collect any orders waiting for me.'

'Scorus' replacement has come from within the Legion, he's due to return to Rome. Make yourself comfortable till you leave. Leave the horse and cart to me. The Legate can pay for them, for what Drusus and the others did,' replied Brachus.

Artorius looked at the group, puzzled. 'Why, what happened?'

The five being worse for wear, all tried to explain what had happened since he had gone missing. Artorius was sure that the ambush story was an embellishment of the truth, but it was an interesting one.

'Any news about that evil bastard Victus?' Artorius enquired.

'We believe he headed to Genua. There's no definite information, but there is a price on his head,' Brachus replied.

'Enough talking, more beer,' shouted Gigantrex.

## Chapter 10

It was a bright but cold start to the first hour of the day as Artorius and his friends rode out of the garrison, the Legate having willingly provided a wagon and good horses. The journey passed quickly, despite the road's muddied surface. Little speech passed between the group, only Artorius remarking at the fallen tree, now mostly rotted away.

As they neared the track to Rosevetha's home, Donor appeared from the forest and Artorius stepped down to greet him. The wolf raised his head and howled, and the forest around them echoed, spooking the horses. Artorius led the carriage and horses forward with Gigantrex following on foot.

'I would like to take Ilona to Rome, but Amoria wouldn't understand,' remarked Artorius.

'Women are strange creatures; you never know what to expect. Another day, perhaps, but for now we must make haste, we have a long way to go,' answered Gigantrex.

No smoke curled from the hut's chimney as they approached, and a pregnant wolf sat by the door. It stepped forward, growling as they approached. Artorius offered his hand, which was initially refused until he spoke, then she sniffed it as Donor joined her. The door opened with Ilona clad in fur and carrying a large bundle.

'Mother is finishing her preparations. You look very handsome in uniform, Artorius.' Ilona offered her hand, which Artorius took gladly, squeezing it.

'We have a wagon for you both. What do I need to load?' enquired Artorius.

'Mine's here and there's more inside,' said Rosevetha as she appeared at the door, a bundle of fur with a head peering from it.

Gigantrex lifted the bundles, light as feathers, and placed them on the floor of the wagon. Gigantrex lifted Rosevetha, struggling into its rear, while Artorius assisted Ilona on to the front seat, Donor and his mate watched. Ruffling Donor's fur, Artorius took the reins and walked the wagon back towards the road where he joined Ilona on the front seat. The group took it in turns to scout forward and cover their rear.

It took three uneventful days to reach Argentoratum. Ilona spent every waking hour beside Artorius as he spoke of his family and the estate in Rome. The others looked on with pity at a very close couple, that could never be.

Rolling into Argentoratum barracks, Artorius left his friends to find accommodation and food for the women, then he went in search of the Camp Prefect. Entering the administrative building, he was surprised to hear Scorus' voice emanating from the Camp Prefect's office. He entered to find Scorus and Scipio, as he had expected. Scorus gave a sharp intake of breath as Artorius saluted.

'I never thought to see you again! Word was, the wolves had seen to you. Looking at your arm, they had a good try. You've caught me just in time as I head back to Rome tomorrow to be handsomely rewarded, thanks to you. Scipio, as you see, is replacing me,' remarked Scorus.

'Congratulations, Scipio, you deserve it. Are there any messages or orders for me?'

'Macro has been informed of your return from the dead. I'm only Camp Prefect by default of you joining the Praetorian Guard, so I thank you for that,' replied Scipio.

'I hope I still have a position to return to. I presume my return orders are valid?' enquired Artorius.

'As you are alive and your mission was completed to the word of the orders, I'd say they are. I'll have a fresh copy drawn up. Do you mind if I join you?' responded Scorus.

'If you don't mind travelling with my friends. We will drop them off as we go. We will be visiting Gigantrex's village and escorting a wagon with passengers. Join us later, I'm sure Gigantrex would love to relive his father's glorious death. The passengers are a seer and her daughter,' related Artorius.

'Not the ones from Mogontiacum? She's well known, even down here,' answered Scorus, clutching an amulet to Mithras. 'Why are they travelling with you?'

'I owe them my life and Gigantrex has offered them his village. The rest is a long story.'

'Sounds like I'm in for a long night,' replied Scorus. 'Is Salinus still here?'

'Strange, that – just after you disappeared they found him and his slave with their throats cut. The locals must have found out who he really was. No great loss,' Scorus replied sarcastically.

Artorius' thoughts were dominated by Salinus as he walked away. Could he be responsible for his exposure?

Drusus' friend from his legion days was running a better than average inn and the whole group had taken up residence there. Artorius found them in a private room, drinking and waiting to eat. The news of Scorus travelling with them was welcomed as the group would dwindle the further south they went. Artorius found a spare seat beside Ilona. Mixed emotions ran through the whole group. The talk, light-hearted, was of the future, which for the most part was to have a family and live out what was left of their lives in peace. It was the fourth hour of dark when Scorus appeared, exhausted.

'I've been looking for you crowd, but I didn't expect to

find you here, where it's a bit well to do, but then you have passengers.' Scorus looked around the group, his eyes stopping at Rosevetha and Ilona. Ilona's beauty shocked him, but it was Rosevetha who took his breath away.

'So, we meet again, Scorus. You have weathered better than I. How long ago was it that we played a loving couple and then you abandoned me?' Rosevetha snapped.

The whole group was taken aback by this and stared at Scorus.

Ilona looked at her mother in total disbelief.

'She can't be mine!' exclaimed Scorus.

'No, she certainly isn't – she knows her father. You weren't up to much, if I remember,' Rosevetha said, waggling her little finger at him and laughing.

Scorus blushed, scratching irritably at his neck. The air was blue with ribald remarks, and Scorus turned the tables back on Artorius by asking about the father of Ilona's child.

'I am, and it's a long story,' replied Artorius.

'Well, that's what I came to hear. Pass the frothy stuff?' demanded Scorus.

The women made their excuses. Ilona touched Artorius' hand and looked deep into his soul and smiled; the electric moment was caught by all.

Beakers replenished, Drusus started his story. Each member of the group intervened to add their perspective, but it was Artorius' story that had them riveted to their seats. It was a late hour of night when the boozy party ended.

Lack of sleep and high alcoholic consumption were reflected in the faces of all the party as they tried to eat the following morning, but the women were unsympathetic. Scorus walked through the inn door, shaved and sober, the epitome of a first-class Camp Prefect, as he presented Artorius with his new orders.

A raggle-taggle group made its way south a short while later, Ilona clutching Artorius at every opportunity as they sat together on the wagon, watched like a hawk by Rosevetha. After four days, the pace being slower than Scorus wished, he decided to press on to Rome alone. As Artorius turned the wagon off the main road towards Gigantrex's village, Ilona's mood changed noticeably, for the time for separation was upon them. As the wagon trundled towards the stockade, the gates opened and a single woman exited. Gigantrex dismounted and strode towards his mother with open arms.

'Did your father, my husband, die well?' asked Breda, fighting back her tears.

'He died as he would have wished – with a sword in his hand,' Gigantrex said, offering his father's blade and ashes to his mother.

'Tonight we will celebrate his passing. I bring the seer, Rosevetha, and her daughter Ilona, who brings her own pack of wolves. She carries Artorius' child, but she will stay here when he returns to his family in Rome,' explained Gigantrex.

'He is too late. I warned him.'

'Warned him about what, Mother?' asked Gigantrex.

'I cannot say, only his son can. Introduce me to our guests.' Breda stepped towards the party.

'Welcome, Rosevetha and Ilona, I saw your coming. A lodging has already been prepared for you. The boy you carry will be a great man,' she said, touching Ilona's stomach.

Rosevetha nodded whilst Ilona looked shocked – she hadn't expected this response.

'I am sorry for your loss, Breda. Herax died trying to find

me and I will always be in your debt,' said Artorius, taking Breda's hand.

'We knew his time had come, but he wanted one last battle. I am sure his son will sing his praises tonight for all to hear, but thank you.'

Gigantrex introduced the rest of the group. Breda looked deep into their souls, and each knew it, before she led the way to the great hall where a meal in honour of Herax was waiting. The food and beer were plentiful as great stories were told of Herax's bravery, and the day slipped away unnoticed. Rosevetha, Ilona and Breda spent much of the night deep in conversation, to the exclusion of all others. Artorius reflected on what the three could collectively see. Meanwhile, Drusus and the others revelled in the hospitality, collapsing once again into a drunken sleep. The ladies slipped away to their newly provided home, joined by Breda.

A heavy morning mist rolled from the forest into the clearing before the palisade, hiding the wolves' arrival until Donor announced their presence with a howl. Gigantrex responded, staggering from the great hall to find Ilona atop the palisade and looking out over her pack below.

'They have arrived, I see,' he said.

'They've been acquainting themselves with your forest. I would like to greet them, if I may?'

'Come, I will open the gate; they should get to know me,' he insisted.

Ilona looked hard at Gigantrex and realised for the first time that it was her wolves she was wanted for. She decided then that he would never have that bond with her wolves – only Artorius and his sons would know that pleasure. Gigantrex wanted the fame and power his father had never had; it was a hidden agenda Ilona had missed and she didn't like it.

Gigantrex lifted the retaining beam as if it were nothing, and as the gate opened Donor walked forward, but on seeing Gigantrex, he stopped. Ilona howled a greeting and the forest around them exploded with the sound of her pack. Gigantrex went to step forward, but Ilona stayed him with her hand on his chest.

'He doesn't know you, but in time he will.' *But not as you would wish*, she thought.

Gigantrex was back staged as the mist cleared, revealing the pack surrounding Ilona. Each wolf approached her in turn, like courtiers paying homage to their queen. A thought struck Gigantrex, that with Artorius returning to Rome he needed a queen, and what better queen than Ilona? He would offer himself as the adoptive father to Artorius' son, and when Artorius departed he would approach Ilona. He was sure in his own mind that both would be happy with the suggestion – he certainly would.

Ilona sat with Donor's pregnant mate's head laid across her lap, while Donor himself sat beside the pair, a powerful guardian. He eyed Gigantrex suspiciously, growling as the man tried to step forward. Artorius, hearing the wolves, found the palisade gate open and Gigantrex filling the entrance. Beyond was a sight he always found amazing: Ilona surrounded by her wolves.

As Artorius stepped forward, Donor greeted him. Artorius took the beast's head between his hands and stared into its eyes; they seemed to smile back as he ruffled Donor's fur. Ilona reached out to Artorius as Donor's mate stood, and Artorius eased Ilona gently to her feet.

She could read Gigantrex's thoughts: they were full of ill meaning and he intended to have his way whatever anyone said. The pack started to growl collectively, Donor stepping beside Ilona.

Artorius looked behind to find his cousin's and friends' mouths agape at the sight before them.

'Ilona, you truly are the Wolf Queen,' Drusus said.

'Thank you, is that what they call me? I am honoured.' Ilona bowed to the group with a smile that lit her whole face.

Artorius couldn't help the deep feelings of admiration he felt for her and he tried to shake away the other thoughts that filled his head daily. They would part today forever, and already he was missing her. The anger at his feelings rose inside him.

Gigantrex took Artorius to one side as the wolves melted back into the forest, watched by Ilona with Donor overseeing the rear.

'I have a proposition that I hope you will consider carefully and agree would be the best option for all concerned,' offered Gigantrex.

'What would that be? Ilona, I presume?' replied Artorius suspiciously.

'You leave today, and in so doing, Ilona will remain in my care. I am now chief and as such I need a queen.'

'Why are you asking me?' Artorius snapped, ashamed of his jealous feelings.

'You are the father of the son she carries. I will look after them both and treat your son as my own,' replied Gigantrex calmly.

'If I were not married I wouldn't think twice about making her mine. I will provide for them both, even though I doubt I will ever see them again. The question you ask is not mine to answer, but if you do and I find either are ever mistreated, my vengeance will be great.'

'Like your vengeance on Victus?' snapped Gigantrex.

Ilona sensed the tension between the two men as both gripped their swords. She took Artorius' arm and eased him away; anger was etched on his face. Gigantrex stomped back inside the gates, pushing past a shocked Drusus.

'Now is not the time,' said Ilona.

'Then I must take you with me. I'm not leaving you here,' Artorius responded.

'He wants me as his queen, doesn't he? And you are jealous? That isn't all – he wants my wolves, too. I hadn't seen it till today.'

'You will come with me and I will find somewhere else for you and my son to stay.' Artorius pulled himself up to his full height above Ilona and blushed, guilty for the way he felt.

'We are here for a reason, or my mother would have declined his offer. Besides, where could you take me where my wolves could go?'

Without thinking, Artorius pulled Ilona to him and held her tight, and her heart jumped for joy. His feelings had betrayed him and she made the most of the moment, clinging tightly to him. Artorius returned to the present moment as a hand touched his shoulder. Turning, he faced Drusus and the rest of the group.

'We must leave,' stated his cousin.

'Yes, I know. Let's eat.' Artorius' head dropped. Taking Ilona's hand, he led her back through the gate, Donor having watched the confrontation.

Within an hour the group were fed and mounted, except for Artorius. Gigantrex absented himself from the group and ignored their departure, much to everyone's surprise. Artorius struggled with his feelings for Ilona as the eagle eyes of Rosevetha and Breda saw and felt every emotion between the couple.

Breda stepped forward and addressed the couple in whispers.

'Fate has dealt you a vicious blow. My son is a fool and his vision of power clouds his brain. He will never attain what he wants.'

'I have a wife, yet my feelings are as deep for Ilona. What do you know? What you say troubles me, and I fear leaving Ilona behind,' pleaded Artorius.

'She is safe here and you will see her again. I can say no more.' Breda wrapped her arms around them both.

'Artorius,' called Drusus.

Artorius nodded and the couple separated. Mounting his horse, he leant down, offering Ilona the knife from his belt. He kissed her hand. She in turn offered him an amber amulet encased in silver.

'It was my father's and I expect you to return it.' Tears filled Ilona's eyes.

Rosevetha wrapped her arms around her daughter and whispered to her, raising a smile. The group walked their horses forward through the gate, Artorius taking a backward glance.

'We love you,' Ilona mouthed, as she held her stomach and Donor joined her, unseen.

Artorius' mind was scrambled with confusion as the group threaded their way through the clearing mist and into the forest. Gigantrex's absence from breakfast and their farewell disturbed him. Talk of families spurred the group on, each thinking of their own. Drusus watched the pain in his cousin's face, thanking the gods it wasn't him.

## Chapter 11

It was an unusually mild end to the year in Rome, which never boded well. The snows had melted early and the coastal marshes misted each morning, signs of an early warmth coming to the land. Marcus urged his mother to move to the estate as a warm spring often brought with it disease, but Amoria stayed any decision. There was only one thought on her mind as the new year started: how soon would Artorius return and how could she make sure he stayed? Tia's thoughts turned to other matters. Her body was changing and she wasn't sure why, it had been a few months since she had suffered her monthly show. She and Marcus had always been sexually active, but she had always been careful with herbs known to prevent any pregnancy. The thought of Marcus as a father warmed her inside, but all in good time, she thought.

The hidden death crawled from the swamps early that year. Like a giant snake, it slithered from the Tiberis through the side streets of filth and vermin that was the Aventine and no family evaded its bite. Marcus argued daily with his mother to move to the estate as neighbours around them started to suffer its poison. The Aventine woke daily to wailing sounds, doors were marked and the wrapped dead were left outside to be taken away, the smell of putrefaction hung heavy in the air.

Verina's friend fell ill with a fever, not uncommon for the time of year. Sores followed, which turned to scabs, and it was obvious to all that the child's life was in the hands of the gods. Out of fear for Verina's life and with the offer of marriage in the air, Amoria sent her away on the Ides of Martius with Lictus' nephew's escort. It was a tearful farewell for all except Verina, who saw it as final recognition of her adulthood. Marcus and Tia wanted to escort her, but it was decided they needed to remain due to Artorius' absence.

It was only days after that Alia started with cold symptoms. Amoria hid it from Marcus and Tia, dispatching them to the estate to prepare for the spring. They pleaded with Amoria to join them, but she refused. Tia had noticed Alia's fever, but not its gravity, and had prepared an herbal mix which Amoria administered.

Marcus and Tia raced to the estate, their hasty arrival throwing the staff into panic. The gates slammed shut and the staff armed themselves before they realized it was the lovers. Georgiakis threw the gates open and was met with a smile from Marcus.

'Now that was an effective response,' he said, sliding from his horse and taking Georgiakis in a firm handshake.

Walking their horses inside the gate, Marcus and Tia greeted everyone they met. Every face held a smile and it warmed the hearts of the couple; everyone seemed so happy.

*

After an uneventful journey, the boat docked unobserved in the outermost part of Ostia Antica in the last hour of night. The harbour quays stank of rotting foodstuffs and a fishy smell invaded the nostrils of three passengers as they carried their own baggage and slipped away, enshrouded in the early morning mist. Only the rats scurried under their feet. Any guards were hidden somewhere warm – after all, who in their right mind would arrive now, by boat?

Victus made his way to a rundown smithy and, dragging its occupant from his bed, retrieved a horse and a small cart before setting off for a small but comfortable farm.

Peter Baggott

Over the following days, Victus made enquiries about the remaining members of the Civilis family and found Honorus of the Praetorian Guard was overseeing their protection, till Artorius' return.

Victus laughed at that suggestion and ordered the Centurion to attend the Praetorian barracks and relate his story, then leave.

Victus saw the Centurion and his prostitute as loose ends, especially once the Centurion had completed his task. With the Centurion on his way to the barracks, Victus decided to indulge himself with the prostitute before sealing her fate. She tried desperately to fend him off until he punched her, rendering her unconscious. Gagging her, Victus tied her naked to the bed, where he used and abused her until she was virtually unconscious, her body a mass of bruises.

'Well, we enjoyed ourselves, didn't we? But all this fun must end. I have no further need of you or the Centurion,' Victus whispered sarcastically in the prostitute's ear, her face a picture of horror. He started laughing maniacally.

As the prostitute screamed, Victus rendered her unconscious again and carried her to a sunken bath which he filled with warm water from the kitchen. Placing her in it, she began to wake, thrashing about attempting to escape, but to no avail. Taking the young girl's arm, Victus cut the venous skin at her wrist and blood poured freely from it. Her eyes rolled in a face white with shock. Victus looked down on the slick of blood as it grew, before turning and walking away.

*

The Centurion had made his way to the Praetorian barracks, and sweat poured from every inch of his body. So, preoccupied was he, that he nearly fell off his horse when a guard challenged him. Requesting Honorus, he was directed to his office where he found him with the Legion accounts, something he hated. Honorus was thankful that at least the clerk seemed to know what he was doing, and now even better, there was a distraction.

'When Centurion Artorius didn't arrive back from a mission I took out a search party and we found him murdered because of an ambush by renegade tribesmen,' related the Centurion.

'Macro will want to be told in person,' explained Honorus, noticing the man's nervousness.

Macro never took to being interrupted for any reason, but when he heard a Centurion had travelled from Argentoratum with news of the death of his envoy, Artorius, he was all ears.

'A few days after Artorius returned from Rome, the Legate took his own life, leaving a list of fellow conspirators led by Victus Antonius Claudian. Some were arrested and some disappeared. Camp Prefect Scorus decided the remaining Tribunes were too young and inexperienced to control the Legion, so he assumed temporary control,' stated the Centurion.

'That sounds reasonable, I'm glad I listened to Centurion Civilis. Carry on,' prompted Macro.

'Centurion Civilis volunteered to travel to Mogontiacum with a dispatch requesting a temporary replacement Legate for the 2nd Augusta.' The Centurion wiped away the sweat as his nerves increased. 'It was a few days later that my routine patrol towards Mogontiacum found his body. His body was returned to the Legion and he had a formal send-off. As a friend, I volunteered to return his armour to his family,' explained the Centurion, paling.

'Are you ill, Centurion?' Macro enquired.

'Sir, I have been ill and I still have a fever,' he explained, showing his blackened and rotting fingertips.

'You should see the senior medicus immediately. Camp Prefect Honorus will take the armour and it might be best that he tells the family, if that's okay with yourself. I am sure the family would like to hear the story personally, when you are well,' responded Macro.

'Thank you. I would like to speak to them before I return to the Legion,' answered the Centurion.

'Take your time to recover at our expense and I will sort out a new Legate. You could escort him back to the Legion. Dismissed.'

The Centurion sought help from the hospital and was informed that they would have to remove his blackened fingers for his own health. He was not happy, but he accepted. With his remaining fingers bandaged, he made excuses to visit a relative and fled to the first inn he could find by the wharf. He felt sick inside for what he had done. He had betrayed a friend, and for what? His mood already dark, the alcohol sent him spiralling into a deep depression.

*

Meanwhile, Honorus had made sensitive enquiries as to Marcus' location. Finding he was at the estate, he set out with the bad news. The sun had long passed its highest point when Honorus slipped from the military road on to the track towards the Civilis estate. As he walked his horse down the final slope, he observed Marcus and Tia putting the male staff through weapons training, oblivious to being observed. The warning bell sounded from the estate, telling Honorus that he was being observed. Marcus broke off and strode towards the lone rider. Honorus, marvelled at the young man approaching him – how he had grown, looking well beyond his years.

ILONA

'What do we owe the honour of this visit, sir?' Marcus said, grasping Honorus' hand firmly.

'I have need to talk to you and Tia in private, if I may?' asked Honorus, slipping from his horse.

'We'll use the bench by the paddock. Georgiakis, could we have some wine by the paddock, please,' requested Marcus, leading the way.

'The estate has grown in population since I was last here,' said Honorus.

Marcus explained the changes and the lack of Hades in the paddock. Honorus was amazed at what had been achieved with the estate – or village, as it had become.

'You came for a reason which you seem to be avoiding. What is it?' asked Marcus, handing Honorus a beaker of wine.

'I have bad news, which I thought to tell you first, so that you can prepare your mother.'

'It's Father, isn't it? What's happened?'

'He was ambushed, but I'm afraid he's dead and a friend has brought his armour home after his Legion honoured him,' related Honorus.

Tia felt for Marcus' hand as she saw him desperately fight back the tears.

'Where is Father's friend? I would like to thank him for returning his armour, the journey must have been hard.'

'He was in the hospital being treated when I left. I will bring him to the tenement, if you like?' enquired Honorus.

'Please, Mother would want to hear from him herself,' replied Marcus.

'Shall we say tomorrow at the tenement? I am very sorry, your father was a great soldier,' responded Honorus, taking his leave after hugging Marcus.

Tia turned and looked into Marcus' eyes and all she saw was a lost soul. She wrapped her arms tightly around him.

'I see Lictus before us and he is shaking his head. He indicates your father is alive somewhere. Let's see what your father's friend has to say tomorrow,' she suggested.

'Please don't give me false hope,' pleaded Marcus.

'I wouldn't,' Tia responded.

As darkness fell, the estate was sealed for the night and the guard set. Marcus called the staff together, explaining what he had been told. Tia explained what she had seen and the majority were receptive, but Marcus and Tia were not sure whether it was through belief or out of hope. The evening meal took on a sombre note, despite some attempts to raise spirits.

Dorina took Tia to one side after the meal. 'You are with child, my dear, aren't you?' 'A few months ago, I thought I might be, but I have had my usual show,' replied Tia.

'When you return to Rome, visit my friend and she will tell you whether you are. Take great care. It has been a long time since there was a child on the estate,' suggested Dorina.

Marcus and Tia settled into their bed, neither able to sleep. Tia could read the questions on Marcus' face. Maybe Artorius' friend would be able to answer the questions, or would he pose more?

The couple had arrived at the estate to smiling faces, but left to sombre ones the following morning. They didn't rush back to Rome. Marcus was deep in thought the whole way and Tia watched him with concern. When they arrived at the smithy to leave their horses, the smithy himself looked more worried than usual and complained of increased gang problems.

Amoria was surprised when the couple appeared,

informing them that Alia had a children's fever which was infectious, but they could see her later. Marcus struggled to withhold the news and found himself rambling about plans for the estate as a knock at the door made him jump, his heart missing a beat. Tia was busy making a drink she knew would be needed by Amoria. Honorus stood at the door as expected, but dressed in a toga.

Amoria looked surprised at both his dress and presence.

'You look as if you are out on the town, Honorus. To what do we owe this surprise?' she said, ushering him into the tenement.

'Marcus, there's a bag outside for you,' replied Honorus.

Without seeing it, Marcus already knew what was in that fateful bag – all that was left of his father. He approached the door with apprehension, which didn't go unnoticed by Amoria. She looked to Honorus, whose head dropped. Amoria let out a blood-curdling scream, collapsing in a flood of tears, asking repeatedly: 'Why?'

Tia knelt beside Amoria, struggling to hold the tears back herself. Honorus stood, not knowing what to say or do as Tia helped Amoria off the floor to a stool by the wall and fetched the drink she had prepared. Amoria raked her hair and tore at her face with her nails as Tia spoke quietly and calmly to her. She tried to entice Amoria to drink the potion, which initially she refused.

Marcus carried in his father's sagum, which was encasing the armour, and looked at Honorus. 'Where's my father's spatha?'

'I believed everything was there,' responded Honorus, looking at the pile that lay before him on the floor.

'What about father's friend, I thought he was coming with you?'

'That's a strange one. He was treated in the hospital and

left saying he was visiting a relative. He hasn't been seen since,' replied Honorus.

'Maybe he's stolen the spatha and run off,' proffered Marcus.

'Don't worry, I've already instigated enquiries.'

Amoria's body shook as she sobbed and curled into a ball, calling Artorius' name. She was inconsolable. Tia's potion took effect and Amoria calmed, but she continued to sob quietly, eventually falling asleep where she sat. With Honorus' help, Marcus carried his mother to her bed. Tia went to look after Alia, recoiling at the sight: the little girl was deathly white and her skin was a mass of pustules and scabs. Tia and Marcus attended to her, fearing for her life, and as they sat together, Marcus' thoughts were miles away to where he thought his father had been cremated.

'Father's friend reported finding him and brought his armour back to Rome, so why would he lie?' Marcus asked.

Honorus shrugged his shoulders and having nothing further to add bade the family farewell.

Tia took Marcus' face in her hands, kissing him tenderly on the lips. They clutched each other tightly and fell asleep where they sat.

It was the early hours of the following day when Marcus awoke, sensing he was being watched. Opening his eyes, he saw his mother, her hair dishevelled and her expression blank. She signed for Marcus to carry Tia to bed while she took over the care of Alia, and as he tried to do as he was bid, Tia woke up.

'Go back to the estate,' Amoria murmured to them. 'I will look after Alia and when she is well, we will come.'

'Alia is very ill. I have seen these signs before and they were fatal,' Tia said, looking at Amoria's tired face.

'It's only a fever, it'll soon pass. Now go, I don't want to be nursing all of you.' Amoria took Tia's hand and squeezed it gently. 'Look after him for me,' she whispered, tears filling her eyes.

'Please, Mother, come too,' pleaded Marcus. 'The fresh air would benefit Alia. You can't stay here on your own. Father will return, Tia says so. Honorus is making enquiries into father's friend disappearing, he'll find us at the estate.'

'Tia is just trying to help you adjust. That was your father's armour, he must be dead. I'm sorry...' Tears flooded from her eyes and she tried desperately to mop them, failing hopelessly.

'If we are to return to the estate, I will send someone to help you,' offered Marcus.

'If you like,' Amoria said submissively.

Her life was collapsing around her, and with it the will to live diminished. In her mind, she had already berated Artorius for leaving her.

'Your sister is very ill and your mother knows it,' whispered Tia, sliding her arm through Marcus' as they left. 'Lictus is watching over her; she senses someone and believes it's your father, but he is not dead.'

The moment was shattered by wailing coming from the street; the body cart was being wheeled away from their neighbours' house. This time it was an adult. *Was there no end to it?* thought Marcus. Amoria was stooped and looked tired as she walked away, shutting the bedroom door behind her. Marcus and Tia observed the plague symbol above their neighbours' door and knew all was lost for them.

'It's no good going there any more, the last one has been taken away,' said a passer-by. 'They are dropping like flies in this neighbourhood, I'd get the family away if I were you.'

The usually packed street was nearly empty, and those that remained looked downtrodden and blank. Marcus tried to hide his fear for his sister's life. Tia knew that all she could do was hold him tight as they walked to the smithy. The sound of metal on metal seemed to ring louder than usual. The smithy was two-handed smashing his hammer on to the anvil in temper. Marcus looked at the man without speaking.

'These bastard gangs are bleeding me dry. I've moving away or I'll do something I'll regret. You should get your family out of here, away from all the disease as well,' he suggested.

Marcus explained the predicament with his mother and sister. The smithy just looked at the couple and clasped the amulet around his neck and wished them well. Collecting their horses, they headed for the Pons Aemilius and the road back to the estate.

Marcus and Tia viewed the chaos on the street as a single horse, barely carrying its rider, tried to negotiate its way along. Marcus, seeing a uniform, rode alongside the Centurion and could tell by the stench of alcohol that he was drunk, but still offered his assistance.

The Centurion had staggered from the wharf-side inn barely able to walk, and had mounted his horse with great difficulty. He now lay sprawled on the horse's back on the Pons Aemilius amidst verbal abuse from those who had to step out of his way.

'No one can help me, I am damned! Don't come too close, it might rub off,' said the Centurion, waving away Marcus's offer of help.

Shrugging, Marcus and Tia continued to the estate.

Back at the Praetorian Barracks, Honorus was informed that the missing Centurion had been seen leaving the city towards Ostia Antica and, thus, he sent two of his best men to make enquiries.

*

Victus lay in wait for the Centurion's return on the outskirts of Ostia Antica. He watched the wobbly rider approach and recognized the Centurion in his drunken state, clinging to his horse.

The Centurion struggled through the haze that fuddled his brain and didn't see Victus until he stepped on to the road and took hold of the horse's bridle. The Centurion fell from his horse in a jumbled mess of arms and legs at the sudden halt. Victus dragged him to his feet by his clothes, berating him for his condition. The Centurion struggled to free himself, instinctively reaching for his gladius. Victus foresaw the movement and, pushing the Centurion backwards, withdrew his sword and slid it expertly into the man's stomach.

As the two Praetorians reached the outskirts of Ostia Antica in the dying light, they saw two figures fighting on the road. Racing to assist, they saw one fall to the floor, while the other mounted and galloped away. The guards reined in their horses by the collapsed body to find the missing Centurion bleeding to death.

He reached out with a blood-soaked hand. 'Victus Claudian!' he wheezed, his words dying with his breath.

'I think we've achieved what we came for. I don't know about you, but I'm not going after his killer,' said the one guard to his colleague, who nodded agreement.

Securing the body to one of the horses, they returned to Rome. In the early hours of night Honorus sent a short missive to Marcus at the estate outlining his discoveries, and that they were still searching for Victus. Marcus was loath to upset his mother further or give her any false hope.

Alia's health spiralled downwards and Amoria sought help from a clinicus, who took one look at Alia and stated there was nothing he could do and promptly left. Amoria lived in hope, but when Alia sat up in a fever and called out Lictus' name, she knew in her own heart that the battle was lost. Leaving Alia momentarily, Amoria ran and sought help from the smithy, who sent his apprentice to fetch Marcus and Tia. On her return, Amoria found Alia in convulsions and holding her tight, she sang to her. As she looked down at her own lesions, she knew she had caught the plague from Alia, but she didn't care, she just wanted to join Artorius. Amoria slipped into a troubled sleep, rocking Alia in her arms, wishing neither would wake again.

By the time the smithy's apprentice had reached Marcus the hour was late, and night was drowning the day in its impending darkness. The couple galloped to the city gates, which were being closed. Marcus begged them to stay the closure, until they were inside. The guard hesitated. 'My sister is inside and she is dying, please let us in.' Marcus couldn't hold back the tears any more. He tried to be strong, but he couldn't – first Cassius, then his father, and now little Alia.

The guards waved them on, clasping their respective amulets and talking to their gods. Marcus had forsaken all his gods; how could they exact such a toll on one family, his family? The streets were virtually empty as the couple pushed their horses as fast as they could towards Amoria and Alia.

Marcus leapt from his horse, running up the steps of the tenement. The door to his mother's room was open, and his mother and sister were on the bed. Neither moved. Marcus felt his heart shatter; he couldn't be too late... Then he saw his mother move. As he stepped into the room he noticed an awful smell, one he would come to know: death! Tia followed Marcus into the room, and she knew straight away. Alia was stood beside her mother, looking at the shell she once owned.

Amoria looked at Marcus, then at Alia, and screamed. 'Artorius, where are you, my love? Take our daughter's hand and wait for me,' Amoria wailed, clutching Alia even tighter. As she lay on the bed holding her daughter, Marcus saw the tell-tale signs on his mother's arm.

'Why didn't you tell us you're suffering too?' Marcus snapped unwittingly.

Amoria looked at him but said nothing. Her eyes were lifeless, she had given in.

Tia chanted an unknown melody to the dead as Marcus eased Alia from his mother. The little girl was cold, her eyes closed tight, and not a breath stirred from her chest.

'Goodbye, little sister, I loved you.' Marcus kissed his sister on her forehead then lay her down.

Taking his mother in his arms, Marcus tried to console the inconsolable. Amoria collapsed on to him, sobbing deeply. Tia lay a clean sheet on the floor and wrapped Alia tightly inside it. She looked like a baby in swaddling. Tia watched the love of her life clutching his mother to him; both lives had been shattered by so much loss. Tia touched Amoria's skin, recoiling at its clammy heat – the pustules were well advanced. Her comment to Tia before leaving for the estate now had meaning – she too had known she was dying. Leaving mother and son in death's embrace, Tia went in search of clean cold water and cloths.

A great depression gripped the house over the ensuing nights, Amoria fading a little more each day, as did Marcus. He looked to Tia, but there was nothing she could do to help but be there. She tried to keep everywhere as sterile as she could, using copious amounts of wine vinegar to reduce the chance of contagion. Marcus and Tia cremated Alia, intending the ashes to be interned on the estate when they could. Tia expected they would have to do the same for Amoria before long.

They took it in turns to care for her, though Tia doubted she knew they were there. Tia sat and watched the ethereal comings and goings of Amoria's family, and occasionally Lictus. She was adamant that Artorius was alive and often spoke to Amoria telling her this, with no response. Marcus hardly spoke, it was all about the touch, the hugs, that let Tia knew all was still well between them.

The day had barely started, its warmth filtering into the house. Amoria roused herself, turning to find Tia dozing in a chair beside her. She reached out and touched Tia's stomach, causing her to wake sharply. 'My dear, you are pregnant, aren't you?'

'How could you know? I'm not sure,' replied Tia.

'A woman always knows. My second grandchild, and to a healthy young woman. I apologise for any bad thoughts I have ever had about you and Marcus. He couldn't have found a better partner. You remind me of his father and I, but even closer. You are so good for each other. Does he know?'

'I wasn't sure, so no,' answered Tia.

'He will make a great father, but I regret I'll not see your child grow.' Tears filled Amoria's eyes as she started to cough, each seizure bringing pain.

'You will be there for it; I know you will,' Tia reassured her.

'I wish I had your beliefs! I thought I saw my parents, but I must have been dreaming,' pondered Amoria.

'It wasn't dreams. Like Lictus, they are watching over

you, they are here to help your transition,' responded Tia.

'I must sleep. I leave my son in your love and care.' Amoria took Tia's hand, and squeezing it tight, she held it to her face. The touch was ice cold.

'Artorius where are you? Have you not come to meet me in death? Thank you Tia...' And with that Amoria took a deep breath and breathed out her last.

Tia closed Amoria's eyes before fetching Marcus, telling him his mother had slipped away in her sleep. Marcus raved in anger that he hadn't been there at the end.

'How can she leave me? First my father, now my mother, what have I done that was so wrong? All I have done these past twelve months is find my family then lose them one by one!' Taking his mother in his arms, Marcus pulled her close.

'Your father is alive. Let us deal with death and inter your mother and sister with your grandparents. Then, we will go in search of your father,' insisted Tia.

Marcus looked at her with tears in his eyes. He smiled at her lovingly and pulled her close. Tia saw the tell-tale marks on Marcus. *The plague shall not have you*, she pledged.

No sooner was Amoria reunited with Alia, then Marcus started to decline, but he wasn't going to give in. The pustules came and went, leaving pitted scars to Marcus' face, scars for life. He was weak, fevered – Tia never left his side for longer than she had to. She was determined nothing would separate them, especially now that she was sure she was pregnant. Honorus visited with a report that Victus had disappeared and still with no news about Artorius. Aaron and Rachel had visited with Cezar, but Tia had turned them away without contact. To all visitors, Tia said the same:

'We will both see you soon.' Never doubting what she said and believed.

Marcus finally woke, he felt alive and strong, but empty. If it hadn't been for the lady, he lay beside; he would be with his family. He had seen his deceased relations in his dreams. He had thought he heard Tia say she was pregnant, but that couldn't be.

She lay with her back to him, and he reached out until their skin touched. Marcus could feel her heat, and she shuddered slightly, burrowing back into him. The effect was instant, his member pressing between her legs, his hand cupping her breasts and squeezing gently. Tia turned towards him, sliding her leg over his, an invitation he couldn't refuse. He found her dampness, slipping one and then two fingers inside her. The effect was instantaneous: her legs spread wider, and she moaned gently as his fingers slipped further into her. The look on her face was always a turn-on.

Removing his fingers, Marcus pulled Tia on top of him, holding her open as she slid down his member. Holding her tight against him, she rocked back and forward, her face filled with sheer pleasure till she screamed through her orgasm. Rolling on to her back, Tia pulled Marcus with and into her, gripping his buttocks till he exploded inside her, meeting his orgasm with her own. Marcus rolled on to his back, pulling Tia on to his chest. She just turned and looked up at him.

'I have my lover back, it seems; I've waited a long time for that,' she purred.

'I feel like I've lived a dream. How long have I been here?' he asked.

'It's the day before the Kalends of Aprilis. Do you remember anything that has happened?' asked Tia.

'I know Alia and my mother are dead. Have they found

my father yet?' Marcus' eyes were watering.

'Now you are well, we can search for him. I have put everything in order with Aaron, and Cezar wants to join us. His mother died of the plague too, and his father drank himself into his grave.'

'I feel strong, but my reactions are slow. We must go back to training and incorporate Cezar. We start today. I have an appetite to quench first, then to Aaron and Cezar,' stated Marcus. Tia smiled knowingly.

Aaron had taken control of the estate in their absence, and the staff were glad to see the young master back from the dead with his guardian angel. Even they hadn't evaded the angel of death, it had claimed three of the eldest workers. At the Praetorian camp, Honorus was one of a number that fell to the plague, and enquiries into Victus had long been forgotten.

## Chapter 12

The sun had long sunk below the horizon when the group wearily entered Octodurus, with Paulinus' horse plodding straight towards its master's inn. Hobbling the horses at the rear, the group, headed by Paulinus, tried to enter the inn from the rear to find it locked. Paulinus looked at his friends in shock and made haste to the front. Stepping inside, he found it half full and no sign of Brunhilda. A young girl who had been propped up against the bar approached the group.

'Can I help you, gentlemen? Will it be bed and lodgings or just food? I can recommend the food – the owner is an excellent cook.'

'Who are you, girl? I am the owner, where's Brunhilda?' demanded Paulinus.

'Here, you great oaf – I thought you got lost somewhere. You have a healthy son.' Brunhilda smiled as she came out from behind the bar, lifting her shawl to reveal a new-born suckling at her left breast.

Paulinus' back became a slap board as the group individually congratulated him. Artorius tried to raise a smile, but thoughts of Ilona clouded his brain. Brunhilda introduced the new helper, a necessity, since Paulinus had been gone so long. He was offered and took his son.

'You take care of your son, I get food for all. Why did it take so long to find your friend?'

'All in good time, but first I need to talk to you about your father and brother,' responded Paulinus.

'I know Father is dead, Mother told me. She saw him die a warrior. Now my big brother is chief, yes?'

'He is, but...'

'Suppose he full of importance now? He needs big sister to slap him.'

The comment was overheard by the group, raising laughter at the thought of the petite Brunhilda slapping the hulk of Gigantrex. Paulinus clutched his son and led the way to a group of empty tables as Brunhilda disappeared into the kitchen. The evening was lost in stories fuelled by copious amounts of beer.

The following morning, Paulinus found his friends exactly as he had left them. Waking Artorius, he gestured for him to follow. Brunhilda was in the kitchen bent over a bubbling cauldron, their son asleep in a basket on the table. Reverting to her natural tongue, she looked straight at Artorius.

'First you must promise that you will not return to my village till the time is right, and only you will know when that is. My mother sent a message ahead of you.'

Artorius nodded with deep trepidation.

'Your lady and child will be safe; her wolves will protect her. The fates await you in Rome, and there you will make the choice that is right for you. Gigantrex fears Rosevetha and my mother for what they see. Your friendship with Gigantrex is finished. He will do anything to have what he desires. Don't forget this – your life may depend on it.'

'What fate are you talking of?' demanded Artorius.

'I don't possess second sight, so I can't tell you any more.'

Artorius' brain was exploding with prophecies and he wanted to scream in frustration at not understanding them. Head down, he joined the others, who were devouring their breakfast. Drusus looked at Artorius, who shrugged his shoulders. Within the hour, the remaining members of the group left, with Paulinus pledging his assistance if required.

The ride to Augusta Praetoria was a forced affair. Artorius was deep in thought as his horse ran with the rest undirected. Augustinian led the party to the rear of his inn, where a red-headed female dressed in a short shift and wearing a bow over her shoulder appeared from his stables like the goddess Diana. He tried to leap from his horse, stumbled and fell at the female's feet, much to her delight.

'You are obviously pleased to see me?' said the female, looking down at Augustinian. His friends howled with laughter, even Artorius.

'This is Velda, my partner,' said Augustinian as he stood up and brushed himself down.

'Partner only because you're too scared to marry me. Have you finished playing soldiers? You still have an inn, thanks to me. You can repay me in the usual way later.' Velda winked.

'Time to settle down,' he replied, slipping an arm around her.

Velda took hold of Augustinian firmly, pressing her lips tightly to his. The effect was all too obvious to the onlookers and, taking his hand, she led the way through the rear door. Copious amounts of locally brewed beer and a poor appetite did little to lift Artorius' growing depression.

He was grumpy and hungover when Drusus tried to rally him the following morning with cold water. Drusus felt for the situation Artorius found himself in, but he knew Artorius needed to restart his life with his family in Rome.

At Vercelum, Tresus was pleased to find his inn busy on their arrival, mostly with soldiers in various states of dress. Slipping into the kitchen, Tresus found Ingrid humming to herself as she prepared vegetables.

'You sound happy. Didn't miss me then?'

She turned, laughing at the shock on Tresus' face when

he saw that a bulging stomach was now in place on his once-slim partner.

'How long have you known?' he asked.

'About the time you left, I wasn't sure.'

Tresus scooped Ingrid into his arms, beaming with joy.

In the bar, Drusus was verbally berating Artorius, who sat with his head in his hands, looking like a broken man. Seeing Tresus and Ingrid entering the room, Drusus nudged Artorius, who looked up to see another happy couple.

Artorius stood, pushing his shoulders back, and greeted Ingrid. 'I am sorry I am the cause of you losing your man for so long; you obviously needed him. Your first?' he enquired.

'Yes. You have children?' she replied.

'Congratulations. I had four, but now three.' Pain etched Artorius' face. 'Some of your best wine to celebrate your pregnancy,' he ordered.

'Suppose I'd better make an honest woman out of you?' suggested Tresus.

'If I'd known it would take a baby, I'd have had one sooner,' said Ingrid, grinning.

'We practised hard enough,' said Tresus without thinking. His ear stung as Ingrid cuffed him.

'Food with our best wine?' suggested Ingrid.

Tresus implored her to rest, but the look she gave him said it all.

'I can cope. I have done these past months while you've been playing soldiers,' she said sharply.

Artorius and Drusus discussed their journey south. Tresus offered to travel with them, an offer which was graciously declined. Memories played heavily on Drusus and Artorius until, with a near-empty inn, Tresus and

Ingrid joined them.

*

Artorius stepped out into the cold morning air, stretching his sore and aching joints. He suddenly felt old. For the first time, he understood how Lictus had felt before his untimely death. Amoria was waiting for his return and the plans they had made before this damned mission. The toll had been a heavy one and he owed a huge debt to all that had come in search of him.

Drawing his spatha, he took up a defensive stance. He felt like a rookie – his arms felt weak, his thrusts without any real strength, and he chided himself for being so unfit. Where was Victus, and would he be there when his son killed him, as had been prophesied? He hoped so.

The muscles in his arms stung with lack of use as he hacked into a wooden post, the reverberations shooting up his arm. He had to put Ilona and their son to the back of his mind or it would destroy Amoria and himself. Amoria must never know, she wouldn't understand – he didn't.

He struck so hard at the post that it held the spatha tight. Pulling the blade free, Artorius turned to find Drusus, who hugged him – he had been watching from the inn doorway as his cousin tortured himself. Tears threatened both before they pulled away.

'They say every man has a soul mate, but you appear to have found two. I can't comprehend how you must feel. One is your life, the other saved it. The fates have been cruel, but they will find a way to keep you all safe,' suggested Drusus.

'If Victus ever finds out about Ilona and my son, their lives won't be worth living.'

'They will be safe at Gigantrex's village, surely?' Drusus

responded.

Artorius shook his head. 'Breda sent a message to Brunhilda. She said Gigantrex dreamed of power, which I had guessed. Breda and Rosevetha will keep Ilona and my son safe, though how, I wasn't told. I was warned never to trust Gigantrex again.'

Drusus looked puzzled.

*

In Rome it was the day before the Ides of Aprilis when Marcus decided the three were ready to go in search of his father. The sun shone bright and warm, spring was well advanced, and damp mornings were a thing of the past. The plague had slowed to a dribble in its toll of death. The training days had been hard on Marcus, Tia and Cezar; today they sweated profusely from the exertion of training the staff in the corral. Taking a break, one of the staff pointed out a visitor who was watching them from the estate track. Marcus and Tia slipped away from the group to meet the man on a mule who was now approaching.

'He looks familiar, but I can't place him,' said Marcus to Tia as he walked forward, reaching over his shoulder to grasp the pommels of his twin swords.

Tia slipped her bow from her shoulder, holding it across her chest. It was then that Marcus noticed Tia's breasts had grown and her clothing was tighter. She looked more rounded, even more desirable.

'It's Gorax!' they said simultaneously, looking at each other.

Marcus drew his twin swords and Tia slipped an arrow from her pouch, laying it across her bow. Gorax reined in his mule a short distance from the couple. Climbing clumsily off it, he looked as fit and mean as their last encounter. He raised his arms and turned a full circle, showing he carried no weapons.

'What are you doing here, Gorax? You were told never to return to Rome,' said Marcus sharply.

'Young master, I come in peace. I need to talk to your father to repay a debt,' said Gorax, bowing to the couple.

'My father is missing in the north after he was ambushed, but we believe he is alive,' answered Marcus.

'Who runs the estate then, your mother?' enquired Gorax.

'I do. My mother died of the plague,' stated Marcus.

'The damned plague took my son, and my wife died in childbirth as well. I work when I can in a gladiatorial school in Ostia. I promised your father I would keep him informed about Victus,' related Gorax.

'I need to find my father first, but where is Victus?' asked Marcus.

'He has recently returned and is living outside Rome. I don't know exactly where yet, but he's currying favour with Caligula through old links. I owe your father and yourself, who spoke out for me. My sword is yours when the time is right, and till then I will track him. I have nothing left in life except to see Victus dead.'

Marcus took Tia to one side. 'If he is free, we have lost staff and he would be a great asset, especially for the security of the estate.'

'Can we trust him?' asked Tia, looking deep into Marcus' eyes.

'Why would he come with this news now? Even if he feels he owes us a favour, it says a lot for him. He has nothing left in his life. We could give him a reason for living and reap the reward,' Marcus said.

'You think beyond your age; you would make a great leader. I agree.' Tia slipped her arm around Marcus and the couple faced Gorax together.

'Are you tied to the gladiatorial school?' enquired Marcus.

'I have an open contract with them, I could leave at any time. Why?' asked Gorax expectantly.

'We have lost staff to the plague and need to replace them. We need free men who will work and, if need be, give their lives for the family and the estate. All of our staff are now free,' Marcus informed him.

'I watched you practise your staff, I am impressed, and for your family to release your slaves says a lot for them. I would be honoured to join your staff.'

Marcus called Georgiakis and spoke to him about Gorax. Georgiakis agreed that if he could be trusted he would be an asset.

'Georgiakis will continue to run the estate, but in matters of security and defence, Gorax, you will have the lead. If there are any problems, then bring them to me. Are you two happy with those conditions?' offered Marcus.

'I am honoured by the offer and would be a fool to refuse,' Gorax said, offering his hand to Marcus then Georgiakis.

'One final thing. If anything should happen to me, Tia will take control of the estate. We are riding north with my friend Cezar to find my father and in the meantime, any problems should be addressed to Aaron. If Aaron requires a bodyguard, Gorax, I would ask that you offer yourself,' insisted Marcus.

'Your wish is my command,' replied Gorax, bowing.

'In that case, welcome to the family. Come and meet everyone,' insisted Marcus and Tia in unison.

As everyone ate, Gorax remarked at how well the estate ran and that everyone was an equal. Marcus brushed the comment aside, stating it was the way his grandfather had always wanted things and that, unfortunately, he never lived to see it, thanks to Victus. At mention of the trip to Rome, Gorax offered himself as bodyguard to the young couple, though Marcus assured him that they would be safe.

## Chapter 13

Marcus and Tia had set out for Rome full of the joys of spring. The birds sang and they talked of a visit to see Hades as they rode towards Rome from the estate.

'Are you able to say where we might look for my father, as you see so much?' enquired Marcus.

'My dreams show only a woman and her pack of wolves surrounding your father,' stated Tia.

'I trust you implicitly, but still, I pray to the gods you are right,' replied Marcus.

'I do too,' Tia added.

Slipping across the Tiberis, the couple went in search of Aaron and Rachel. Rachel was at their jewellery stall, soaking up the sun and oblivious to being watched by the couple. Marcus slipped up behind her and tapped her shoulder, startling her enough that she fell off her seat. Rachel chastised him before throwing her arms around him. She went to do the same to Tia, but momentarily faltered, a pause missed by Marcus.

'Do you have something to tell me, pretty one?' asked Rachel, placing her hand on Tia's stomach. 'Well?'

'What do you mean? How does everyone know? Amoria guessed before she passed.' 'How long?' enquired Rachel.

'Dorina's friend said about two months, and no, Marcus doesn't know yet,' replied Tia.

'I think he needs to know before you travel north,' insisted Rachel.

'He'll try to talk me out of the trip, but I need to be with him. I will tell him when we are travelling, he won't send me back then,' responded Tia.

'What are you two whispering about, and where's Aaron?' asked Marcus.

'He said he'd meet you at the tenement a little after midday.' Rachel smiled.

'We'll return with Aaron later; is there anything you need?'

Rachel waved the request away as Marcus and Tia walked their horses toward the Aventine. Life had returned to the city after Sejanus's execution, his family's slaughter and the end of the plague. The vendors seemed to shout louder than ever and the streets seemed cleaner. *Perhaps in the aftermath of the plague someone thought to clean things up*, Marcus thought. The smithy was still there, but was preparing to leave for Ostia to help his sister, who had lost her husband. Marcus secured a cart from him to move their belongings from the tenement to the estate before it was sold. New neighbours had already replaced the old ones and they looked to be of dubious origins.

Marcus was glad that his Aventine home was to be sold. It seemed like a lifetime since they had visited the tenement, and a thick layer of dust covered everything. Marcus wrote endearments in it for Tia, much to her amusement. They both started packing with the best of intentions, but each box and cupboard revealed a memory that weighed heavy on them both. A simple job became a heart-breaking task. Tia fought back the tears as she watched rivulets of them run down Marcus' face. She needed to lift him. Was this the time to tell him of his intended fatherhood? Gritting her teeth and wiping away her own tears, Tia took Marcus' hand and sat him down.

'We need to finish this before Aaron arrives,' he said weakly.

'No, sit. I have something very important to tell you. We have been together some time now and my head still spins from where I was to where I am now. I love you, as

I've said so many times before, like no other, which makes me so proud to tell you that we are expecting a baby.' Tia placed Marcus' hand on her stomach.

His mouth dropped open in shock, which frightened Tia until that beaming smile she loved filled his face. He lifted her off the floor, swinging her round as best he could in the space around them.

'How? Marcus asked.

'Do you really want to know, words or pictures?' she said, laughing.

'I thought you were taking something?' Marcus asked, and Tia's face dropped.

'Don't be sad, I can't believe how lucky I am. How long?' Marcus kissed Tia passionately as tears of joy rolled down her face.

'About two months. Your mother guessed before she died, but I had to be sure,' Tia stated. 'Are you able to travel north? You could always stay and look after the estate?' Marcus suggested.

'I'll be okay to travel; I'll just have to be careful.'

Marcus hugged Tia so tight, and so wrapped up in each other were they that they didn't hear an unwelcome visitor enter the tenement.

'Very touching, the whore and the whelp,' the voice snapped.

Tia's eyes flew open. In front of her, over Marcus' shoulder, was Victus. The hairs on Marcus' neck stood on end at the sound of the voice, and he pushed Tia away from him. Spinning around, he reached for his double swords. He was just in time; Victus had already levelled a doublehanded blow at his head. One sword was blocked by two as Marcus pushed the single blade backwards. Victus tried desperately to hold his ground, but found himself sliding across the dusty floor. His blade slipped downward as he slid under the two blades, striking at Marcus' calves with a freshly drawn pugio. Marcus spun one blade to block the pugio while the second blade sliced down at Victus.

Victus stumbled away from the attack, but Marcus' blades whipped through the space he had occupied – his sword was no match for the finely-honed weapons that Marcus wielded. Victus worked his way around the room, trying to reach the door. Seeing Tia without a weapon, he feinted at her, distracting Marcus. His blade sliced at Marcus, cutting across the skin of his stomach. Tia screamed, thinking Marcus was seriously injured. She drew her own knife and threw it at Victus, who swept it aside. Marcus lunged at Victus, who blocked the blades, spinning away.

Seeing Tia undefended and with nowhere to go, Victus stabbed his sword towards her, revenge etching his face. She rolled away, colliding with the wall in the confined space. Two blades spun once more at Victus, who desperately tried to block them with his sword and a stool whilst manoeuvring around the room, his back against the wall. Victus found Tia to his right, still dazed, and stabbed at her, his blade sliding easily between her ribs and into her chest. Shock and horror filled Tia's face as Victus ripped the blade free. Blood poured from the wound and she clutched at it helplessly.

Marcus' scream shattered the air when he saw what had happened, and his blades lashed out in a mad frenzy towards Victus. Tears of love and rage trickled from Marcus' eyes. Tia sat crumpled against the wall, blood pouring from her fatal wound.

Marcus stood trembling before Victus. A red mist of rage filled his whole being, and the two swords were strong in his hands as he stood over the dying body of his first love. Blood trickled from the cut across his stomach. It wasn't deep. It didn't matter anyway now.

Victus edged towards an open door and his escape, desperately fending Marcus off. Pieces of wood flew from the stool held by Victus as Marcus' blades hacked at it until one lodged itself and wouldn't move. The second blade sliced at Victus' head, the tip of the blade scratching his face. Marcus discarded the other sword and the stool in which it was embedded. His remaining sword spun in circles, slicing at Victus' undefended arm. Victus paid dearly for his slow reactions; he instinctively raised his arm as the blade sliced sideward. Two of his fingers flew and he screamed in pain, hammering his blade at Marcus.

Blade smashed into blade, and sparks flew where they met. Victus struck out in a life-or-death frenzy as blood dripped from his hand. Marcus stepped back, slicing low at Victus' legs, only to be blocked. A sound distracted Marcus – was Tia still alive? Victus saw his chance to escape and slipped through the door, slamming it shut behind him. Marcus dropped to the floor beside Tia, her eyes still open, but the pool of blood she lay in was growing rapidly. Marcus leaned forward, Victus forgotten, as blood bubbled from Tia's mouth.

'I've always loved you.' Tears ran freely from Marcus' eyes as he cradled Tia's head.

'And I've always loved you too,' she whispered, then she was gone.

Marcus traced the blood line on his stomach and, touching the bloodstained fingers to his lips, he tasted the iron in it. He grimaced, remembering Victus, and he stood, flinging the door open and carefully peering out. There was nothing but a sole rider with his head down driving his horse through the human tide in the street. It was too late. There would be another day, then revenge!

His heart was full of grief as he returned to his love. Sitting on the floor, he cradled her to him for the last time, wiping the blood from her lips, and he kissed her as he always had. He heard a 'thank you' and, looking down, he knew she had gone.

Two fingers lay on the floor. Victus was marked for life if he survived. *May the gods let him live so that I can take revenge*, thought Marcus. His head dropped forward as the spasms of grief struck home. He didn't want to live any more, but he had to, to find his father and see Victus die. 'Holy God, what's happened here?' asked Aaron at the tenement door.

Marcus lifted his head, acknowledging Aaron, then his head dropped again to gaze upon Tia. Clutching her tight, he rocked back and forward.

'Marcus, who did this?' demanded Aaron.

'Victus!' he spat.

'Where is he?' enquired Aaron.

'Love has died in me. I will live each day till I kill the bastard who took Tia and our child away,' Marcus snapped.

'A child? Tia was pregnant? I didn't know,' replied Aaron sympathetically.

'Nor I, till moments ago,' answered Marcus. 'Aaron, watch her body for a few moments.'

Marcus disappeared, emptying the half-full cart into the street, much to the amazement of the passers-by. Returning to the tenement, he scooped up Tia's body, carrying it to the cart where he lay her gently, her bow and pouch across the fatal wound.

'Aaron, sell the tenement and its contents and use the money for the estate. I am taking my love home.'

The journey back to the estate was slow, Marcus talking to Tia as if she were alive beside him as tears rolled

116

freely from his eyes. Travellers stared at the strange young man talking to himself till the cart passed, then they understood, shaking their heads.

Gorax was the first to see Marcus driving a cart on his own and raised the alarm. Marcus didn't notice Gorax, the horse and cart plodding on towards the open gate as the staff ran towards him. Marcus was still talking to Tia as he wound his way through the gate. Georgiakis took the reins, slowing the cart to a halt, and peering into its rear he recoiled at the sight of Tia covered in blood. Cezar looked on, hoping that what he already feared to be true wouldn't be so. Cezar walked away, unable to watch, as tears trickled down his face. Tears he had never shed even for his parents, tears of heartbreak for his friends.

Marcus lifted Tia gently in his arms.

'Master Marcus, let us take her,' Georgiakis and Lucretia asked simultaneously.

'She is mine to care for,' Marcus snapped unintentionally, walking past the pair towards the house.

As he walked past Dorina she screamed, though it was unheard by Marcus. Placing Tia down on their love nest, he returned to the kitchen, where he found Dorina sobbing at the table. Scooping hot water from a cauldron into a bowl, he returned to the bedroom. Marcus stripped Tia's blood-soaked clothes from her and sponged the clotted blood from the fatal wound. He laid his head on her swollen stomach that had housed their child, his tears of grief started again, turning to sobs as he lay beside her.

Lucretia stood in the doorway, afraid to say anything that might destroy their last moments together. She had never seen a love like theirs and she envied them. She walked away, pleading with all who asked to give them space. Tears filled the eyes of all, and hardly a word was spoken. Dorina offered to take Marcus a meal, then sat back down and cried. Gorax couldn't believe that one person could mean so much to everyone and sat on the outside of the group craving their closeness. The question on his mind as was everyone else's: what had happened?

No one slept that night. The screams emanating from Marcus' room were unnatural, almost animalistic, and furniture was thrown, smashing against the walls. Cezar wanted to go to his friend but couldn't, sharing some of his grief.

The morning was cold and dull when Gorax decided he needed to approach Marcus. On reaching the doorway to the room, he looked in. It was full of matchwood that was previously furniture. The only piece standing was the bed on which Tia lay in her best clothes, her bow held in her hands on her chest. She looked asleep, defeating death's face. Marcus was collapsed on the floor, laying in his own wine-induced vomit, a flagon smashed beside him. Gorax entered the room, climbing over the debris, and seeing water in a bowl, he threw it over Marcus who shuddered awake. He looked up through red, hate-filled swollen eyes.

'What do you want?' he demanded sharply.

'I know how you feel; I know what it's like to lose everything,' stated Gorax.

'How can you know how I feel? I should have killed him, I couldn't even protect the one I loved,' spat Marcus.

'Who should you have killed?' enquired Gorax.

'Victus, of course, but I have scarred him further. I am killing him piece by piece.' Marcus laughed maniacally, producing two fingers from a pouch on his belt.

Gorax lifted Marcus from the floor, pulling him close. Marcus struggled then collapsed on to him. Gorax carried him outside, dumping him in a trough of cold water and leaving him coughing and spluttering.

'Now go and change. You need to celebrate your love's life, and in style. I know that's what you really want,' ordered Gorax.

With water dripping from him, Marcus staggered back to his room, appalled at what he saw. Tia lay sleeping in death's grip, as white as snow. He touched her face. Her skin was cold and lifeless; it was then that he knew where he would scatter her ashes. Dressed, he returned to the kitchen where the staff had gathered. No one knew what to say, though their faces said it all.

'We have a final act to honour the one I loved,' said Marcus.

'We loved her dearly as well,' answered staff around him, many with tear-filled eyes.

'Thank you for those kind words. Let us prepare her pyre. Let us send her off in the style of her tribe, then Lucretia, we will take her ashes to the lake and to Hades.'

'Perfect, she would have loved that,' said Lucretia, struggling to hold back her tears.

The sun had reached its highest point in the sky as Marcus solely cradled his love to her pyre. Gently he laid her on top, slipped her bow from his shoulders, placing it alongside her, and taking her sword from his belt he kissed the blade before placing it in her hands. He kissed her one final time as he fought back the tears.

Marcus spoke of the special lady before them and how she had touched everyone's lives and now, with child, she was taken from them. There was a collective intake of breath at the mention of a child. All control collapsed, man and woman alike couldn't hold back any longer. Gorax was reminded of his own wife, taken in childbirth, and strong as he was he brushed aside the tears.

Dorina held a firebrand from the house. Marcus reached out for it and, drawing himself to his full height, he stepped forward, plunging it into the pyre.

'Goodbye, my love, I will never forget you. May our child grow with you?' Marcus stepped back as the flames exploded around the pyre.

A lone eagle circled above and called out to its partner, with no response. Marcus saluted in homage. A feast like no other was enjoyed in honour of a great woman and Artorius' best wine toasted a warrior queen. Cezar, struggling with his own emotions, took Marcus to one side.

'Marcus, I have a confession to make. I may have implied that Tia and I had a relationship in the past, but it's a lie.'

'You don't have to lie to make me feel better on this day,' replied Marcus.

'But it is true. We were good friends, nothing more, I am still a virgin. You were her one and only love, a love I am so envious of. If I ever find anyone half as good as Tia, I will be a very happy man.'

'Thank you for those kind words, though they make my loss even deeper,' said Marcus, hugging Cezar to him, and sharing tears to a lost friend.

## Chapter 14

Using his papers, Artorius acquired horses for Drusus and himself from the mutations as they continued south. The first hour of night had passed as the two rode into Placentia and the welcoming arms of Helga. Artorius made himself scarce in the bar with a jug of wine. Magda joined Artorius at his table, and he noticed that all eyes watched the dark-haired, green-eyed shapely young woman, oblivious to the attention, as she sat beside him.

'I am told you have a son about my age. What are his weapon skills like? I was brought up to use a sword and bow.'

'He was taught by my father's foreman, an ex-gladiator, to fight with two swords. His girlfriend Tia is a Scythian ex-slave and she taught him to use a bow. As a couple, they are formidable opponents,' responded Artorius.

'He has a girlfriend then?' Magda's mood changed noticeably.

'If he didn't have Tia, I am sure you would be well matched,' offered Artorius, though Magda didn't reply.

Brushing talk of Marcus aside, Magda enquired about Rome, a place she dreamed of visiting. Artorius talked of its glory, its sordid and sinister sides, which didn't appear to dissuade Magda from her wishes.

'Does the plague happen often in Rome?' she asked.

'Strange question, what made you ask that?' enquired Artorius.

'Travellers have spoken of it being particularly bad this year.'

'It comes and goes, some years worse than others. It's the result of the swamps surrounding the river Tiberis and poor living conditions in parts of the city.'

'Is the Tiberis as big as the Rhenus?'

Artorius nodded. The Spring sicknesses were always a worry to him, being so far from home. Once again, his thoughts turned to how much he missed his family, and his need to return. These feelings crashed when Magda asked how he had survived, and once more images of Ilona, with the beautiful smile he loved, filled his head. He had gone silent without realising until Drusus reappeared with a fresh jug of wine.

'I see Magda has kept you company; she is a likeable and skilled young lady and is like a daughter to me. It's a shame your son has someone. From what you said, they would be well suited. I am sure she will find a man, but he'll have to face my approval. I know you will be the same with my nieces Verina and Alia?' smiled Drusus.

'I certainly will be. Magda has just informed me of a bad plague in Rome.'

'Yes, Helga mentioned it too. I hadn't intended to say anything, but she said the death toll in the Aventine has been high. One of the soldiers heading north mentioned that the second most senior Praetorian had died of it.'

Drusus called out to Helga, who appeared at the kitchen door looking flustered. 'Was there any mention of the senior Praetorian's name, the one who died?'

Helga shook her head.

'Honori, or something like that,' interjected Magda.

'Honorus?' suggested Artorius.

'Could have been.'

'Honorus was my supporting link into the Praetorians. I wonder if Macro will keep to his promise to make me Primus Pila of the 1st Century, 1st Cohort of the Praetorians? I must prepare myself for whatever happens, and I won't step down without a fight,' stated Artorius.

Helga and Magda fetched some food for the men and then left them to their own counsel. Drusus tried to talk to Artorius about his situation, and it was with a heavy heart that Artorius struggled with his emotions – especially after what Helga had told him. The alcohol fuelled his growing depression and he begged solitude, slipping away to his room and into an uneasy sleep.

His mother, father, Amoria and Alia appeared before him, and Artorius wondered what this could mean. Collectively they were telling him to hurry home. He eventually slipped into a heavy, but troubled sleep.

\*

Marcus had kept vigil at the pyre till all that was left were ashes. Thrusting his twin swords into the earth, he knelt in front of the embers. Cezar watched from the side lines, craving a love like theirs.

'If it takes my whole life, I will avenge your death,' pledged Marcus, collecting the remaining ashes in a prized family urn that was fit for a warrior queen.

'Remember me as you loved me, not as a reason for revenge,' said a voice from behind, and turning, Marcus saw Tia in all her glory, smiling, with a child in her arms. He reached out to touch her as she blew him a kiss and vanished.

'Tia, don't leave me,' Marcus pleaded.

A firm hand touched Marcus on his shoulder, bringing him back to the moment.

'Marcus, the staff have asked to travel with you to scatter Tia's ashes if they may, as a sign of love and respect,' stated Georgiakis.

'Thank you, but we must leave some to protect the estate. With Victus still about, though with further injuries, I suspect he will go into hiding again. Gorax would be my pick to remain and oversee the estate. The choice is yours to stay or come with the staff.'

'I will speak to the staff and I will leave a strong team with Gorax,' said Georgiakis, bowing to Marcus.

It was the first hour of day. The ground was wet with dew and the air heavy with the solemnity of the task ahead as the staff assembled. Marcus stepped forward with the urn and placed it into a saddle bag on Tia's horse. Everyone either rode or mounted the cart, leaving a strong contingent behind with Gorax.

It was a slow, snaking trail of mourners that left the estate and headed for Lucretia's village, the lake and Hades; barely a word was spoken throughout. Lucretia spoke to her father on their arrival at her village, before the group resumed their journey to the lake. It was late afternoon, the sun shimmering off the placid waters, but there was not a sight or sound of Hades or his herd. Marcus called out as loud as he could, without response. His heart dropped that he would scatter Tia's ashes to the wind without Hades present.

'Hades!'

Everyone looked around for the source of the voice – was it the wind? Across the lake, a single black horse appeared, rearing on to its hind legs before racing out of sight. Moments later, breaking free of the trees, he raced at the gathered group. Hades skidded to a halt in front of Marcus, showering him with dirt, then reared high above him. Marcus had no fear of him anymore.

Hades walked towards Marcus, nudging him with his head.

'Yes, Hades, she is gone, but her spirit will always be here with you.' Marcus reached out to touch the creature's head.

Hades dropped his forelegs to the floor, and a tear filled each eye as he considered Marcus' face, who shared his tears. The gathered group stood in awe of the scene, Cezar bemused at the way the great horse was acting. Hades rose to its full height and walked alongside Marcus to the lakeside. Saying a prayer to his forefathers' gods, Marcus opened the urn. Hades nudged Marcus again. He stroked the horse's mane then scattered the ashes on to the lake.

'You were stolen from the great plains and I give you this as your final resting place, with Hades to watch over you the rest of his days. I love you, Tia,' Marcus murmured, fighting back the tears.

The peace was broken by a strong gust of wind. 'Thank you,' it whispered. The gathered group looked at each other in shock.

Hades reared on to his hind legs, and crashing back to the floor, he pawed at the ground. The group stood, each with their long and short memories as the sun slid down behind the trees.

Marcus led the way back to the cart and horses, accompanied by Hades. As they all remounted to return home, Hades laid his head-on Marcus' lap, gazing up one last time into the young man's eyes, before turning and galloping away.

'Who does that horse belong to?' said Cezar, incredulous at what he had seen.

'Firstly Marcus' grandfather, then Tia – the only two to ride him. I doubt anyone, ever will again,' said Lucretia.

*

Artorius could hear his name being called and felt someone shaking him. His eyes were open, but his brain couldn't comprehend where he was.

'Artorius, are you all right? You were shouting in your sleep.' Drusus bent over him, his face troubled, holding a lamp.

Peter Baggott

Artorius recognised his cousin and forced himself back into reality. He sat on the cot edge and looked around the room as Drusus offered him water, which was cold and welcoming. Artorius related his nightmares, and with talk of a particularly bad plague in Rome, his thoughts had turned to the warnings he had been given by Rosevetha and Breda.

Drusus was unable to offer solace or advice, but over breakfast he made a suggestion. Having spoken to Helga, he thought to ask Ilona and Rosevetha to move to Placentia. Artorius mentioned the wolves, but not to be put off, Drusus suggested there may even be a way around that.

Once again, the battle between Amoria and Ilona took over Artorius' mind... Would it ever be settled for all concerned? Thanking Drusus and Helga, he said he would think on it. Having already taken up Drusus' offer of hospitality for a further night, Artorius took some air.

He stumbled his way through streets that reminded him of the Aventine – a small market with stallholders, making what they could to survive. Finding a fountain, he sat and drank deep of the cold waters, watching the populace go about their business. He reflected that their lives must be so uncomplicated compared to his, and he tried to come to terms with what he had to do. Returning to the inn, Artorius found Drusus, Helga and Magda deep in conversation. He needed a drink, but his spirits sank with each emptied beaker until Drusus appeared in front of him with a piping hot bowl of meaty smelling stew.

'The rabbit is courtesy of Magda, she thought you might enjoy it,' Drusus answered the unasked question. 'Because you insist on my remaining here, Magda has asked to accompany you to Rome. She is an exceptional warrior and I wouldn't hesitate to have her accompanying me, if I were travelling alone.'

'I don't know her, and do you really want her in Rome?' enquired Artorius.

'It's a dream of hers and we think she will be safe with you and your family. She will be company for you on the journey and her abilities will add to your safety.'

'You have told him of Magda's request?' said Helga, appearing at the door. 'I heard your reservations, Artorius, and I'm hoping that in your care she will see Rome for what it is and will return with her thirst quenched.'

Magda stared at Artorius with a pleading look that made him smile; it was an expression he had seen many times on Verina's face.

'Against my better judgement, the company will keep me sane. Okay, if you are sure. Verina would welcome her,'

All three hugged Artorius.

Drusus held counsel over Artorius as the women began to prepare for the following day. He pledged to keep a watch on any developments and promised to remove Ilona and Rosevetha if they were at risk. With his spirits lifted and feeling more positive about his future, Artorius sought his bed and a good night's sleep.

\*

Artorius woke with a start, so deep was he in sleep, when Drusus shook him. 'Food is ready and waiting and I have had the mutatione provide you both with a fresh horse for the start of your journey.'

'Is Magda awake?' enquired Artorius.

'She is already up and waiting.'

The sky was crimson red, not a good sign as Artorius and Magda sat mounted, saying their goodbyes. Tears rolled down Helga's face as she was held tightly by Drusus.

Magda smiled and turned her horse away to hide her own tears.

Taking Drusus' hand in a firm grip, Artorius smiled at the couple. 'She'll be okay and you'll soon see her back,' he said reassuringly.

'Safe journey both,' called Drusus.

## Chapter 15

On the Civilis estate the day had dragged for the remaining staff, but Gorax kept a close watch on the surrounding countryside. The sun was dying in a blood-red sky as Gorax posted the night guard and an archer on each wall. The braziers crackled into life, but nothing stirred and an uneasiness grew amongst the staff.

\*

Victus had gathered the five surviving speculatores and they in turn brought wharf rats, persuaded with the promise of wealth in a raid on a Senators estate. Victus had been informed that only a skeleton staff remained. He was in pain from his lost fingers and it was this pain that fuelled the need to destroy everything that had the Civilis name to it. Dressed in black, six on horse, the rest in a wagon, the group headed away from Ostia Antica as the sun set, without a moon to lighten the night. Victus wanted maximum surprise as he sought out the alternative track to the estate walls, directing the wagon to the main gate.

Hobbling their horses by the river, Victus and his speculatores set off quickly and quietly on foot for the estate walls, conveniently highlighted by the braziers. The wagon turned on to the estate track, proceeding down it as directed, till they had cleared the briar.

Gorax was the first to see the wagon, but could only make out six figures and it didn't look like Marcus and the staff. The call of 'Attack!' spread around the walls.

The wagon moved slowly towards the gate on the slope before stopping. Gorax ordered a fire arrow, which arced up high before plunging into hidden straw within the cart. Ignition was instantaneous, causing bodies to leap from the vehicle. Gorex watched the horse being removed and the fully ignited wagon released towards the estate gate, followed by the six running alongside.

Victus and his colleagues slid along the estate wall unobserved, watching the fire arrow's trajectory into the cart. A rush of air above them, as bows launched death at the running males, two falling immediately and a third collapsing as the cart crashed into the gate, demolishing one side, the other left hanging. The three ran on as Victus and his speculatores edged toward the shattered gate. Three staff stepped beyond the gate with pila and round shields as a fourth runner fell, an arrow protruding from his chest.

'You three take the shield wall, the rest with me,' Victus said, leading his group.

The staff were slow to react to the foe from the side. Swords swept forward and were buried deep into the backs of the estate staff as Victus and two men entered the inner compound.

Gorax leapt from the wall into the path of Victus.

'My chance at last, you bastard,' shouted Gorax, as he swung his sword with full force and was blocked, the force knocking Victus backward into those following.

One speculatore swept around Victus and rushed at Gorax, who dropped to one knee and slashed at his target, ripping the man's stomach apart. Victus sidestepped them, making for the house and finding the door open. He entered warily to find it empty. Victus raked embers from the kitchen fire on to the floor and, finding an oil lamp, smashed it in an explosion of flames.

Egressing the house, Victus found himself facing a battle between a speculatore and a staff member. Stepping forward unobserved, he grabbed the staff member from behind, drawing his sword across the man's throat, and blood fountained over the floor as he dropped him. Victus surveyed the scene; bodies lay dead or bleeding as Gorax ran towards him covered in blood. His target was obvious: himself. One of the remaining speculatore stepped in front of Gorax, only to be swept aside by the ex-gladiator's sword buried in his ribs. Seeing his chance, Victus slipped through the broken gate as his last speculatore made a final stand. Victus slipped back along the wall, the home now an inferno, making day out of night. Taking a horse for himself, he scattered the rest and, picking his way carefully, Victus disappeared into the night.

*

Marcus' returning party had skirted around Rome, with barely a word spoken. Smoke trailed skywards from the direction of the estate and Marcus' reaction was instant, as was that of everyone on horseback, and Cezar, on his right, matched his speed. Reaching the top of the estate track, Marcus looked down the slope at the scarred remains of the villa. Bodies scattered the ground inside and outside the walls; winged death had taken its toll. One gate hung from its hinges, the other shattered by a discarded burnt-out cart. Reaching the damaged gate first, Marcus found Gorax splattered with blood and propped against the wall, surrounded by two dead.

'What happened?' enquired Marcus calmly.

'It was Victus,' replied Gorax.

'Where is he?'

'The devil protects him, he alone escaped,' Gorax responded.

Lucretia tended to Gorax with tear-filled eyes: her partner lay torn in two. Marcus touched her shoulder and looked around the estate, where only the stables stood intact. There had been little wealth left behind except the hidden pot, which Marcus recovered.

'Cremate our dead and drag the rest into no man's land and let the wild take its fill. I need to find my father, then finish Victus. Collect anything salvageable from the ruins. Looks like we're all sleeping in the barn tonight,' shouted Marcus as the rest of the staff arrived.

After a restless night and with the stench of smoke biting at their throats, everyone rose to start the task of rebuilding the estate.

*

With a sky, full of pink clouds, Victus was once again counting his blessings and cursing the Civilis family in one breath, as he settled back on to his farm over a hot wine under his assumed name. He was torn between travelling north or remaining to build on his new acquaintance with Caligula. The dust needed to settle, and so he formulated plans to return to Genua and the delicious Naomi.

## Chapter 16

The crimson dawn didn't take long to change into a fine drizzle, Artorius replenishing a horse at each mutatione. Artorius found Magda to be a bright and intelligent young woman and a good travelling companion as she taught him about the wildlife around them. Their first night was spent at a village where Magda and her sister were well known – the reception was welcoming and it was a bonus to not be sleeping in the elements, which had turned worse as the day extended.

By late afternoon of the following day, the pair reached Bonnia, where Artorius seconded two horses for the next day with a small bribe. Entering the Stag Inn, Artorius found it noisy but not very busy. As Magda entered, she was exposed to the lecherous looks of the clientele, but she was oblivious to them. Artorius mentally noted the looks and decided that a change of dress was necessary as two young females – obviously prostitutes – looked Magda up and down with contempt. Artorius sat by the door and laid his spatha on the table, sheathed, as a warning.

A grey-haired male, almost bent double, hobbled towards them. 'Welcome, Centurion, which legion do you hail from?'

'The best – the 2$^{nd}$ Augusta, of course,' Artorius answered with pride.

'A fine legion, and one I served in as a Centurion myself until I damaged my back and was left for dead. Here I am alive and still enjoying life. What can I do for you and your slave?'

Artorius felt his hackles rise at the implication and spat his response in anger. 'Why do you assume that a young female travelling with a soldier is automatically a slave?

My *cousin's daughter* is travelling with me to Rome. You will treat her with respect or you will see the point of my spatha at your throat.'

'Call her what you want, we are all men of the world,' replied the innkeeper.

The table was propelled forward as Artorius rose, drawing his weapon in anger. Grabbing the innkeeper's throat, he placed the point under the man's jaw, where it drew droplets of blood.

Magda stood nearby, awestruck, not comprehending the situation. 'Uncle, what is it that has so enraged you?' she asked, laying her hand on his arm.

Artorius felt his mood subside as Magda pulled his spatha from the man's throat. Artorius released his grip on the innkeeper and scanned the room for any movement: there was none.

The innkeeper slipped to the floor, choking. He looked up into Artorius' face. 'I am sorry. It is rare to find a man, let alone a soldier, with such morals these days. May we start again?' He offered his hand to be assisted to his feet.

Artorius hesitated at first, then helped the man up. 'I am also sorry; my anger lives on a short leash these days. I have two daughters, one of similar age, and it makes my blood boil to see them offered for a piece of copper. We need good food and a drink. Do you have two rooms together?'

'You will have the best of the rabbit stew and my own wine. However, your niece would be safer sharing your room. I can move a cot from one of the other rooms if you like?'

'If that is the safest option, thank you,' responded Artorius.

'The room is free to a man after my own heart. I'll bring

the food and wine.'

'What was all that?' snapped Magda after the innkeeper had hobbled away. 'You told Drusus and my sister that I would be safe with you!'

Artorius explained it all to an angry Magda, who flushed red as she tried to cover herself with his sagum, suddenly so aware of how the clientele were looking at her. She looked around the room, and everyone looking tried to hide the fact and turned away sharply.

'You have a lot to learn before we reach Rome. This is little more than a large village. Rome, on the other hand, will crush you.'

'Is your son noble like you?' asked Magda.

'I believe so.'

'Tia is very lucky then,' she replied.

Artorius explained how the two young lovers had met, and how Marcus' grandfather had paid for Tia's freedom at his grandson's request. Magda had only ever known one Roman: Drusus. The others she had come across tried to buy her attention with false offers and cheap baubles, and then tried to grope her. Magda's response had always been the same – the lightning production of her knife, which always had an instant response. She had always thought she could protect herself, but could she? This wasn't the enclosed world of Drusus' inn or Placentia any more.

The room was clean but spartan, and the two cots were better than Artorius had expected with the blankets barely used. Placing his cot across the door, he oversaw Magda, who slept well, whereas he woke at the slightest sound as he slept with his spatha in hand.

*

Morning came all too quickly as a tap on the door heralded an early rise. Magda woke to the sound of

Artorius sliding his cot from the door, and she clearly noticed the lack of sleep on his tired face. A mix of warm milk and oats awaited the pair, washed down with warmed wine. The innkeeper once again apologizing for the previous evening's assumptions by providing travelling victuals for the pair.

Artorius purchased a pair of riding trousers, acquired from some old military stock, for Magda. Despite the trousers, Magda's looks still caught the attention of every full-blooded male, which she shrugged off with a grimace. Artorius was warming to the young lady accompanying him, and in so many ways he saw a lot of Tia in her.

The pair set off at a brisk pace, Artorius aiming to make Florentia by the first hours of night. Magda's eyes were everywhere and her questions flowed as they headed south with frequent changes of horses that added to the speed of their travel. She was like a child, awestruck with the newness of her surroundings.

The pair cantered into Florentia for an overnight stop as the lanterns swayed from their holdings in the third hour of night. They travelled more leisurely the following day, and Artorius watched as Magda killed two hares with the expertise he had seen in Tia.

Reaching a small and insignificant village shortly afterwards, Artorius went in search of shelter and they were offered space in a small barn. The hares didn't go unnoticed by the farmer's wife, and after negotiation they were cooked and shared in the warmth of the farmer's home to the delight of all. Artorius marvelled at the simplicity of their lives compared to his father's estate outside Rome, whereas Magda melted amongst the farmer's children. Leaving the following morning, they were provided with fresh thin bread and cheese from the farm. Artorius slipped a sestertius into the smiling farmer's hand as he shook it.

\*

Marcus walked out into still smoke-filled air on a new day, Cezar and a recovering Gorax accompanying him. Dew covered the ground, the Civilis villa was a skeleton of its former beauty, but Marcus knew it would rise from the ashes. Tia was his dominant thought. He wanted – no, needed – revenge, but at what cost?

'Georgiakis, I need to start the search for my father. Aaron will take care of you all and I will see you on my return, if the gods will it.'

'May I come with you as far as my village, as my man is dead?' asked Lucretia.

'It would be our pleasure to escort you,' replied Marcus.

Marcus stood straight and tall; two blades crossed his back and his bow slid easily between them.

Would he return? Did he want to return? Finding the truth about his father's fate would determine that.

The four mounted amid sad farewells walking their horses through the damaged gates as the sun shared its warmth with the new day. Marcus cast a look back at what had been his grandfather's villa. The mists from the river rolled over it, obscuring the scarred wreck from view. His party topped the hill, approaching one of Rome's arteries, and a lone eagle launched itself into the air in front of him, calling as it flew. In the distance, a second eagle responded and soon the two of them were circling overhead.

It was the signal Marcus wanted, and nodding to his group, he led his horse forward and broke into a trot. The group were soon galloping across the Tiberis via the Pons Aemilius towards the Forum, and Aaron.

## Chapter 17

At the third hour of day, a single horse entered the track to the Civilis estate. The rider was middle-aged and his clothing was smart and clean, speaking of time and rank in the legions. A vexillum hung on his belt alongside a trophy spatha as his mount trotted down the slope. Stopping briefly, he surveyed the estate with its burnt-out villa – *therein lies a story*, he thought. A bell tolled as he got closer. Damaged gates lay before him, as did a group armed with pila and shield. Stopping his horse ten paces distant, he hailed the group.

'I've come to speak to Gorax, I believe he may be here?'

Georgiakis stepped forward. 'Gorax and the young master left earlier to travel north and I don't know when he will return. Can I help?'

'I owe Gorax a favour. He was trying to find an ex-Praetorian known as Victus Claudian, and I've come with information.'

'As I said, he's left. The damages you see is due to Victus Claudian. I believe there is a warrant for his arrest for treason – you could take this information to the Castra Praetoria.'

'Thank you, I will.' The horse was turned and began to trot away.

*

A short time later, a straight-backed causarius limped slowly up the hill towards the Castra Praetoria, the honours on his belt glistened in the midday sun. He stared up at the gates before him, wishing he was still a part of Rome's greatness: the Legions. A guard stepped towards him.

'I need to see Macro. I have information on the whereabouts of the treasonous Victus Antonius

Claudian.'

'Guard Commander?'

A squarely built Optio appeared from the gatehouse. The vexillum was the first thing the officer saw. The guard spoke to his superior in a whisper, who in turn extended his hand in greeting to the visitor.

'Victus Claudian is still wanted for murder, but more importantly, for treason. Macro is currently occupied with his new friend, Caligula, and you would be kept waiting all day. Can I pass on your information rather than have you wait?'

'Victus Claudian is living on the old olive farm just past the first mutatione on the Pisae road from Ostia. It sits high on a hill overlooking the coast, and the only way to get to it without being seen is via a goat track from the beach below. He lives alone.' The causarius looked at the Optio, saluted, turned, and limped away, his duty done.

The Optio scurried away into the administrative building and Macro's outer office, where he collided with the senior clerk who tried to block his progress. Fortunately, Macro's office door opened as the heated discussion was taking place, and Macro stepped out. The Optio insisted he had information of the highest level for Macro's ears only, and was ushered into an empty office.

Macro's face lit up at the mention of Victus' name, the only man he believed was outstanding from Sejanus' conspiracy. When asked for the source of the information, the Optio could only say that it came from a causarius bearing a vexillum.

'Fetch our best two speculatores to assess the location before we take Victus Claudian alive at last,' requested Macro, smiling as he wrung his hands.

The Optio marched briskly away to find the required speculatores, and having briefed them, they immediately left the barracks incognito.

\*

Aaron and Rachel were deep in discussion as Marcus' group approached slowly through the growing throng of the populace. It was Rachel who saw the group first, her face filled with foreboding.

Slipping from his horse, Marcus hugged Rachel whilst Aaron's eyes questioned those with him. Marcus introduced his companions and briefly explained the attack on the estate. Aaron's face turned white in shock at the news of the destruction.

Marcus took Aaron's hand firmly in his. 'I go in search of my father – Tia insisted he is alive. I know not whether I will return, but in case I do or don't, I'd like Grandfather's villa rebuilt. If I do not return, contact father's cousin Drusus in Placentia, and ask him to inform Verina in the Alpes that the estate is hers.'

'I am sure you will return, and I will visit the estate tomorrow to discuss the building work with Georgiakis,' responded Aaron. 'A safe journey to you all, and I hope you find your father.' Aaron clutched the amulet that hung from his neck, with his arm wrapped tightly around a tearful Rachel.

Marcus' group travelled the Via Flaminia and then on to the Via Cassia. Gorax and Lucretia rode close beside each other with unspoken glances. The sun soon reached its highest point and as the road circled the first of the lakes, the group rested and watered their horses. The sun reflected off the rippled waters, inviting the group in. Marcus and Cezar abandoned their weaponry and clothing and dived into the lake's cool waters.

Marcus surfaced and looked instinctively for Tia – though he knew she was gone, he was sure he felt her close. A poor swimmer, Cezar struggled to the surface.

Marcus seemed fixed in the water, bathed in an unreal light. Gorax and Lucretia had seen the change in Marcus and called out as he slipped below the surface.

Lucretia was in the water in an instant, surfacing to look around before diving. With her lungs at bursting point, she found Marcus with his eyes closed, hanging below the water, bubbles from his mouth rising to the surface. With every last ounce of her strength, she dragged him to the surface.

Gorax waded chest-deep into the water and, seeing Lucretia surface, snatched Marcus' limp body from her. Cezar waded out to stand over his white-skinned lifeless friend. Lucretia slid from the waters and proceeded to pump Marcus' chest, causing his body to convulse. The two men looked on helplessly, each questioning without asking: why?

Water erupted from Marcus' mouth as he heaved, his eyes shooting open. Lucretia turned him on his side, tears of relief trickling from her eyes as more water poured from Marcus' mouth amidst a coughing fit.

'Tia, wait! Don't go...' muttered Marcus, reaching out.

Gorax sat Marcus up, colour returning to his pain-filled face. His head drooped forward, his eyes full of tears. Lucretia took him in her arms and hugged him, and he gave way to sobbing.

'I thought it was too soon. He's trying so hard to hide his feelings,' suggested Gorax.

'I felt her around me... I just want to be with her,' responded Marcus.

'Of course, you do, but you must let her go. You will never forget her, and yes, there will be times when you will think you see her. Your love was special and no one can ever take that away,' replied Lucretia, stroking Marcus' forehead as he looked blankly into her face.

Cezar assisted Marcus to stand, his own thoughts floundering at what his friend was feeling. Gorax took Lucretia's hand as she too stood, and their eyes locked momentarily. They found themselves hugging each other before Gorax, stumbling with his speech, apologised and offered Lucretia his cloak to dry herself with, which she gladly accepted.

\*

The party continued in silence, reaching Lucretia's village in the late hours of day to the surprise of the residents. Seeking out her father, the village elder, Lucretia related the final hours of her lover and Gorax's defence of the estate. She discussed her future options, her father noting the frequent mention of Gorax's name, and he knew that he would soon lose his wild and independent daughter again.

The men were already in the community hall warming themselves when Lucretia floated in on the arm of her father. The emerald green of her dress, worn tight around the bodice, accentuated her small breasts whilst her waist-length auburn hair was interwoven with wild flowers, and her brown eyes sparkled in the firelight. A leather belt around her waist held a short-sword and in her free hand she carried a bow.

The vision of beauty stunned Gorax, and with his mouth wide open, he choked on his beer. Lucretia had never been so radiant.

Taking a seat next to her father, Marcus nudged Gorax – a blubbering wreck – to the seat beside her. Lucretia took Gorax's hand in hers and squeezed it, causing him to blush.

Lucretia's father looked at the man beside his daughter, who had resumed his composure. 'So, you are the gladiator who has caught my daughter's eye. When will you give up your wandering, Lucretia, and give me a grandchild?'

'Father, you presume too much,' she insisted, blushing.

'You forget that your mother was my third wife, and the best I ever laid eyes on. Seeing you tonight reminds me of her, and you are as strong-willed and independent as she was, may the gods bless her,' replied her father with a smile that lit his worn and wrinkled face.

Gorax looked at Marcus and Cezar, shrugging his shoulders. Lucretia stood and walked in front of the trio. Removing her sword, she laid it with her bow and quiver on the table in front of Marcus.

'My man is dead and my brother returns from the Legions to take his rightful place in the village. I cannot settle back into this gentile way of life. Marcus, you are still recovering from a broken heart. You are brave and skilled in weaponry beyond your age, but you are still a boy playing the part of a man. You have Gorax by your side, and though your skills are greater than his, he has survived where most would have died and your choice to accept him back is a tribute to your leadership. Cezar, you are a street fighter, but you lack the skills of the other two. I have fought alongside my father on many occasions with short-sword and bow, though not with the proficiency of Tia. Marcus, I ask that I may join you in your quest to find your father, as Tia said you would.'

Marcus was shocked by Lucretia's comments – and a little hurt – but he reflected on how she had held him earlier as he sobbed, and he knew she was right. Gorax gazed into Lucretia's face, full of admiration, while Cezar was both stunned and offended by her comments.

'It is not my decision alone to make, even though – as you say – I lead this party,' Marcus said, pointing to Gorax and Cezar.

'Lady, you are twice my age, but you are wrong if you think you know me. I killed my first man when I was twelve years old, as a matter of honour for my sister. I will not be found wanting in any confrontation,' Cezar responded angrily.

'Another sword, and especially another bow, is always welcome,' replied Gorax, still trying to take in Lucretia's transformation.

Marcus, looking at Cezar, went to respond, but Lucretia took Cezar's hand and shook her head. 'I did not mean to offend, but I spoke as I saw. Yes, I am old enough to be your mother, Cezar. We cannot have a fracture in the group and if you are not happy, then I will withdraw.'

'I have never known you with weapons, Lucretia. Maybe you could demonstrate your prowess, if your father will allow?' prompted Marcus, looking to Lucretia's father, who in turn beckoned to the centre space.

Lucretia looked at Cezar; he was no longer the scrawny youth Marcus had first met. Her face was calm whilst Cezar's was etched with anger.

'If I am to be judged, and rightfully so, then it must be with sword and bow and I choose to start with the bow.'

Lucretia, recovering her bow and quiver, walked to the end of the hall, calling on one of the villagers to stand at the far end of the hall with a candle.

Marcus watched as Lucretia went through a series of exercises, as he had so often seen Tia do. Choosing an arrow, she took aim as the man held the candle at arm's length. In the blink of an eye, the arrow thudded into the hall wall. Lucretia ordered the man to stay as he was and a second arrow snuffed the candle out, to the rapturous applause of the villagers.

The candle was placed in Marcus' hands: the wick was gone from the top of it and he gazed through a hole left by the first arrow. He knew she had the expertise of both Tia and himself, and smiling, he handed the candle to Gorax, who felt the hole and whistled.

'You sell yourself short, Lucretia. Cezar, we all have strengths and weaknesses, but I know that if I asked you to die for me, you would, and I for you. You and Lucretia are both an asset and I would be honoured to have you both ride with me,' stated Marcus.

Marcus took Lucretia's hand in his and reached out to Cezar, who hesitated before seizing his friend's hand. Placing the two together, Marcus raised them as Gorax reached in to join them. The hall erupted in cheers and the thuds of knife handles on wooden tables.

'I take it you are leaving again, daughter,' responded Lucretia's father. 'You should have been a son, but I am proud to call you mine.'

The night was one of celebration and much discussion of Lucretia's archery prowess. The lady herself left the trio in the hall, where they slept – except for Marcus, who sat staring into the hearth fire, his thoughts only of Tia.

*

Two speculatores slipped into Ostia unnoticed, opting for the Anchor Inn on the waterfront, where their dress and demeanour meant they were not out of place. Ordering food and wine, they slipped into conversation with the locals about strange goings-on. Locals spoke of young women disappearing from the village, some of whom had been found washed up in the cove beneath a mysterious farm. The old olive farm overlooking the sea was believed to be haunted by demons, and this was just what the speculatores wanted to hear. An old fisherman took up the tale, stating he had heard screaming and seen strange coloured lights at the farm while he was night fishing in the cove below. He related that there was only one track from the north road, but his grandson knew of another from the cove.

'Has anyone been up to the farm?' asked Remus, the senior speculatore.

He was firmly told no, out of fear. The speculatores needed to assess it for themselves and asked the old fisherman if his grandson would show them the cove path. The old man hesitated, but he was assured they only wanted to be shown the path and would pay well. Arrangements were made.

*

As the sun rose the next day, the innkeeper rapped hard on the door of the room housing the sleeping speculatores, before returning to the bar downstairs. Both were already awake and slipped stealthily down to the bar, surprising the innkeeper with their speed.

'That's the fisherman's grandson in the corner, he has just arrived,' pointed out the innkeeper.

A scrawny youth, barely out of his teens, with dishevelled dark blond hair and olive skin sat with a steaming bowl of food. On hearing the innkeeper, he turned to find two rough and imposing figures in front of him. He was in no doubt they had served in the legions, judging by their stance and the numerous evident scars on their arms and legs. Remus had a slight limp, though it was hardly noticeable, and his slightly deformed left arm was evidence of a historic fracture.

'Are you sure you want me to show you the cliff path to the demon's house?' the boy asked. 'We can travel to the cove either by boat or around the cliff base, but you must watch the tide doesn't cut you off. The path from the cove is steep, but it shouldn't trouble you.'

Remus nodded briskly and then turned around. 'Innkeeper, food and wine and a bag of victuals to go, if you would,' he ordered.

The youth, riding a mule, led the way through the stench of the fish market at the northernmost part of the harbour. Following a coastal path, he led the speculatores through a small stand of Mediterranean spruce before hobbling his mule to one of the trees at the edge of a small rocky beach. The speculatores surveyed each end of the beach – there appeared to be no way off it. Reading their minds, the youth laughed, gesticulating to his right as he set off across the sand, which soon gave way to sharp black rock. The calm sea stretched out of sight with only an occasional ship breaking the monotonous view. The youth climbed higher as he rounded the cliff, which opened out in a small but perfectly formed sandy cove, perfect for even a medium-sized vessel to moor in. The youth pointed upwards, where the outline of a building hung precariously atop the cliff.

'That's the barn you can see, and that's the track just below it. It's a stream-bed when it rains. You can't be seen till you reach the barn and this is as far as I go,' the youth informed them.

Remus reached into a small pouch and extracted a sestertius, placing it in the youth's palm. 'If you'll mind the horses, I'll double it.'

The youth, grinning, nodded agreement and departed to await the speculatores' return.

They strode across the beach, struggling across the soft sand, before they both noticed a strange object at the cliff base. As they drew closer, the flies gave the final clue. At the foot of the cliff, like some discarded doll and twisted out of any normal shape, lay the battered, naked body of a young girl. Other than knowing the body was female, no one would ever recognise her again, her head pulped by the impact of an obvious fall. Between them they laid the cadaver out, covering it till their return.

Sweat dripped from every pore as the speculatores struggled up the stream-bed path. The rock beneath was sharp and unforgiving, and toes were stubbed with frequent slips.

*

Marcus' breath rose like steam as he looked over the settlement walls. The day had barely reached its first hour. This was where Lucretia found him, deep in thought. She was dressed for riding with warm trousers and a leather jacket, every bit a warrior and unlike the maiden of the night before. She placed her arm around his shoulder, and he turned to see her knowing smile as tears filled his eyes and she pulled him close.

'You will never forget her, but you must move forward. You must say your goodbyes at the lake. Your father awaits us,' she suggested.

By the second hour of day, the four had retraced their steps to the lake and as the sun caught the surface of the water, it shimmered. There was an eeriness about the place; nothing stirred, until a sudden breeze lifted their cloaks.

Marcus called out for Hades with no reply and dismounted, making excuses to be alone. His request went unquestioned as he slipped to the water's edge. He thought he felt the warmth of the sun on his head and, looking up, had to shade his eyes. The water before him stilled as the image of Tia emerged – she was smiling. Marcus reached out, but the spirit shook her head.

'Your father travels towards you. Never change, despite what life holds for you. I will always be beside you.'

Marcus' concentration was broken by the snap of a twig behind him and he instinctively reached for his sword. Hades nudged him in the back. Marcus turned to find the great beast in front of him, head bowed. Running his hand along Hades' mane, Marcus talked in whispers of Tia and the horse whinnied in response. Marcus called out to his friends, who appeared almost instantly.

Cezar looked on in amazement. 'I'd give anything to possess such a creature,' he exclaimed.

'Possession of a creature like Hades is built on respect between man and beast and is quite unique,' responded Marcus, with Lucretia agreeing.

'I leave this lake in the care of you and your mistress, Hades. I know not if I will ever see either again,' Marcus murmured, touching Hades' forehead with his own.

Hades stared into Marcus' eyes, his ears pricked up as a breeze whispered: 'You will.' The group looked around for its source, but Marcus didn't need to. He felt Tia one last time, wrapped around him as he whispered 'goodbye.' He stroked Hades' mane one last time and bade him go. Hades walked away and, looking back a final time, rose on to his hind legs and bellowed before galloping into the distance. Four sets of eyes watched Hades run before turning towards each other and clasping hands, drawing each other close.

'To the horses. My father rides towards us,' Marcus said, pointing north.

*

By midday, the speculatores were huddled under the overhang just below the barn. In whispers, the pair made their assessment of the climb and the reality of bringing a troop this way. Neither believed it to be a viable reality. Both agreed on the need to assess the farm, so one at a time they crawled from the path to the barn wall.

The barn was a lone wooden building away from the farmhouse with nothing blocking its view. There was certainly no chance of reaching it unseen in the daylight. A door to the farmhouse opened, and a sole male exited, limping. Both recognised the ex-Camp Prefect Victus Claudian. He surveyed the path that ran from the door to the north road about a half mile away, then hobbled towards the barn. A creaking door indicated that he had entered it. They heard the scream of a young female, which was silenced immediately. Moments later Victus reappeared, dragging a scantily clad semi-conscious young female back towards the farmhouse.

'I'm going to have a look in the barn. Cover me,' requested Remus, as the two crawled along the barn edge.

The barn door hadn't a lock, which was a sign of Victus' confidence. Half standing, Remus lifted the outer latch and slipped inside; the smell was horrendous. He stood momentarily, allowing his eyes to become accustomed to the dark. The floor was covered with old straw and the predominant smell was of excreta – human excreta. There was a trough filled with water and a wooden bar on either side, for animals to be tethered, which ran down the centre of the barn. A lone horse was secured to it along with three dirty and dishevelled young females, secured by their hands to the poles. As Remus reached out to the first one, her eyes shot open and as she went to scream he slipped his hand over her mouth.

'Don't scream, I've come to help,' he whispered, easing his hand from her mouth.

'He'll kill you if he finds you! One of the girls' lovers found her, and he tortured him in front of her,' she said, indicating one of the recumbent figures.

'Are there any others?' he asked.

'There were ten, but we are all that remain. One he has just dragged away,' she responded.

Remus cut her bindings with his pugio. Rubbing her wrists, the female moved to the remaining two, shaking them carefully. Their eyes opened, wide with shock.

As the three huddled together, shaking, Remus addressed them. 'I have a colleague waiting outside. You need to be quiet and you must do what I tell you if we are to escape. I will let one of you out at a time and you must crawl round the barn to Adolfi and wait for me to join you.'

Opening the barn door a crack, Remus peered out. There was no movement from the farmhouse. The first female crawled quickly out of sight, followed by the second.

'What about my sister? He has just taken her, I can't leave her,' said the final girl, tears trickling down her filthy face.

'We can't save her, she is buying your life. Now go, like I told you,' snapped Remus.

She slipped out of the door as a gust of wind caught it. Remus lost his grip on the door and dropped his pugio. As the door slammed against the barn wall with a loud thud, the girl seized her chance. Snatching up the pugio and rising, she ran towards the farmhouse followed by Remus. Adolfi and the other two girls watched in shock as an act was played out in front of them.

'There's a path to the beach over there,' ordered Adolfi. 'Now go – you'll find a fisherman's son waiting, you must tell him what's happened. I need to help my colleague.'

As he turned back he saw the running female tackled by Remus amid shouts from the farmhouse door, which now stood open. Victus appeared, spear in one hand, sword in the other. Spear raised, Victus let fly as the female gained her feet and ran towards him. On a powerful flat trajectory, the metal tip punched through her stomach, the point exiting her back and stopping her dead. Shock filled her face; the exit from life was too quick for a scream. Remus stood, his sword sliding easily from his well-greased scabbard as he adopted a defence stance. Victus laughed as he limped towards Remus, rotating his sword in a warm-up.

'I'm right behind you, Remus,' shouted Adolfi.

'No! Get the other girls away safely. If I don't make it, tell Macro. Go!' ordered Remus.

'You think you can take me, Remus? I could take both of you with an arm behind my back. You're all brawn, and not a brain between you.' Victus' face contorted as he closed the gap.

Adolfi joined Remus, standing shoulder to shoulder with him as they faced Victus.

'I told you to go, save yourself! That's an order,' spat Remus, causing Adolfi to hesitate.

'Do what you're told and I'll catch you presently, when I've finished with Remus,' suggested Victus.

Adolfi turned and ran to the overhang where the two girls were already making their way gingerly down the track. He looked back momentarily.

Victus sliced at Remus, who spun away, deflecting the blade easily, then undercut at Victus' exposed stomach. Victus, with lightning reactions, twisted and blocked, sending shudders through both combatants. Remus swung out with his spade-size fists crunching into Victus's jaw, stunning him momentarily. Spinning full circle, Remus slashed at Victus' stomach again but was blocked with a counter strike, though not before taking first blood, albeit a scratch.

Victus, purple faced, hammered strike after strike at Remus, forcing him backwards towards the cliff. Remus slipped below a strike, sweeping his leg at Victus, and bones juddered. Victus fell badly and lost the grip on his sword, laughing manically. He rolled forward, knocking Remus from his feet as he sliced down with a killing stroke.

Victus recovered quicker than Remus and, slipping a blade from his belt, he leapt on top of Remus, driving the short blade into his neck. Blood sprayed as Victus' blade parted an artery. Remus choked and spat blood as he drowned and bled out at the same time. Rising, Victus pulled the spear from the dead female and hobbled to the overhang.

Adolfi was already halfway down the track, urging the females to hurry as Victus launched the spear. Rock splinters exploded into Adolfi's face as the spear skidded off the cliff wall beside him, but he continued downward. A knife followed shortly thereafter, falling at Adolfi's feet amidst curses from above. Reaching the beach, the two girls had already found the cadaver; they screamed and threw themselves on to the sand beside it.

Adolfi stared up at Victus as he rolled Remus's inert body over the cliff edge. It bounced off the rocks to fall in a mutilated bloody heap at the base. Dragging the women to their feet in hysterics, Adolfi slapped them both, urging them towards the fisherman's son who stood wide-eyed and open-mouthed in shock.

Mounting the two girls on to Remus' horse, Adolfi wrapped Remus' recovered body, tying it across his own horse. The fisherman's grandson led the way from the carnage back towards Ostia.

\*

Victus returned to the farmhouse where a young female lay battered and bleeding. Barely conscious, she never felt the fatal thrust to her heart. Discarding his sullied clothing and packing quickly, he set a small fire in the farmhouse. Flames licked around him as he exited, making for the barn, where moments later he rode his horse from it. *Once again fate has decided my destiny*, Victus thought as he headed for the north coastal road.

*

As Victus was departing, Adolfi reached the Ostia wharf and the Anchor Inn, a crowd following the procession. A scream ripped the wharf-side air as a middle-aged woman clutching a child to her breast ran towards the two girls as they slipped from Remus' horse. One turned and in a flood of tears hugged the woman and child to her.

'Who's that?' enquired Adolfi.

'It's her daughter, one of those who disappeared about a month ago,' replied one of the crowd.

'Does anyone know this other girl?' shouted Adolfi at the crowd.

'It's Antonius' daughter – he was a causarius from the 2nd Augusta. I found him dead by his own hand yesterday, she was his reason for living. She's been missing for nearly a month. Where have they been?' enquired the innkeeper's daughter.

'Fetch the vigiles immediately and bring them to the Anchor,' ordered Adolfi to a young boy in the crowd.

The innkeeper's daughter led the way, and once inside, the innkeeper provided wine as they waited for the vigiles. The crowd stood expectantly as other parents arrived, enquiring about their lost daughters. The sound of marching feet caught everyone's ears, announcing the vigiles' arrival, at which Adolfi explained the situation. The tale rippled out to those waiting outside the inn, to sounds of gasps and mutterings.

'I need to report to Senior Praetorian Macro immediately, and you need to secure the farmhouse and prevent Victus Claudian's escape. He is wanted for treason!' stated Adolfi.

'We need you to come with us and identify this Victus Claudian,' insisted the senior vigile.

'My orders are from the most senior man after the Emperor. I must return to Rome, and you must secure the farmhouse. He is the only one there,' stated Adolfi as he stood to leave, to spontaneous applause and cheers.

Adolfi galloped the horses carrying himself and Remus to the Castra Praetoria, where the duty Optio promptly responded to his arrival, Macro being sent for. Adolfi explained the incident in full, including his request that the vigiles secure the farmhouse. Macro's face turned purple with rage and he screamed for the Camp Prefect, who appeared at the double.

'I want the best ten mounted and dispatched to the farmhouse in Ostia with Adolfi immediately. Victus Claudian must be brought back here alive,' spat Macro.

The Camp Prefect saluted, spun around and doubled towards the barracks.

*

As the troopers departed for Ostia at a gallop, Victus was already making good time on the Via Aurelia towards Graviscae, the Etruscan port of Tarquinii, arriving in the late hours of night. Slipping on to the wharf side, the moonlight danced on the rippling waves. Few boats were moored, and those that were there were fishing boats, newly returned with their catches.

The fishermen didn't notice the dark-cloaked figure that stood in the shadows and watched them. An elderly weather-tanned man was spreading his net to dry before retiring to his home with his catch when Victus approached him. He tapped him on the shoulder, making him jump, and the older man reached for the gutting knife on his belt.

'You won't need that. I'm seeking transport up the coast to Pisae. Can you suggest anyone, yourself perhaps?' enquired Victus.

'To come looking for a boat at this hour you must have something to hide. It will cost. How soon do you wish to leave?' asked the fisherman.

'As soon as we can. It's a secret mission for the Emperor, no one must know,' replied Victus, smugly jingling money in a purse on his belt.

'Ready when you are.' The fisherman invited Victus on to his boat.

Moments later the small craft was being rowed out of the harbour to acknowledgements from other fishermen as Victus lay flat in the hull as a precaution. A light breeze filled the small sail as the fisherman pointed his boat north and Victus sat upright, the smell of fish invading his nostrils.

The fisherman hugged the coastline as the breeze grew stronger. Victus requested to be left on a beach just outside Pisae, where the fisherman suggested he might procure a horse. Victus had brushed aside all enquiries about his mission.

Early afternoon, the small boat was aimed at a secluded beach with a path leading up the cliff. As the boat scraped the shingle, a final wave lifted its bow on to the beach and the fisherman jumped out. Victus dropped over the side on to the shingle with a loud crunch. The fisherman offered a hand for payment whilst holding the boat with the other. Victus reached for his purse, but grasped his pugio and in a flash of light embedded it in the fisherman's throat. In horror, the fisherman instinctively grasped at his neck as blood pumped from it and he collapsed.

*I can't afford any witnesses*, Victus pondered, as he

pushed the boat back into the sea with its dying occupant within.

Victus struggled up the stony cliff path, cursing the Civilis family for the injury to his leg. *I really should exercise more*, he thought to himself as he headed for the nearest buildings. The familiar dull thud of metal on metal suggested a smithy, where Victus enquired about procuring a horse and an inn for the night. The local market on the edge of Pisae oversaw the Raven Inn, a reasonable hostelry for its location, where the food was plentiful and wholesome, though the rooms weren't of the same level.

Having indulged himself in a light breakfast the following morning, the new day Victus beheld was misty as he proceeded north on a long and laborious ride along the coast towards Genua.

## Chapter 18

The short ride to Volsinii was a leisurely one for Marcus' group. Arriving in the late hours of day, the group settling for a busy inn. They were eyed suspiciously and the clientele spoke in whispers as they entered. The innkeeper enquired as to their destination, and in a voice loud enough for all to hear, Marcus related the destruction of the family estate and the quest to find his father from the 2nd Augusta.

The atmosphere changed in an instant, with enquiries into his father's name by obvious ex-legionaries. Many knew Artorius and spoke highly of him. Talk then turned to a renegade gang ambushing travellers and raiding estates, of which Marcus' group made a mental note. Taking two rooms, Lucretia was given her own, which Gorax insisted on sleeping across the doorway.

*

Perusia was reached with ease by the last hour of day, and finding the best inn, Artorius and Magda again shared a room. Magda felt a growing respect for Artorius, something she never thought she would have for another Roman. He was so similar in his ways to Drusus. At the same time, she watched the clientele of the inns, noticing that they appeared rougher as they rode closer on Rome. It was now only two days away, Artorius told her. Magda felt excitement for the new experience, but trepidation based on his warnings.

The following morning, the innkeeper warned Artorius about the marauding gang who were targeting travellers on the Via Cassia. As the Via Cassia passed through Etruscan land, no one seemed interested in policing it. The traffic to and from Volsinii had reduced to a dribble, the last attack happening only days before. Artorius, forewarned and prepared for any eventuality, chose the best horses from the mutatione.

The swirling mist clung to the ground as Artorius and Magda left Perusia behind. The sun's warmth soon turned the countryside into a blaze of colour as the spring flowers burst from their winter hiding places. Travellers were few and all those they met avoided contact. Artorius viewed the approaching forest with foreboding, and reining his horse in, he expressed his concerns to Magda. Stringing her bow, Magda slipped it over her shoulder as Artorius slid his spatha in and out of his well-oiled scabbard whilst scanning the horizon. Nothing moved.

\*

Marcus and his group set out from Volsinii at first light, the road before them obscured by thick fog. As they travelled, the rising sun cleared the fog to reveal an incline into a thick forest. The road that rose forward as it sliced between the trees was empty, and Marcus called a halt at its edge. The trees were like dark sentinels and the ground mist clung to the ground below them. Lucretia slipped from her horse, removing her bow from her pack, and strung it. Gorax produced a small hand axe he had hidden, securing it to his saddle. Cezar checked the throwing knife in his right boot, and tested the ease of drawing his sword. Marcus watched in interest as each went through their unspoken preparations. Standing in his stirrups, Marcus reached back and swiftly withdrew his two swords, rotating them in his hands before replacing them.

'Are we ready?' he enquired as Lucretia climbed back into her saddle.

With Marcus leading and Lucretia in the centre of a triangle formation, the group trotted forward. Four sets of eyes pierced the partially hidden undergrowth for any movement. The quiet was deafening as two groups entered the forest from opposite ends, completely unaware of the other.

*

Ten damp and poorly clothed souls stirred in the partially derelict hovel that was their home, deep in the forest between Perusia and Volsinii. Most carried scars of a minor nature from the skirmishes they had had, but their rewards were few and far between these days. The group were deep in discussion about moving location when the barn door flew open and a youth entered, sweating.

'What is it, Hatto?' demanded the leader.

'A soldier and a young female have just entered the forest from Perusia.'

'Just the two, are you sure?' demanded the leader.

'Just two. He's dressed in fine armour and she's a pretty thing and would fetch good money from the slaver – and they are both riding good horses,' responded Hatto.

'Has anyone seen Tegan this morning? We'll take them on cliff bend. We want the girl alive; kill and strip the soldier,' ordered the leader, pointing to the door.

The group picked up their discarded assortment of weapons and left. The leader ruffled the youth's hair and followed.

Tegan had fallen asleep huddled into the remains of a damaged tree at the opposite end of the forest. He woke with a shock as a group – what appeared to be parents and two youths who were a similar age to himself – passed him. They were well dressed and all armed. Four against twelve: the leader would be pleased.

Slipping from his hiding place, Tegan crept away, heading for the hovel. He ran as fast and as lightly as he could, but when he found the hovel empty, he surmised that there were other targets and set off for the gang's favourite ambush location: the overhang.

*

Marcus sensed movement and raised his hand. His group stopped, looked and listened.

'Thought I heard something,' said Marcus.

'Probably just a fox,' offered Gorax.

Marcus wasn't convinced. Pulling Egorix's sword from his back scabbard, he prompted his horse slowly forward. Lucretia slipped the bow from her shoulders and tied the reins to her saddle, and as she controlled her horse with her legs she selected a quarrel. Gorax and Cezar looked across at each other and shrugged, but still checked their weapons.

*

Meanwhile, in another part of the forest, the hairs on the back of Artorius' neck stood up. His eyes struggled to pierce the darkness around them and the mist swirled at their horses' feet.

Sensing Artorius' tension, Magda slipped the bow from her shoulder and notched an arrow, scanning around her. Their pace slowed to a walk as they descended the slope towards a bend.

*

Tegan found his gang at his favourite location, looking down over the metalled road, the sound of hooves echoed off the stones in what would otherwise be a deafening quiet.

The gang had assembled with their leader on the overhang, looking up the hill towards Perusia.

'Where have you been?' the leader demanded in a whisper.

'My usual hiding place, and a good job too. There's a family of four heading this way and they're all armed.

What's happening here?' responded Tegan.

'A soldier and his young female slave will be here shortly. How far behind are the family?' the leader enquired.

'Probably not far. I ran as fast as I could.'

'Warn the rest, and hurry. I want you down on the road behind them.'

*

Tegan had just slipped away when Artorius and Magda rounded the overhang to find their way blocked by a tree and three large heavily armed males. Artorius pulled his horse up abruptly, followed by Magda.

'Magda, flee. Now,' ordered Artorius.

'No, you don't. Tegan, Hatto!' came a rough voice from above.

Magda turned her horse to find two armed youths facing her. Without prompting, she dispatched her first arrow, lifting Tegan from his feet with blood pumping from his throat. A second arrow sped towards a screaming Hatto, who was brandishing a short-sword. A lucky stumble meant the arrow ripped into his shoulder, sending him sprawling backwards, screaming in pain.

'Take them now. You'll pay for that, little missy!' shouted the gang leader, jumping down and dragging Magda from her horse as she tried to release a third barbed death.

Landing on top of her, she was swiftly rendered unconscious and then he turned his attention to her companion. Artorius screamed at the top of his voice and charged head down towards the leader. Artorius felt the breeze of an arrow from behind puncture his horse's neck, and as it stumbled, he jumped clear.

*

Marcus' party were cautiously plodding up the steep incline towards a bend when their ears collectively heard a war cry, followed by a clash of metal. Marcus launched his horse forward and the rest followed, Lucretia beside him. Rounding the bend, a lone soldier stood beside a dying horse, surrounded by four attackers. Marcus charged towards the lone soldier.

Lucretia's first arrow skewered the back of the nearest attacker and the gang recoiled at the sound of hoof beats from behind. Two turned towards the riders, leaving their leader to deal with Artorius.

Marcus charged and, slicing down at a raised sword, separated the arm from its body, blood spurting from the fatal wound. Cezar knocked the remaining male from his feet, and leaping from his horse, the now sword-less male tried to crawl away, pleading for his life. Cezar gave no quarter, driving his sword into the man's chest.

Gorax's horse leapt the tree and stumbled, dislodging Gorax, who hacked down at the gang leader but missed. Hatto, having regained his composure, snapped the arrow in his shoulder as he stood guard over an inert Magda. The flying bulk of Gorax took Hatto unaware, flinging him backwards into a tree and snapping his spine.

The swoosh of an arrow erupted from the forest darkness, penetrating Lucretia's arm. Snatching at the reins, her horse veered and fell sideward, throwing her. Rolling in pain, she sought her bow and quiver as a second arrow lodged in the tree beside her. Seeing Lucretia rise with loaded bow, her attacker dropped his own and turned to flee. Lucretia buried an arrow in his spine, stopping him dead.

Artorius shared blow for blow with the gang leader, forcing him backwards. Marcus stared at the soldier before him in disbelief – it was his father, alive. As

Marcus called out to him, he was dragged from his horse from behind. Crashing to the floor, Egorix's sword skidded across the stone road, and Marcus stared into the faces of two bearded males with axes.

The leader seized on Artorius' momentary distraction and tried to run, but Artorius' spatha slid easily through the leader's stomach wall. Twisting the sword, Artorius then wrenched it free and leapt on to the tree, screaming at the two who stood over his son. They half-turned to face the caller, and Marcus rolled into the roadside moss, ripping Jorgan's sword free. The taller male rotated his axe as he approached Artorius.

Gorax, in full flight on foot, rolled over the tree, pushing Artorius aside and knocking the remaining axeman to the ground. He sat astride his male and punched down with every ounce of strength at the semi-conscious axeman, smashing his jaw. The smaller male now found himself caught between Artorius and Marcus. As he turned to run, Marcus swept his sword two-handed at the male, who half-heartedly tried to block it. Failing, he was swept off his feet with Jorgan's sword invading his innards.

Magda, now conscious, sat against a tree tended to by Lucretia, who in turn was having her arm bandaged by Cezar. Magda stared as Marcus and Artorius threw their arms around each other, neither wanting to let go.

'Who's that hugging Artorius?' enquired Magda.

'His son, Marcus. Who are you?' asked Lucretia.

'He was very brave to charge the robbers. I am related to Artorius' cousin,' answered Magda with her eyes locked on Marcus. Lucretia smiled.

'Make sure they're all dead,' ordered Artorius, as he held Marcus at arm's length. 'What's happened to you?' he asked, looking at the faded pock marks on his face. 'What are you doing out here, where's Tia?'

'I survived the plague, thanks to Tia. We were told you were dead, but Tia insisted you were alive. Victus killed her and raized the estate to the ground. There's not much left in Rome.' Tears filled Marcus' eyes at his painful memories.

Artorius looked with foreboding at his son, dreading to ask the question in his head. 'How is your mother, and what of your sisters?' he enquired, bracing himself for the answer he didn't want to hear. *He had been warned.*

'Verina was sent to your cousin in the Alpes to marry. Mother and Alia… died of the plague.' Marcus reached out to his father, his eyes full of tears.

Artorius drew his son close, fighting back his own tears and gritting his teeth. His first image was of Amoria and Alia, but it was quickly superseded by one of Victus. With the image came the knowledge that Victus had destroyed his family bit by bit and that he, Artorius, had been unable to stop him.

Inside Artorius cursed himself for not listening to the warnings, but then he blamed Scorus for sending him north to where Victus had waited to kill him. Without thought for where he was, Artorius screamed Victus' name in anger and pledged his life to killing him, knowing fate had other plans.

Marcus considered his father's pain-filled eyes and watched as he sank to his knees, his head bowed. Gorax stepped forward with sympathy for a soul like himself, who had had everything and lost it.

Artorius looked up, tears streaming from his eyes. 'Thank you for saving my son's life, but what are you doing here, Gorax?' he snapped.

Gorax offered his hand and let it fall when there was no response. He explained the loss of his family and how, as promised, he had visited the estate with news of Victus.

'Where is that evil bastard now?' snapped Artorius.

'He lives somewhere outside Ostia,' replied Gorax.

Marcus helped his father to his feet. Deep furrows cut his father's face and his hair had silvered. Lucretia stepped forward with Magda, still a little dazed. Cezar's eyes soaked up Magda's visage.

Marcus introduced each of his group with a brief background, leaving Gorax till last. Taking Gorax's calloused hand in his, Marcus thanked him for his timely intervention. He related how Gorax had fought Victus and his men in defence of the estate and had volunteered to help search for Artorius. Taking his father's hand, Marcus married it with Gorax's. Artorius faltered at first, then gripped it tight.

The tension eased further as Artorius introduced Magda, Marcus barely noticing the beautiful young woman who gripped his hand and stared into his eyes, hoping for an acknowledgement.

'I must return to Rome, but I don't think it's safe for you to go any further, Magda. I think you should go back with an escort,' suggested Artorius, clenching his fists so tight his knuckles went white.

'I'm not going back this close to Rome, and besides, there is strength in numbers,' responded Magda, her eyes devouring Marcus who was oblivious to the attention.

'Father, I must take you to the lake where I scattered Tia's ashes and released Hades. He never recovered from Grandfather's death.'

Artorius nodded, his head too full of internal grief to suggest any alternative.

Gorax stared at Lucretia with enquiring eyes. She took his hand and smiled a reassuring smile as he pulled her closer. Magda offered her horse to Artorius and, looking around, she was disappointed when it was only Cezar and Lucretia who offered her a seat. Gorax sifted through the unwanted weaponry from the robbers, taking only the axes, offering one to Marcus with the promise to instruct him in its use, if he desired to learn. Lucretia took the discarded bow and quiver; the bodies were left where they lay.

Clearing the road, the enlarged group headed towards Volsinii, arriving as the sun set in a blood-red sky. Making for the inn Marcus' group had previously used, Marcus informed the innkeeper that his father was found and a celebration was called for. Artorius tried magnanimously to refuse as he descended into depression, but the clientele wouldn't hear of it. As the talk turned to the attack on Artorius and Magda, the group achieved celebrity status for implementing the gang's demise. Drinks flooded the table as Lucretia diplomatically took Magda away against her wishes, leaving the men to enjoy their popularity.

Magda wanted to return, but Lucretia refused to let her. She knew she needed to talk to Magda over her obvious growing adoration of Marcus. She described the strength of Tia and Marcus' relationship. An angry Magda rose to leave, but Lucretia blocked her way.

'The wound he feels is deep and fresh, he needs to heal. You are young, beautiful and you have time. Make the best use of it, befriend him. Rush him at your peril. Give him time to grieve, prove yourself worthy and let fate decide,' suggested Lucretia, taking Magda in her arms.

'But I have never had such strange feelings for a man before,' Magda replied.

Lucretia only smiled.

The two females tried to settle down for the night, but the noise from below grew in volume.

Marcus watched as his father buried his grief in alcohol, not knowing how to help him. Gorax was recognised for the famous gladiator he had been, eventually winning his freedom. Stories were demanded of him by all present, the gorier the better. Marcus and Cezar left Gorax to his stories while they dragged Artorius away to sleep.

It was the late hours of night when the last survivor crashed to the bench. Cezar slept, dreaming of Magda, while Marcus kept vigil over his father, striving to come to terms with his father's injuries and how he had aged. Artorius hovered between sleep and wakefulness, calling out to Amoria and someone called Ilona. Marcus puzzled at the name. He finally slipped into sleep in the last hours of night, missing his father's exit.

Artorius raised the sleeping staff at the mutatione and returned to the inn with a fresh horse, refreshing himself in the ice-cold waters of a trough. Shaking the water from his head, he didn't hear the soft foot-falls of Lucretia behind him. She touched his shoulder, shocking him back to the present, her whole presence calming. He imagined Ilona, and with it came a realisation that he could finally do right by her without damaging Amoria's memory. Artorius cursed Rosevetha under his breath, grasping the amulet around his neck. He recalled Breda's comment that he would see Ilona again – they all knew!

'How's your arm?' Artorius asked Lucretia, returning to the present. 'I am remiss for not thanking you for your part in our rescue, you are very skilled with the bow. What are your plans now that my son and I are reunited? Marcus and I must seek out Victus and impose our own summary execution. My future in the Praetorians is uncertain now that my is mission complete.'

'It is a clean injury and will heal well in time, thank you. My future is as the wind; I know not where it blows me or how strongly. I have no one, and though I love my father and my village, it is not for me. What will happen to your estate?'

'That depends on Marcus, but I would like to rebuild it and have somewhere to return to when I retire. There are many considerations I must contemplate, but for now we must return to Rome,' replied Artorius.

'Then with your permission, I will accompany you as a chaperone for Magda until you have made your decisions.'

Artorius nodded his consent.

Behind the two, the inn clientele was escaping from the previous night, some still barely able to know where they were going or who with. Gorax stepped out into the morning air, fresh as a mountain stream until he saw Lucretia, the sun's first rays turning her hair the colour of polished wood. Struggling, he offered her his hand, and she stepped forward and embraced him. His arms easily encompassed her svelte body.

Artorius nodded to Gorax and re-entered the inn, arranging for food and drink. Marcus, bleary-eyed, left his room and walked into a very pale Magda, much to her delight. He flustered and attempted to apologise, a gesture which was brushed aside. Regaining his composure, Marcus enquired after her well-being in the manner of a well-meaning brother. Magda smiled, lacing her arm through his.

Cezar sat with Artorius as the rest of the group joined them; seeing Magda's arm linked with Marcus', he felt deflated. Marcus guided her to the seat beside Cezar, who couldn't believe his sudden change of fortune, whilst Magda looked shunned. Every look and expression was monitored by the ever-watchful Lucretia, while Artorius looked at the gathered group, pondering on the discussion he must have with his son.

The journey to the lake was a delight on the eye, the roadsides a myriad of colours as nature exploded for another year. Hades' herd grazed near the lake as a light breeze rippled its surface and rustled the trees, but there was no sign of Hades himself. The wind hailed the arriving party and Artorius looked on at the beauty of the place.

'Son, you chose well for Hades. Where is he? As a last resting place for Tia, it is unsurpassed of all the places I've ever seen.'

Artorius' ears twitched. Sensing movement in the trees to his left, his hand slipped to his spatha. Hades strolled from cover in the company of a white mare. Artorius sat in awe of the beauty of the moment as Hades approached him.

'It seems you are a match maker as well, Marcus,' he remarked.

Marcus nodded, trying to hide the tears he fought back as he promised the memory of Tia that she would never be forgotten.

Hades nudged Artorius, who ran his hand down his mane; memories of Lictus stirred in him.

Magda was dumbstruck by the wonder of the location and the grand creature that stood before them. Slipping from her horse, she reached out with an open hand to Hades, whispering to him. The stallion turned, eyeing Magda from head to foot, Looking back at Marcus, he whinnied. Marcus went to call Magda back, but something inside told him it was okay. Hades stood at his full height in front of Magda, allowing her to caress his mane, but he looked at Marcus as if he was trying to gauge the situation. Cezar stared in growing admiration, of Magda as Hades, joined by the mare, walked away and approached Marcus. They offered their heads, which he rubbed tenderly.

'Hades must be going soft. There was a time only your grandfather could have done that,' remarked Artorius.

'Circumstances change everything, Father, sometimes for the better.'

Artorius wondered if Marcus would think the same when he told him of Ilona. The midday sun reached out to every member of the group, bathing them in warmth and light. Artorius looked on at the son who had become a man, and marvelled at how he had risen from the loss of Tia. Could he do the same with his bereavement of Amoria and Alia?

At the lake, Hades' herd hung back. Hades alone rose on to his hind legs in a final gesture, before turning and racing away, followed by his herd.

As the group enjoyed the moment, Lucretia spoke: 'I will go ahead to my village and warn them of our arrival. You know the way, Marcus.'

'I will accompany you,' offered Gorax. 'For safety,' he quickly added as the couple set off.

Marcus and Cezar looked at each other and smiled.

'Who does that beautiful horse belong to?' Magda looked to Artorius for the answer.

'He belongs to no one. He is as free as the wind, till the day he dies,' interjected Marcus sharply.

Cezar and Magda were taken aback by the abruptness of the response. Each connection to Tia was a dart in Marcus' heart, so deep was the abyss of her loss. Recouping his composure, Marcus looked at his father then turned his horse in the village's direction.

*

171

Lucretia was deep in thought as Gorax rode quietly beside her. He looked at her, wrestling with the thoughts and emotions she unknowingly caused, and went to speak, but was beaten to it.

'What are your plans, Gorax, now that Artorius is found?'

'I had wondered the same about you, after the speech in your village. All I have is what I wear and carry with me. If Artorius keeps the estate, I am hoping Marcus and his father might allow me to remain. What about you?'

'Lasa, your Fortuna has treated me harshly for my independence. I have outlived two partners, but I am alone once more. I have my village, but I want to be more than just a wife, a mother. I want to be equal to the man I choose. My father taught me well with sword and my mother the bow. I await the next turn of fate.'

Lucretia reached across the narrow gap between them and, taking Gorax's hand, squeezed it and smiled.

He stared back at her and wondered, *Is she feeling the way I am?*

It was a surprised father that welcomed Lucretia back in the sole company of Gorax a little while later. Having explained the good news, a welcome was prepared. A short time later Marcus led the remaining group into Lucretia's village.

The dark closed in around Lucretia's village, where the greeting was as warm as the great fire in the community hall. Artorius' survival was the talk of the community and it fell on Lucretia's father to ask him to entertain the gathering with his story.

Artorius hadn't expected to have to relate his story so openly to his son, and so soon. He set the scene from Argentoratum, with the events that led to him being sent to Mogontiacum but omitting his visit to Ilona and Rosevetha.

Marcus sensed there was more, especially when he looked directly at his father and he looked away.

Victus' ambush and Artorius' escape thrilled the congregation, but it was the talk of the wolves that had everyone transfixed as he bared his disfigured arm for all to see. At a late hour and after much drinking, Artorius brought the proceedings to a conclusion with his first memory after his rescue. The story of Ilona and Rosevetha was for Marcus' ears only, when the time was right.

Artorius slept poorly, reminded of the guilt of leaving his pregnant rescuer behind in Gigantrex's village.

As he sat by the fire being recharged in the first hour of the following day, Breda's prophetic words flooded back to him. He knew then that he must return north as soon as he could, hopefully with Marcus.

## Chapter 19

On the outskirts of Rome, Artorius continued alone to the Castra Praetoria while Marcus led the remaining group to the edge of the Forum to stable the horses.

Magda's eyes were everywhere. The smells were horrendous, far worse than any farm she'd ever known, and the streets were filthy and the populace ignorant. When she commented on it, Marcus laughed and welcomed her to Rome, asking her what she had expected.

Rachel was the first to see Marcus and opened her arms to him, Aaron being firmly ensconced with a prospective buyer. Marcus took her in his arms and lifted her off the floor, and Aaron's face lit up as he turned to see what the commotion was. Marcus introduced his companions, and Magda immediately caught Rachel's eye with the way she watched Marcus.

'I had thought it would be a long time till we saw you again, if at all,' remarked Aaron, taking Marcus' hand.

Marcus smiled at the couple. 'For once I have good news. Father is found and he's at the Praetorian barracks as we speak.'

Aaron and Rachel wrapped their combined arms around him, tears evident in their eyes.

'Does he know?' asked Rachel gently.

'Yes, I told him everything, but his experience has aged him, as you will see,' replied Marcus.

Aaron looked at Rachel and then, because of the lack of interest from the populace, he gathered up the jewellery from his trestle and led the group back to their home. The smell of honey cakes caught Marcus' nose as Rachel opened the door, and as he sniffed at the aroma she saw his eyes glaze over. Taking his hand, she squeezed it and smiled. He in turn, with a saddened face, shrugged his shoulders and tried to smile.

*

Artorius snaked his way around the ever-expanding city, new buildings signifying someone's new wealth – whether it be real or borrowed, mattered not.

It was with trepidation that he entered the huge gates of the Porta Documana and returned the crisp salute of the guard. On the far side of the central crossroads lay the administration building, where he hoped to find Macro. Twelve towers broke the huge walls – two at each gate and one at every corner – each holding their own contingent of Praetorian guards, the grandeur due to the late Sejanus. The sound of wood thudding on wooden stakes continually floated on the air, as half-naked guards in loincloths practised their gladius techniques. The strong smell of sweat was also evident, as rival Centurions barked orders at their men, practising their defence capabilities. Each legionary was looking to win favour by finding a gap between the opposing scutum with their wooden swords. It could have been a permanent camp anywhere in the empire, but this was the Castra Praetoria, a place of elitism.

Artorius relinquished his horse to a groom and entered the administration building. In the clerk's office, Artorius found to his delight that clerk Alexander was missing and when he enquired after him, he was delighted to find that he was missing, wanted for crimes against the state. Addressing the new senior clerk, Artorius handed over his orders and requested a meeting with Macro.

The clerk lifted his eyes from the scrolls. 'You were reported missing, presumed dead, a few days since we were informed that you have in fact risen from the dead. I will speak to Macro; take a seat, he has company. The emperor's adopted grandson Caligula is in the city on a visit, and Macro is a close friend.'

The clerk knocked on the office door behind Artorius, and as it opened, laughter escaped.

Artorius sat expecting a long wait, but was surprised when moments later the clerk reappeared, beckoning Artorius into Macro's office. Marching in, Artorius saluted, a gesture which was waved away as Macro looked him up and down.

'You look well for a dead man, Centurion. A fellow Centurion from the 2nd informed us that you were murdered in Germania. That same Centurion was later found dying at Victus Claudian's hands in Ostia. Ex-Camp Prefect Scorus has already briefly outlined your survival.'

'What's the current situation with that bastard Claudian? I believe he is hiding near Ostia?' enquired Artorius.

'That is all in hand,' Macro said, dismissing further comment as a figure stepped out from the shadows behind Artorius.

'I would love to hear this Centurion's story,' said a youthful voice.

Artorius turned to see a thin, pale-skinned youth, a little older than Marcus. He was thin-haired, with dull eyes sunken into a broad furrowed forehead and spindly legs; quite an ugly specimen.

'This is the emperor's adopted son, Gaius Julius Caesar Germanicus,' Macro said, pointing to the youth.

'So long winded! Caligula, the troops' nickname, suits me better. So, you are the soldier saved by a witch and a wolf queen?' interjected Caligula.

Artorius saluted, 'Sir, I cannot say whether what you have heard is truth or tale,' added Artorius.

'Centurion Civilis – sit, my guest wishes to hear the truth of your adventure and I too am intrigued,' responded Macro, calling for refreshments and pushing a chair towards him.

Removing his cassis, Artorius took the seat that was offered, and before he had time to start he had a beaker of wine thrust on him. He made a great story of the predicament that Longinus' suicide left Scorus and himself in. Having identified the conspirators and detained the majority, he volunteered himself to travel north in search of a new temporary Legate for the 2nd.

'You certainly are a fine and brave Centurion to suggest such a course of action, and to volunteer as well. I am sure Grandfather would love to meet such a devoted soldier, Macro. Continue, please,' remarked Caligula.

The suggestion of meeting the Emperor was not something Artorius had foreseen – in fact, it would only delay his plans. He resumed his tale with the ambush by Victus and his associates, leading up to him being stripped and left for dead even after the young tribune had set him free.

'Goody, I hope we're getting to the juicy bit with the wolves.' Caligula grinned.

Artorius related the wolf encounter as best as he could remember, even uncovering his arm at the request of an excited Caligula. He described the two-legged wolf he saw due to his delirium and the fact that she was his rescuer, who took him back to Rosevetha's home where the two women nursed him back to life. Caligula, in his excitement at the talk of Ilona's ability to control the wolves, demanded to have the women described to him in explicit detail. Having to describe Ilona in such detail rankled Artorius, but he continued. He finished with the arrival of his friends, after which Caligula jumped to his feet and applauded Artorius, like some common actor in a show.

'Macro, what can we do with such a fine and loyal soldier? He deserves a reward for his privations in the pursuance of the Emperor's orders.' Caligula unfastened a pouch from his belt and tossed it to Artorius. 'This will be a start, and I am sure there will be more to follow from the Emperor once I have spoken to him,' he added.

Macro looked from Caligula to Artorius and took a deep breath. 'You have certainly completed your task in an exemplary manner, but I am afraid I have already appointed a successor as I was informed you were dead. I will, of course, ensure you are paid accordingly for the lost time. However, I have no vacancies left in the guard for a senior officer—' Macro was cut short by Artorius.

'I was under no illusion that you would replace me, and rightfully so, with the information laid before you. With that in mind and the fact that my wife and daughter died while I was away, might I make a request?'

'Before you do, I can offer you two options. Firstly, an early retirement, as you are back in Rome and I am sure Caligula, as the Emperor's grandson, would agree that you have earned the right. However, you may not wish to retire, and in that case perhaps you would like to finish your final years as a Camp Prefect in Germania?' offered Macro.

'Sir, I have only ever known the glorious 2$^{nd}$ and they have a new Camp Prefect,' replied Artorius.

'I am sure with the support of Caligula here we can rearrange things to your liking. I think you need time to grieve and put your house in order. I suggest you take, shall we say, ten days from now and you can return with your answer? In the meantime, take this note to the treasury clerk. Dismissed.' Macro quickly scribbled a note on the back of Artorius' orders and handed it back to him.

Caligula, smiling, held the door for Artorius as he replaced his cassis and saluted both of his seniors. Somewhat in shock from the abrupt ending to his interview, Artorius walked in a trance to the paymaster's office, where he received further funds. Collecting his horse, he slowly made his way down the Vicus Longus to the Forum, passed by a troupe of mounted Praetorian Guard heading for the barracks.

Inside the barracks a short time later, Macro exploded as he was informed by Adolfi that despite a search at the farmhouse and the surrounding area, Victus Claudian had once again escaped.

Finding no signs of Aaron or Rachel in the Forum, Artorius lodged his horse and made his way to their house on foot. There was a party atmosphere within when he knocked on the door. Rachel answered it, offering condolences for the loss of Amoria and Alia. Artorius stood tall, but he was shaking inside as he fought with his feelings, and his eyes began to water. It didn't seem appropriate to celebrate.

Marcus couldn't help himself; at least his father was alive, and he thanked Tia's memory for giving him hope, which brought his inevitable tears. Magda gazed on at him lovingly, trying to understand her own feelings. Lucretia and Gorax sat together with a beaker of wine. Cezar felt surplus to the occasion until Marcus gathered himself and explained that Cezar was orphaned. Rachel responded by throwing her arms around him, and Cezar surrendered to the grief of his own life.

It was some hours later that the group withdrew from Aaron and Rachel's and made the journey Artorius had been dreading. Cezar, with renewed confidence, engaged Magda in conversation although it was obvious to all except Marcus that she only had eyes for him.

Turning off the metalled road, Artorius faltered, inviting the others to continue. Marcus remained as Lucretia encouraged the rest to proceed onwards. With the party having moved past them, Artorius looked at his son and with tears welling up inside, he dismounted from his horse and Marcus followed suit. Artorius fell to his knees, as his emotions finally imploded. Marcus knelt beside his father, holding him as best he could, and succumbed to his own grief.

'Why!' screamed Artorius repeatedly, his arms flailing in frustration.

As the rest of the party crested the hill, Lucretia, Gorax and Cezar couldn't believe the sight in front of them. The ruined villa had been cleared, except for the central fireplace, and had been replaced by a new wooden framework. The burnt remains lay in a pile beside the barn. Inside the walls was a hive of activity, but not at a loss to security, for the gates were shut. As the horses were walked closer to the walls, Gorax called for Georgiakis, who appeared almost immediately. His recognition was instantaneous. Both gates slowly opened and Georgiakis strolled from between them, reaching up to take Gorax's hand as he looked for Marcus and feared the worst.

Lucretia read his thoughts and responded. 'Marcus and Artorius are following. This is the daughter of Artorius' cousin,' she said, pointing to Magda.

Georgiakis' face lit up at the news and beckoned the group in, looking back up the hill for father and son. As the group entered they were greeted like long-lost family, and news of Artorius was on everyone's tongues. Georgiakis called out to male and female staff alike to prepare a feast for the returning master.

Artorius' face was filled with shock and horror when he eventually gazed down on the ruined villa. Marcus' face was one of surprise to find that the rebuilding had already started. The repaired gates lay wide open, and in two columns on either side of the entrance stood the staff. Artorius looked at the many strange faces and their numbers and turned to Marcus.

'The staff were freed and I allowed their partners and children to move here,' stated his son. 'Many have brought trades, and financially the estate was doing very well until Victus attacked it.'

Georgiakis stepped forward, bowing to both Artorius and Marcus. Artorius took the man in a strong embrace as he slid from his horse to the sound of united cheers. Georgiakis took the two masters around the skeleton of the new building and pointed out the new homes that were starting to line the walls.

'I hope you don't mind the new homes that are springing up inside the wall line? I thought it best that they should be inside, for safety for all. I am sure young Marcus has informed you of how well the estate is doing? We have our own forge and smithy behind the barn, and his weaponry is superb and attracting a lot of interest. Most of the ladies are more than proficient with a bow and the men are well drilled to protect the estate should there ever be another attack.'

Artorius looked around in disbelief. His father's estate had become a self-supporting village, and outside the walls land was being cultivated for food, an addition Marcus hadn't yet seen. In the few days Marcus had been away, Georgiakis and the staff had truly started to raise the estate beyond its former state.

'I don't need to ask how you all feed yourselves. Between Marcus and yourselves you have created something my father would have been proud of. Thank you,' announced Artorius to the gathered staff.

It was then that Artorius and Marcus saw the family tomb adorned with flowers; the staff parted and their eyes followed father and son. Artorius stumbled, his head dropping as he attempted to hide the deep feelings welling up inside him, but Marcus supported him.

Father and son stepped slowly forward, and Artorius reached out to touch the cold marble that surrounded all that was left of his life's love. Unable to hold back the tide of tears, he turned to Marcus, crushing him to his chest. Both sobbed uncontrollably in shared grief. The staff looked on helplessly, Georgiakis shuffling them away. Magda stood silently, tears wetting her eyes, and Cezar slipped his arm around her to offer his shoulder, which wasn't rejected.

Georgiakis took Gorax aside. 'Gorax, someone came looking for you while you were gone. I told him I didn't know when you would return. He said he knew Victus' current location. I told him that he should inform Macro and the Praetorians, as I believed there might still be a warrant out for him. That was the day after you left.'

'You did well, Georgiakis. I don't think we need to tell the masters, they have enough to deal with for the present,' responded Gorax.

Darkness engulfed father and son without them being aware, until Lucretia swept towards them carrying hot spiced wine. Artorius thanked her and offered some to the family altar before downing the rest. Lucretia walked away, the men following.

A table stood filled with celebratory food, but some feared the sombre mood had destroyed the moment. Unbuckling his spatha, Artorius called out for the staff to join Marcus and himself to celebrate the passing of their collective loved ones.

'My wife, my daughter, Tia, and all those you lost in the

attack deserve a proper send-off. We need a pyre.'

Burnt timbers were dragged together and Artorius added a libation before sprinkling it with oil. Dorina offered a firebrand and as the first flames licked at the tortured timbers, Artorius raised his beaker.

'To all of those who gave joy to our lives and were taken too early – we salute you.'

Artorius and Marcus whispered their own private salutations to their lost loves.

As the new family celebrated in the heat of the pyre, memories filled the gathering with laughter and tears alike. Marcus and his father remained wrapped in blankets as the staff eventually slipped away, and Magda looked on until Lucretia suggested that she retire for the night.

Artorius explained Macro's offer to Marcus, but he decided that talk of Ilona would have to wait; nerves were too raw. Marcus listened and reflected on the possibilities that lay ahead for them both, unaware of his father's hidden agenda.

The pair sat watching the last embers as the sun rose in a cloudless sky. Georgiakis approached them with fresh hot wine, and the question on everyone's lips was: *What happens now?*

## Chapter 20

As Artorius and Marcus settled back into the estate, a saddle-sore and dusty Victus skirted around Genua and headed for the Villa Aphrodite, where he was guaranteed a welcoming embrace. The main gate was brightly lit by monsters breathing flames, and music floated over the walls from unseen instruments. Posted either side of sealed wooden gates, with broad curve-bladed swords, stood two of the tallest and darkest-skinned Egyptian males Victus had ever seen. Both blocked his path, their swords now held across their chests as he made to ride towards the closed gates.

'Step aside for your master and open the gates,' demanded Victus, but neither moved.

'There is only a mistress here, and judging by the state you are in, I suggest you turn around and find a cheaper location,' boomed the closest male.

Victus' hand slipped to his sword pommel. 'I suggest you call your mistress Naomi and inform her that Victus Claudian – *her partner* – is here.'

The name appeared to jolt their memories. Looking at each other, they stepped aside and opened the gates, bowing to Victus as he passed. He struck out at the nearest male with his riding whip, leaving a red welt across the man's face; he stared back defiantly and spat blood from a cut lip.

The garden interior was ablaze with light, and small buildings were scattered about the grassed area with scantily clad females either being chased by men or carrying wine and fine glasses. Victus was amazed by the changes; it was like a large garden party. Hobbling his horse, he strode towards a lone figure sat with her back to him on the edge of the sparkling fountain, where stone nymphs decanted water into an enlarged pool. He knew it was Naomi, but she seemed different from the distance between them. Then he realised why, when she turned to face him: she was pregnant!

He stopped suddenly. *Have things changed that much since I last saw her?* he thought.

Naomi had turned and stood at the sound of footfalls, her face lit up, but then it dropped as she saw Victus' response. *He doesn't know I'm carrying his child*, she thought. As quickly as she could, she closed the gap between them. Victus' face was red with anger and before he could say anything she snatched his hand and held it against her stomach as he tried to pull away.

'This is your child. I was pregnant when we last parted. I didn't intend it, but then I thought, if you never returned, what better memory could I have of you?'

'Why didn't you tell me? When are you due?' Victus demanded.

'You weren't in the right state of mind to know, and you still would have gone – your mission was too important. I'm due in Iullius.' Naomi took Victus' shocked face in her hands, kissing him firmly.

Taking her in his arms, Victus carried her towards the villa, which was a storey higher. She nuzzled into his shoulder, staring into his face and seeking an answer that wasn't forthcoming.

Slipping carefully through the open villa door, he was faced with stairs rising in front of him that weren't there before.

'The top floor is ours,' Naomi indicated.

The stairs were of fine pink marble and three rooms led off the landing. Naomi reached out for the central door's handle, pushing the door inward. The room was decorated sumptuously, with fine material hanging from the ochre-coloured walls. A marble table took central place in the room, and a silver wine jug and beakers adorned it. A balcony lay before the couple, with fine drapes drawn aside.

A stunned Victus placed Naomi on a padded seat in front of the table. He turned slowly around the room, each alcove and corner was filled with a bust or figurine. Everything, he knew was of the finest quality.

'You like?' Naomi asked. 'You may have seen some of the pieces before – they once adorned the houses of late senators, courtesy of Sejanus. I bought them at a knock-down price and stored them for such an occasion as this. The room to your left is our bedroom, the other is my surprise.'

Victus walked towards the right-hand door and pushed it noiselessly on oiled hinges. He stared inside. It looked every bit a torture chamber, but he knew that it had been designed to be anything but. He turned to see Naomi smiling, and he returned the look.

'I am afraid it will be a while till I am able to indulge, but this doesn't mean you can't indulge till then. We must be gentler for now, but I am sure I can arrange a demonstration of the room,' she offered, as Victus stepped forward into her arms.

Shock and horror filled his brain. *I have never considered children, thinking they would be a hindrance. I'm not sure if I am ready for this*, he thought.

Outwardly he played his part well over the coming days, being the attentive father-to-be, and in settling back into the villa it gave him time to think. From his hiding place, Victus collated information on the survivors of Sejanus' plot. Only Publius Pomponius Secundus had somehow avoided death or execution, though he languished in the Mamertine Prison in Rome. *My vendetta is incomplete and I need to place it on hold. I need to escape from this wilderness by furthering my contact with the heir apparent, which looks to be Caligula. But Macro is cultivating the same idea,* Victus considered.

For Naomi, her thoughts were purely maternal, and she didn't see through Victus' façade.

## Chapter 21

Five days had passed since Artorius' conversation with Macro. He watched the staff, committed to rebuilding the villa and the continued economic growth to everyone's benefit. He had avoided giving Georgiakis any idea of where his complicated plans lay. Marcus took great delight in showing Artorius how productive the estate was and the justification for retaining it. Artorius needed to confide in someone, someone he could talk things through with, without being judged. There was only Aaron and Rachel, but he wasn't sure how they would respond to his news; he needed help, not condemnation. With five days before he must present his decision to Macro, he had to have the conversation with Marcus soonest.

The day was barely an hour old, and a mist rolled off the river hiding the paddocks as Artorius rode from the estate. The road towards Rome was busy, with a myriad of carts laden with all manner of items heading for the city's populace. Without realising where he was going, Artorius found himself in the Aventine, gazing at where the local smithy had been. The yard and building was now occupied by Rome's great poor and unwashed, seeking shelter wherever they found it. Struggling to ride through the strengthening tide of humanity, Artorius found another smithy, and was surprised by the inflated prices.

Walking was no easier as he made his way through the throng that was making for the Forum and the surrounding temples. Passing through at this hour, even on foot, was difficult as the first stalls were opening and the night slops were thrown from open doors without a care for passers-by. With no sign, yet of Aaron or Rachel, he pressed on. Reaching their house, he found it a hive of activity. Knocking without reply, Artorius knocked again and all went quiet inside before Aaron's face peered around a crack in the partly opened door.

'Artorius, come in! We were just preparing to walk to the Forum – will you join us?' said Aaron as Rachel stepped forward and hugged him.

'I have need of good counsel, and you two are the best I know.'

'The only counsel, I'd wager. Take a seat. If it's counsel you need, you'll have privacy here,' responded Aaron jokingly, as he was cuffed by Rachel.

Artorius explained how he had sought refuge on the night of a blizzard and found the hut occupied by Rosevetha and Ilona. As he described Rosevetha and her gift, Rachel clutched tightly at a religious amulet around her neck. Artorius tried to explain that he had been expected, and whilst in a drug-induced sleep had made love to Ilona at the two women's instigation. Aaron looked at Rachel and she, in turn, at him in disbelief. Artorius related the details about Victus' ambush and being left to die in the snowy wilderness with wolves stalking him. Expecting death, he had crawled to a cave where Ilona and her pack of wolves found and rescued him.

'That's a trifle far-fetched. A woman with a wolf pack? Did you take a knock to your head?' enquired Aaron suspiciously.

'I thought at least you would believe me,' replied Artorius, but he continued with his tale.

Rachel was enraptured. Aaron was growing more sceptical at the fanciful story, especially when Artorius described being accepted by the alpha male and hunting with it.

'Didn't you give any thought for Amoria and your

family?' snapped Aaron.

'Aaron, let him finish. You know he would have made his way back if he could – and he obviously couldn't, could you, Artorius? Ilona is pregnant, isn't she?'

Artorius' head dropped. His face reddened and he felt the frustration growing inside, and questioned whether he should have come at all. He explained that when he came around he had refused to share a bed with Ilona out of respect for Amoria, but the scene was already set.

'I was too weak and the weather too bad to make it back to the nearest barracks. Twice I had been told to return to Rome before it was too late, but I never knew what that meant. I was trapped between duty and my family, then fate stepped in! Rosevetha and Ilona saved my life, and yes, I was tricked, but I am as much to blame. The son she carries is mine.'

'Where are they now?' enquired Rachel.

Artorius explained about their current location and what he had planned for their future, that was until Marcus had broken the news to him about Amoria and Alia. He felt responsibility for both Ilona and their son, and combined with Macro's offer, there was only one solution: return to the 2nd Augusta.

'So you haven't yet told Marcus about Ilona?' asked Aaron snidely.

'I was foolish to think you wouldn't judge me,' responded Artorius angrily.

'Stop it, you two! Aaron, I've never seen this side of you before, enough. Artorius, you and Amoria were made for each other for life, but the fates decided otherwise. There is a young woman out there carrying a son she obviously wants. Is it love, or responsibility that drives you north?'

'Both. I could not help myself. Amoria was always in my thoughts, staying any relationship except friendship with Ilona. Before I knew of Amoria's passing, Ilona showed me an image of the three of us together, of what might be, but now I know it is meant to be. I need to tell Marcus and I hope he will come with me, but would you oversee the estate for us if we left?'

Rachel hugged him and whispered, '*It will be okay.*'

Aaron, however, looked stern-faced at Artorius, considering what had been said and the history between them all. He couldn't comprehend what his friend had gone through, and what he must be suffering because of his losses, but still with the chance of a future.

'The estate goes without saying, it will be our pleasure to help. But you need to be fully honest with Marcus, as you were with us. I cannot say how he will respond, but you are the only family he has left. If he chooses to remain then we will look after him, but don't condemn his choice. We wish you luck,' said Aaron, as he drew Rachel to him and held out his hand to Artorius.

Artorius thanked them both and set off towards the Forum, blundering through the populace and toying over the best way to tell Marcus. He wondered whether he should seek the support of others close to him first.

Retrieving his horse, he trotted back to the estate. The road was sparsely filled. He stopped at the crest of the hill by the gorse, to once more look down at his parents' estate. Inside the walls, he could make out two people that he took to be Marcus and Cezar, giving some of the male staff a hard time with sword and scutum, and overseen by Gorax and Lucretia. For fun, Artorius, with spatha drawn, galloped down the hill. The alarm bell rang out and the practising parties dispersed to their positions. Marcus, Cezar and Gorax ran for the gate as it was secured, while Lucretia ran for the wall, arming herself with bow and quiver as she went.

Artorius, laughing, skidded to a halt as a single gate opened. A sweaty but impressive Marcus appeared, spinning his double swords, closely followed by Cezar and Gorax. Artorius leapt from his stationary horse and clapped the presentation before him.

'Where have you been, Father? It must have been important, leaving so early,' enquired Marcus.

'I had to discuss a few things about our future with Aaron and Rachel.'

'So you've made a decision then?' asked Marcus.

'Not quite; I need a little more time and we need to talk. Gorax, could I have a moment of your time, and where's Lucretia?' enquired Artorius.

Lucretia stepped spritely from the wall and joined Gorax. The pair looking questioningly at Artorius.

'Walk with me, please, the pair of you,' Artorius said, heading for the paddock.

'Marcus has accepted you back, Gorax, where I probably would not have. It was a smart move on his part, as with many other things. He has his grandfather's brains and skills beyond most I have ever known. I have noticed that you and Lucretia are close and I wish you well in wherever it takes you. I need your counsel now, as my son's friends, before I speak to Marcus. You have heard how I was rescued, but the story doesn't end there...'

Artorius sat with his back against the paddock railings, looking out over the killing ground, and invited Lucretia and Gorax to do the same. The couple looked at each other and sat expectantly. Artorius reminded them about Rosevetha and Ilona, and nervously related the rest of the story. His friends formulated the reasoning behind this conversation, but when Artorius informed them that Ilona was pregnant, their stunned faces said it all. Artorius told of the predictions and the night he was first stranded.

'Typical woman, seeing a good opportunity and making the best of it,' interjected Gorax.

'Is that what you see me as?' snapped Lucretia. She made to stand, but was prevented by Gorax.

'Of course not,' he stumbled.

'Please, you two – fate has many strange routes to fulfilment. Breda and Rosevetha both foresaw what would happen. I was too late, and because of that I was unable to react. I loved Amoria very deeply and I don't know if I will ever be able to love another in the same way. However, Ilona carries my child. She is a lovely woman, a good friend, and she will make a good mother. Before you ask, when I return north – yes, when – it won't be out of duty alone. I have strong feelings for her,' related Artorius.

Gorax looked stunned and turned to look at Lucretia. He swallowed carefully before speaking. 'Fate rules our lives, and for the most part we have to accept it. I have growing feelings for Lucretia and I never thought I would have such feelings again. Like you, Artorius, I had a wife and family, and fate took them all from me. I was in despair of life. If you are asking for my humble counsel, then I suggest you speak to Marcus. You have a second chance and another son on the way – grasp it with both hands. If Marcus refuses to go, it will be hard to leave him, but you know he will be well looked after here.'

'I thought of you only as a friend, Gorax,' Lucretia responded. 'I feared to hope for more. I agree that Ilona is a special woman – a seer and a controller of her own wolves, and she carries your son, Artorius. I think you should only travel north, maybe with the loss of your son, if you truly love her. Marcus needs to know, and soon,' she added.

Artorius thanked them for their counsel and wandered down to the river as they returned to the villa. *Could I bring Ilona and her wolves to our forest? It would certainly keep away unwanted visitors...* He laughed momentarily. *But what of the prediction that it will not be me who has the satisfaction of killing Victus – which son will it be?*

His thoughts were terminated by his name being called. He had lost track of time, and darkness now wrapped its cloak around him as he saw his son bounding towards him.

'Father, you look deeply troubled. Is it Mother and Alia?'

'Partly. I have decisions to make, and with them are consequences for everyone. We must talk, but the hour grows late. Hunt with me tomorrow, father and son?' requested Artorius.

Marcus nodded and clasped his father's hand.

*

The day started early for father and son. To Artorius, sleeping on hard ground was a lost memory of the early days in the legion under canvas. He brushed away the deep sadness that was drowning him, and as an image of Amoria appeared to him, smiling, he felt ashamed. He wished she were there just once more, so he could explain. His head dropped and as he closed his eyes, tears escaped.

Marcus, noting the quietness from his father, didn't know how to react. He knew how he himself felt over Tia, but his father's loss must be a hundred-fold. Marcus collected a bowl of hot oats, and adding a little honey, offered it to his father. He explained in detail what Tia and himself had planned. For the first time, he mentioned their unborn child.

Artorius was stunned. *Maybe he will understand about Ilona after all*, he thought.

Artorius, with a food satchel, collected a pair of pila and a shield. Marcus had his double swords strapped to his back and chose his bow and quiver, before they headed towards the forest on foot, watched by the eagle-eyed Gorax and Lucretia.

'A fine sight, father and son going hunting,' Gorax murmured, fighting back tears in memory of his own son.

Lucretia threw her arm around his shoulder, and turning him towards her, drew him close, his head resting on her shoulder.

'Maybe I should follow them for safety, with Victus about?' suggested Gorax.

Lucretia shook her head and, taking his hand, led him towards the river where they stripped, slipping into their own embrace as the waters wrapped around them.

*

Marcus matched his father's pace as they strode towards the metalled road and the forest beyond. There was little traffic as the pair crossed the road and as they found an ancient track, the forest sucked them in. The edge was thinly filled and light spilled over the ground, displaying its green finery, and the air around them exploded with birdsong. Each was deep in thought as the deeper forest devoured them in its darkness and their footfalls lightened. Their combined eyes pierced the forest for any movement, but everything that moved was above them in flight.

The sound of water running and a blaze of light brought the pair into a clearing. Crystal-clear water cascaded over large rocks; moss and lichen covered the surrounding banks. Artorius sat on the streamside rocks and opening the food satchel, tossed a portion of cheese to Marcus and bade him to sit. Finding a wine sack, Artorius took a large gulp for courage.

'You have something to tell me, Father?' queried Marcus.

'What do you mean?'

'I've sensed untold words since we met, and I know it has to do with you being missing in Germania,' explained Marcus.

Artorius swigged another mouthful of wine before passing the sack to Marcus. Drawing himself up, he began to relate his tale of the snowstorm and the first time he saw Ilona. With care, Artorius described Ilona and her mother, and the second warning to return to Rome as soon as he could. He retold the episode with the wolf pack and how Ilona and her pack had saved his life, though he didn't know it at the time. He described the dreams that haunt a person when life is in the hands of the gods. He explained in detail how Ilona and her mother had done everything to keep him alive, but how he was trapped by the snows for many days. He described how, in regaining his strength, he had hunted with Ilona and her wolves.

Marcus sat wide eyed, as if he were listening to a storyteller. Artorius tried to explain how he had learned to respect and admire Ilona, though in every sane moment he thought of Amoria and the family.

Marcus' face changed as he started to think through the tale that was being related. 'You slept with Ilona, didn't you?' he asked, sitting upright.

'It isn't as simple as that,' responded Artorius. He started his explanation of the dream he had had: his seduction.

Marcus scoffed at the idea that a man could be seduced when he wasn't willing. Artorius was at a loss as to what to say, but he insisted on the truth of the tale. He spoke of the day when he noticed Ilona was pregnant, when she told him the baby was his, from the night of the storm.

Marcus stood, throwing the wine sack at his father, disgust written across his face.

Artorius' head dropped. 'What can I say? It was as much a shock to me. I loved your mother so much and I felt I had betrayed her – and you all – but what could I do? Rosevetha told me that the pregnancy was due to the fates and that my new son's life would depend on me. I tried to make provision for them both and left them in Germania to return to you and your mother.'

Marcus walked up to his father and punched him full in the face. The forces of it shocked Artorius. Blood trickled from a cut on his lip as he stood and faced his son, tears filling his eyes as he set his jaw.

'If it will help, hit me again – I deserve it. In all my years I have only slept with one woman: your mother, and she knew that.'

Marcus stood shaking, fists clenched and knuckles as white as snow, in front of his father. He wanted to punch and kick him for desecrating the memory of his mother, but he was all Marcus had left, and though he didn't want to, he believed what he was being told.

'So where is she now, and how do they know it will be a boy?' questioned Marcus.

Artorius took up his story again, explaining where Ilona and Rosevetha were and what he had been told. He added that, on finding Amoria dead, she would have wanted him to look after both his sons.

'I feel duty bound to take Macro's offer of a return to the 2nd Augusta to look after my new son, your brother, but I want you to come with me. The fates have decreed that one of you will have the satisfaction of ending Victus' days, but I know not which of you, or when. Ilona said that the wolves would accept you and your brother as equals. I have known what it's like to walk and hunt with her pets – the leader, Donor, is beyond explanation. Your mother will always be a special part of my life and nothing can change that, just as Tia will always be a part of yours, even though you will love again one day.'

'I will never love anyone as much as I loved Tia, so don't try to cloud my judgement. If you wish to return to Ilona, I will understand – he is, after all, your son, but I will remain at the estate. Maybe one day I will meet my brother, when the tear in my heart has healed, but till then I cannot forgive you. I'm sorry.'

Marcus turned his back on his father and with a stooped back, started to walk slowly away. Artorius' head dropped in despair and tears filled his eyes. Once again he must choose.

A twig snapped, and both father and son froze and looked up as they sought the intruder. There was snorting sounds followed by squeals, and a sow and her piglets broke cover, noses burrowing in the undergrowth. The sow raised her head, displaying a fine pair of tusks, and stared directly at Artorius and Marcus. The piglets ran around squealing, oblivious of the danger their mother had perceived. Artorius and Marcus spun around at the sound of something large running towards them - it was a boar, half as high as Marcus, and it had one target: them.

Artorius lowered his pila and taunted the creature, beating his shield to draw him. 'Step back, this one's mine,' he shouted as Marcus drew an arrow.

The boar and Artorius collided, and the pila point snapped and lodged in the creature as head and shield impacted. Artorius was thrown backwards and the boar continued goring at him as he rolled instinctively away.

198

There was a hiss and a thud as Marcus' first arrow buried itself in the creature's neck, but still its tusks swung at Artorius, ripping at his leg guards.

Dropping his bow, Marcus walked calmly towards the incensed creature, rotating his swords. The boar's energy was weakening, but the fight in him was as strong as ever as it dipped its head and charged at Marcus. Marcus could smell the creature's foul breath as he swung away and sliced down with Egorix's sword into its neck. There was a scream of pain as metal sliced into the boar's neck, and it collapsed in death throes.

'Look out,' screamed Artorius as the sow charged at Marcus from behind.

Marcus spun and sliced at the charging sow as it tossed him aside, slipping beneath his blades. Artorius, in full flight with pila and shield, charged, screaming as he ran. His pila ripped into the sow's bulk, splitting her heart, and as it collapsed the piglets gathered around its dying mother.

Breathing heavily, Marcus sat tending to a cut on his shin, inflicted by one of the sow's tusks. Artorius looked at his own bruised legs, then to his son.

'Just a scratch. Shame we had to kill the sow,' acknowledged Marcus.

The piglets nudged the sow, its life spent in their defence as Artorius dragged the boar from the forest. Marcus rounded up the squealing piglets and, lifting the sow over his shoulder, he dragged it after his father, the piglets happily following behind.

Sweat poured from both father and son with the exertion. Artorius struggled, observed by Marcus. Thinking on his feet, Marcus dropped the sow on the roadside, suggesting his father remain where he was, and the suggestion was readily accepted.

Artorius pondered as he took several deep breaths: *I've not recovered as well as I thought, my exile has taken a heavy toll on me.*

Marcus returned with a cart and Gorax, to find Artorius dozing in the afternoon sun. He looked down on his father who was deathly pale, his mind confused. The sight reminded him of the last days of his grandfather. *Am I betraying my love for Mother if I go with him? What would Tia have done?*

Marcus felt a breeze on his face and Tia's voice whispered in his ear: 'Think of the living, the dead are at peace.'

Gorax, struggling with the boar, looked at Marcus. 'Did you say something?'

'Why?'

'I thought I heard you speak,' replied Gorax.

Marcus shook his head as he grabbed the boar's rear legs and pushed the bulk on to the cart.

'This will be welcome fresh meat and we can rear the piglets,' suggested Marcus. Gorax nodded.

With the two carcasses and the piglets loaded, Artorius shuddered awake and was aided to his feet and on to the cart by Marcus.

The trio were greeted by Lucretia, who read Artorius' colour straight away.

'A jug of wine for the hunters. Sit, and I'll bring it. Then I'll see to your wound, Marcus,' suggested Magda, gripping his hand in hers and smiling.

Artorius slumped on to a bench, watched by Marcus, who felt a hand on his shoulder. Lucretia stood behind him, and having placed a tray of wine and beakers on the bench, she beckoned Marcus away.

'Your father has suffered more than he thought. The

stresses will have weakened his heart, he'll need you more than ever,' she offered.

'He's just had the audacity to tell me he has another woman, and that she is pregnant. How could he have done this to the memory of my mother?'

'The fates control us, who are we to fight them?' responded Lucretia.

'You don't seem surprised.'

'Your father asked Gorax and I for our advice.'

'And what was your advice?' snapped Marcus, thinking, *I'm always the last to know anything.*

'He was left to make his own choice, but we said we would look out for you if you remained,' said Gorax as he joined Lucretia.

'When he told me, I was angry and ashamed of him. I lost my temper and hit him and I wanted to continue hitting him. I told him to leave and that I would remain, but look at him now – he reminds me of how grandfather was before he died.'

'He hasn't fully healed, and perhaps he never will, which makes your decision harder to make. I have seen it in many gladiators – they lose the will to fight,' suggested Gorax.

'I am sorry for snapping,' said Marcus. 'The estate will remain in the family and it will be rebuilt in memory of all those we have lost. Will you both stay?'

'The fates have drawn us together. I for one will remain, if Lucretia does.' Gorax took Lucretia's hand and squeezed it. She returned the grip and smiled.

\*

The glow of the fire matched the bloodied sunset, and the smell of roasting boar, turning slowly, filled the air. Everyone looked on at the feast before them, mouths watering.

Artorius had slipped away to the family tomb, where he sat talking to Amoria, expecting her to answer with forgiveness. Taking the amulet Ilona had given him from a pouch on his belt, he gripped it tightly before tying it around his neck. *Maybe this will help*, he thought.

In that instant, he felt cold as a host appeared before him. His mother and father stood with their arms around Amoria and Alia, and Cassius with his arm around Porcia, holding their son. Tears poured from Artorius' eyes. *Is madness finally taking over? I can't take much more...*

Amoria reached out to him, and even though he knew he must be dreaming, his arms reached for her too. She smiled as her voice filled his head, telling him to seek happiness in the north. It was the sign he needed.

He longed for a final kiss, but it was not to be as the group faded at the sound of footsteps from behind. Artorius felt lost, his enthusiasm drained.

Marcus called out to his father, and Artorius heard his voice, but struggled with its origins.

'The boar is cooked and the staff are awaiting your decision,' his son said.

Marcus aided his weakened father to walk towards the feast. Gorax stepped forward with a beaker of wine for both, then resumed his place beside Lucretia.

'Georgiakis, please call the staff together, I want everyone to hear what I have to say,' requested Artorius.

With everyone gathered together, Artorius thanked every member of staff for what they had done while he was away. Foreboding crept on to the faces of many as they listened to his words. Artorius turned to Marcus and suggested that he should be the one to give the good news.

Marcus stood, ahead of his years, in front of the gathering. 'The news you all want to hear is that the villa will remain with the family. There is a place for all of you who want it.'

Marcus looked to Gorax and Lucretia, hand in hand, and the staff cheered before Marcus quelled them to continue.

'My father returns to Germania to finish his time in the 2nd Augusta and to follow his destiny.'

Marcus looked to his father. Artorius' head dropped, and the staff looked shocked, with murmurings of '*No*' rippling through the crowd.

Marcus offered his hands to both Georgiakis and Gorax. 'Georgiakis, you will remain in joint charge with Gorax, who will oversee everyone's safety. Aaron will take care of the finances as he always has, and he will have the final say. Yes, I see by your faces that you have guessed – I will be travelling with my father, and I intend to join the 2nd Augusta. What say you, Cezar, will you join me?'

Artorius stepped forward, tears of pride filling his eyes. *What made him change his mind?* he wondered, as he crushed Marcus to him. Rapturous applause and cheers erupted from those around them.

'You are all I have, Father. My destiny lays out there, maybe it's time to find it,' Marcus whispered.

Cezar offered his hand to Marcus, who took it firmly. Stepping back, they drew a sword each and punched it into the air. 'To the Legion,' they both shouted, to more cheers.

Magda looked on, amazed at the revelations – she was going home, and Marcus was going too.

Marcus strode towards Dorina and hugged her. 'No matter what happens to any of us, we would be honoured if you would remain and spend the rest of your life here.'

Dorina clung to Marcus, sobbing as Artorius joined them. She pulled away, wiping her tears. 'I'm still the head cook and the feast is going cold, but thank you both.'

## Chapter 22

The first hour had barely started and the staff were all about their respective jobs when Artorius slipped out of the estate, heading for Rome and Macro with his decision. He had misgivings still, especially in pushing Scipio aside to become the 2nd Augusta's Camp Prefect, a position his father had craved but never reached.

Marcus and Cezar toured the estate. The staff were happier than Marcus had ever known. Magda tagged along to Cezar's delight, but she only had eyes for one and Cezar had noticed it wasn't him.

As they reached the river, Marcus suggested a swim. Magda was more than keen, leaving Cezar with no choice. Stripping to his undergarments, Marcus ran and dived into the cool waters. Magda stood, admiring Marcus' body, but hesitated before diving into the river fully clothed. Cezar stripped and slowly walked into the waters till he was waist deep, watching as Marcus and Magda raced each other across the river and back.

Marcus strolled out of the water, his thin underclothes clinging to every contour. Cezar awaited Magda's emergence. Her leather clothing clung to her also, but spared her embarrassment, though the sight of Marcus brought a flush to her face.

'Have you never seen a man before?' Marcus laughed at the red-faced Magda before him.

She didn't know where to look when Cezar struggled out of the water, his erection quite evident. She turned and ran back towards the barn, her emotions in overdrive. She couldn't understand her feelings or the dampness between her legs. In tears, she sought out Lucretia and explained what had happened.

Lucretia smiled and drew her close. 'Everyone has these

feelings at some time, they are a normal part of becoming an adult. There are many more to come.'

'But why would Cezar be like that?' Magda asked.

'I know you have eyes for Marcus, but haven't you noticed the way Cezar looks at you?'

'But I don't like Cezar that way.'

'You have a lot to learn, young lady. Come you need to dry yourself, you're shivering.' Lucretia led her away.

*

With Macro duly informed, and Aaron and Rachel appraised of the situation, Artorius headed back to the estate, assured he had made the right decision now that Marcus was accompanying him. He was pleased to see that security hadn't been forgotten – the alarm bell rang out as he trotted down to the gate to be met by Marcus and Cezar.

'If you two are to join my Legion then you need to hone your skills, and I like the idea of my men being proficient with the bow if they are to be in the cavalry units. Cezar, you have three of the most proficient archers I've ever seen to teach you, and we have three days to make a start.'

Artorius' heart was already lifting at the thought of seeing Ilona again, though guilty thoughts of Amoria still hovered in the background.

Walking through the gate, Artorius was taken aback by the young woman with Lucretia – he couldn't recall having seen her before. With long flowing dress and hair tied up, he didn't realise at first that he was staring at a very different Magda.

Cezar too stood, mouth open at the sight, whereas a smiling Marcus tapped him on the shoulder and whispered to him to close his mouth.

'I have suggested that Cezar should learn the skill of the

bow before joining the legion cavalry,' said Artorius.

'An extra skill is always an asset. We could start today,' responded Lucretia.

'I'll change,' added Magda.

'Don't change on my account,' was Cezar's instant response, until Marcus whispered in his ear. 'But if you'll be more comfortable...' he added.

Marcus' mind filled with images of the first time he had seen Tia with a bow, and how he had loved her in her short tunic. His eyes misted. He was so ensconced in his memories that he hadn't heard the others talking until his name was called. He felt the tears of his lost love on his cheek, and there were worried looks in front of him.

'Memories,' remarked Marcus, to collective smiles and sympathetic looks.

Artorius placed his hand on his son's shoulder as they walked to the sleeping barn, where Marcus collected his bow and quiver. Lucretia and Magda appeared with theirs, both wearing short tunics; Cezar didn't know where to look and gave a wink to Marcus, who shrugged his shoulders and smirked.

Cezar was a poor pupil, or at least he pretended to be, to get closer tuition from a frustrated Magda. There was little difference between the two women, though Lucretia's skills just took the edge to rapturous applause from Gorax.

Magda asked Marcus to teach her his sword skills, and Tia once again came to mind. He tried intimating that Cezar was as good as he, but Magda saw through his poor deflection.

By the end of three days, Cezar could hit a large target, much to the delight of all. Magda sought closer contact with Marcus, who continued to be oblivious to her looks and lingering touch.

Artorius had been armed with his orders: the time had finally come to depart for the north. Lucretia and Gorax's offer to travel with them was brushed aside by both Artorius and Marcus.

\*

The first hour of day had barely started, and a mist clung to the ground as Artorius took a final walk around the estate. *I doubt I will ever see this place again, unless I can return with Ilona and the wolves*, he thought.

Marcus was saying his goodbyes when Lucretia begged his indulgence; she looked troubled.

'I must make you aware of Magda's feelings before you travel.'

'I know how Cezar feels about her,' he replied.

'No, Marcus, your mind is blocked with thoughts of Tia. It is you she desires, not Cezar.'

'That can't be. I've never encouraged her. She is like a sister, no more than that,' he responded.

'I have already spoken to her of your love for Tia, but she sees only you.'

'Cezar would be devastated, and I cannot love another. I must talk to her,' Marcus insisted.

'I have counselled her and I hope she has listened, but please, be gentle with her feelings.'

Marcus' thoughts were interrupted by his father calling for everyone to mount up. Marcus rode alongside him, determined to keep his distance from Magda, who followed behind with Cezar.

Slipping across the Tiberis via the Pons Aemilius, they made a short stop to say their farewells to Aaron and Rachel at the Forum. Turning north through the Mons Capitolinus and on to the Via Flaminia, the pace quickened as they headed towards Tia's lake at Marcus' request.

There he begged a moment alone, striding to the lake's edge where he sat on a rock. Gazing into the cool waters, he said his goodbyes to Tia, promising to return whenever he could. He felt a cold presence beside him, but there were no words. He knew then that Tia would always be there, wherever he was.

Marcus stood and turned to footfalls from behind: his father. They scanned the lake with no sign of Hades or his herd, and headed back to Cezar and Magda before heading north towards the Legion.

Six days of hard riding brought them into Placentia in the late hours of the day, where the horses were left with the mutatione. Drusus sat on a bench outside his inn, enjoying the afternoon sun, his son on his knee and a large cold frothy beer at his feet, oblivious to anything else.

'We'll have three of them when you're ready,' shouted Artorius, pointing to the beer.

Drusus looked up, taken aback by the shout. He grinned and called Helga: 'We have visitors!'

Magda ran and hugged Drusus and her nephew, and when Helga appeared the sisters embraced in tears. With his son in his arms, Drusus reached out for Artorius' hand and was pulled to him. Marcus and Cezar, in turn, were introduced by an excited Magda. They all took a space on the bench, with beers arriving shortly, brought by an attentive Helga.

The men were soon deep in conversation to the exclusion of Magda, much to her disgust, so she got up and left, seeking the counsel of her sister to discuss the new arrivals. There was little news from the north for Artorius, who had decided to settle back in the Legion before making formal enquiries about Victus. What was known was Gigantrex's growing anger at Ilona's continued refusal of his marriage offer. He had forbidden anyone, including traders, from speaking about his guests and his problems.

Artorius began to formulate plans for her rescue, though what of the wolves, where could he take them? *They could return to their old forest and I could improve the farm for them with Marcus' help*, Artorius pondered.

Cezar sat in awe of what was being discussed: predictions, wolves... *What sort of world am I entering?* he thought. Marcus watched his father closely, satisfied with his decision to travel with him, but the news of Gigantrex and his village worried him. Artorius decided they should make their way to Octodurus and speak to Paulinus and Brunhilda. Drusus' offer to travel with them was considered and then brushed aside.

Helga was in no doubt that her sister was smitten by Marcus. Magda related Lucretia's discussion with her, which Helga wholeheartedly agreed with. When Helga broached the subject of Cezar, Magda snapped at her.

'When Marcus and his father leave, I will go with them,' she stated.

'Sister, you are still so young. Artorius is returning to his Legion, and as you know, Marcus and Cezar are intent on joining too. A soldier's life is a hard one, talk to Drusus.'

'He would only try to discourage me,' snapped Magda.

'I need to talk to Drusus,' retorted a frustrated Helga, who tried to distract her sister with serving in the inn to prevent her intervention in the men's talk as the evening drew on.

When she had a moment, Helga called Drusus away and explained her sister's intentions. Drusus agreed that Magda accompanying Artorius was a bad idea, especially because of the rumours surrounding Gigantrex and Ilona.

'Artorius has already been warned that Gigantrex will stop at nothing to get what he wants. The only solution I see, and which I am sure Artorius has seen, is to recover Ilona by force if necessary. I don't want Magda anywhere near that confrontation. What do you suggest?' said Drusus, drawing Helga to him. She just shrugged and sighed.

Drusus returned to his cousin's group with a smile and more beer. Artorius was relating some of his war stories. Magda's eyes never left the men, and her temper only increased as Helga kept her busy. Out of earshot of the boys, Drusus related his conversation with Helga to Artorius, which he found disturbing. Both knew the relationship was a non-starter. Marcus put on a good act, but inside he grieved.

\*

In the last hours of night, Magda slipped from her room unnoticed and collecting her horse, she walked it through the side streets that linked up with the Roman north road. Mounting on the outskirts, she rode hard to clear the town until she trotted within sight of the first mutatione. She took up an observation place and reached into her saddlebag for the dried food she had packed for her breakfast. Helga and Drusus would be angry, but she didn't care. There was nothing back there for her, surely, they would understand that?

\*

The day had barely begun when Drusus roused the three men, providing them with victuals for the journey. Only Cezar enquired after Magda as the sun rose above the small town. Helga found Magda's bed empty and her clothes missing; she ran to inform Drusus. He checked his stables, already knowing what he would find. Magda's horse was gone, so he immediately approached Artorius. The decision was taken that Drusus would accompany them until Magda appeared and he would then escort her back.

The group trotted out of Placentia, leaving a tearful Helga behind. They settled into a long but comfortable ride, playing with suggestions of how to resolve what lay before them. Drusus was deep in thought. So engrossed were they, that they didn't notice a lone horse and a hooded rider waiting near the first mutatione. As the four stopped for the change, it was Cezar who recognised Magda and called out to her.

Magda braced herself, sitting upright in her saddle. 'Firstly, you're not my father. I am a woman and as such I can do whatever I like and go wherever I want.'

'You are a child and you're like a daughter to me,' stated an injured Drusus.

'You won't be welcome where we are going and you'll get in the way,' added Artorius. 'We have a dangerous task we must complete, then we travel to Argentoratum and the 2nd Augusta.'

'I am here to make sure you return,' said Drusus. 'Once Marcus and Cezar start their training in the Legion you won't see them for months on end. Come home, Magda.'

'Let me speak to her, Father,' said Marcus, approaching Magda and taking her hand. Cezar hesitated.

'Magda, I must speak plainly. I do not and cannot love you. I know Lucretia told you about Tia, and in some ways, you are like her. She was my life and her memory is burnt deep within me. There is no place in my life for you or any other. My father and I face a hard task, and somewhere out there is a man who would kill you just for knowing us. Return with Drusus. One day someone special will appear.'

'But in time maybe you could grow to love me – we could be so good for each other,' pleaded Magda, tears oozing from her saddened eyes.

'But I love you, Magda. Isn't that enough?' offered Cezar, taking her hand, having dismounted and approached her.

'Thank you, Cezar, but it's Marcus I want.'

'Now is not the time, Magda,' suggested Drusus.

Cezar stepped back, deflated. 'Sorry, Marcus, I am not ready for the Legion. I will return with Drusus and Magda if I can.'

Drusus nodded.

Marcus reached down and hugged his friend. 'Feel free to return to the estate. I will be waiting for you to join us. Take care, friend.'

Drusus embraced Magda, and through tear-filled eyes she sought Marcus with outstretched arms. With farewells completed, father and son trotted away.

Drusus stared down at his wife's sister and felt for her, but she would recover.

Marcus gazed back momentarily. He was sorry for Magda's feelings, but he felt nothing other than friendship.

Artorius quickened the pace and Marcus, detecting the sound change, followed suit. Stone chippings flicked up as the pair broke into a gallop. Distance had to be travelled, and fast.

## Chapter 23

Gigantrex paced up and down in the great hall, his face purple with rage at a further refusal by Ilona, who awaited Artorius' return. Her wolves prowled outside the stockade at night and were frightening the villagers, who wanted Ilona and her mother gone. They feared the three females more than Gigantrex's wrath, especially Rosevetha and Breda, not knowing if Ilona also shared the gift. Food was sparse, as traders to the village were becoming scarcer, frightened by the wolves' presence.

He cursed the day he had taken Ilona and her mother in, and since he had refused Ilona any further access to her wolves, the situation had worsened. He wouldn't venture outside any more, after an incident when the wolves refused his exit and two were killed. Gigantrex had begged Ilona to talk to her pets from the walls, but she had refused and he had confined her to a hut.

Breda had now sided with Rosevetha and Ilona, refusing all contact with him. His mind turned to how he could rid Ilona of the hope of Artorius' return. *I need to contact Victus Claudian, but where was he, and would he even listen? I have to get out of this village first, and that will mean some deceit.*

It pained Gigantrex to have to eat humble pie, but if he gained the result, his loss of face would be temporary. Forcing a smile, he strutted across the compound to the lone hut and struck the door with his knife handle. It irritated him that there was no reply, yet he could clearly hear the women talking inside in veiled language.

'Ilona, I need to talk. I fear I have offended you,' offered Gigantrex.

'No, your anger cost two pointless deaths. I will never give in to your requests,' she shouted.

A closed door did little to make Gigantrex's task easier. 'Maybe I have been hasty?'

'You are cursed, and we know what you plan, so go away,' snapped Rosevetha.

'Mother, talk to them! Our people are starving because of the wolves,' pleaded Gigantrex. The silence was deafening as he strode back to the hall. *Maybe I could starve them into submission.*

Their continued well-being with food and drink was assured, and Ilona hoped Artorius' return was all just a matter of time. The three women discussed the predicament that faced the village and there seemed only one solution: Ilona and Rosevetha had to be allowed to leave now, rather than later. Breda insisted she would accompany them, as she felt she had no further place in the village. She sought out her son, finding him deep in thought in front of the hall fire, beer in hand and a foul mood brewing.

'You must let Ilona and her mother leave,' she demanded.

'I must do nothing. Eventually the village will turn on her because of her wolves.'

'Your stubbornness and demands have led to the problem, and they no longer accept your hospitality,' stated Breda.

'Rosevetha can go, and good riddance – you can join her if you like,' Gigantrex suggested.

'You cannot keep Ilona here against her will, the problem won't go away if you do. For a chief, you are a fool, and you are a disgrace to your father and I,' Breda screamed, slapping her son hard across his face, leaving an imprint.

Without warning, Gigantrex swept his arm forward and knocked his mother off her feet. Collapsed on the floor, Breda's eyes burned deep into her son as she shuffled backwards towards the door.

'That is the final straw,' she screamed, struggling to her feet. She flung the hall door open, leaving her son behind. Striding across the compound, the villagers appeared from their huts at the sight of their once-queen, tears streaming from her eyes, and clutched at the talismans that hung from their necks.

'Open the gates! I am your queen and I demand my freedom,' shouted Breda as she reached Ilona's hut, where the door stood open.

'We are leaving,' Breda insisted of Ilona and her mother.

The three walked towards the gate. The village elder bowed to Breda and lifted the retaining bar from the gate. As it opened, the trees filled with eyes. Donor stepped out from the tree line.

'Shut the gate! I order you,' shouted Gigantrex, striding towards them, sword in hand.

The village elder walked away from the open gate. As Ilona stepped into the gap, Gigantrex ran towards her. Rosevetha stepped in front of him with Breda, and both were sent flying as Ilona waddled forward to meet the advancing wolves. Donor crouched, moving slowly forward, flicking his head left and right, indicating that the pack should split.

'Shoot the wolves, she is not to escape,' ordered Gigantrex of the guards. As one, they turned their backs on him.

Donor bounded forward, racing past Ilona and hitting Gigantrex in full flight, knocking him off his feet before he could strike. Donor rolled forward and turned swiftly to face Gigantrex, snarling, saliva dripping from his jaws.

Ilona continued out of the gate, followed by her mother and Breda. Every movement was watched by Donor as

Gigantrex walked towards him, slashing right then left. The villagers stepped away, creating an arena for the two.

'Step away, Gigantrex. You are finished, look behind you.' Ilona's voice, clear and sharp, boomed from behind him followed by a growing cacophony of growls.

He turned to face a line of dribbling, snarling wolves, with Ilona, her mother and Breda at their rear.

'You have disgraced yourself and the village, Gigantrex. Leave now – you are banished,' spat the village elder.

'Who will come with me?' enquired Gigantrex.

As one, the villagers turned away from him.

'The people have given you their answer, son. Leave,' demanded Breda.

Gigantrex growled as he turned back towards the great hall and entered it. Exiting moments later with spear, shield and a large shoulder bag, he walked to the hobbled horses where he mounted his own, walking it to the gate.

'You know I will return and have my revenge, Rosevetha,' he cursed.

'You have a choice: one of death and the other, a long life. Choose well, one decision is all it takes,' interjected Breda.

As Gigantrex passed the village elder he swung his round shield, forcefully knocking him off his feet. As he did so he charged at the wolves and the trio of women. Ilona let out a howl, Donor continued the call, and the wolves quickly surrounded the women.

Gigantrex's thoughts were to strike out at Donor, who faced him in defiance, but he decided not to. Racing past, Gigantrex took the path he had previously taken with Artorius, heading for the Roman road, where he lost no time in racing to Octodurus to plan his route to Victus.

The village elder was assisted to his feet by Ilona.

'Have no fear of me or my pets,' she said. 'They will protect the village. Send out messages to merchants that the village is open for trade and safe to all. We will provide meat for you all this night.' Ilona reached down and ran her hand through Donor's thick fur. His face was one of pleasure; his mistress was safe.

As the sun reached its highest point, Ilona was astride her pony, Breda walking beside her and a gang of nervous village youths accompanied them both as they returned to the stockade with meat for all. Their pride and joy was a full-grown stag, brought down by an elated Breda. As the procession entered the village, Ilona slipped from her horse and watched as her pack disappeared amongst the trees, leaving only Donor. As she knelt before him, he placed his head in her hands and gazed into her eyes as she whispered into his ear.

'Artorius is coming, Donor, we'll all be together again.'

## Chapter 24

Four days of hard riding saw father and son closing on Octodurus in the late hour of day. They had paid their respects and declined assistance from Artorius' rescuers on the way. Lodging their horses at the mutatione, Artorius, followed quickly by Marcus, picked his way through the familiar side streets to Paulinus' inn. He and Brunhilda would be best placed for information about Gigantrex's village, which had been bitty and confusing up to now. Marcus' head still lurched from the rough travelling experience and the friends his father had accumulated.

Brunhilda sat outside the back of the inn with her son at her breast, soaking up the last of the day's sun. Artorius, not wishing to embarrass her, slipped round to the main entrance where he found Paulinus leaning against an outside table discussing strategy with two soldiers, one being an Optio. The soldiers watched Artorius' approach. One recognised him immediately, and he in turn, from the 2nd Augustus cavalry.

'The dead man returns!' Decurion Julian stood and reached out to Artorius as Paulinus turned.

'Back so soon? I thought you'd re-joined the Praetorians?' enquired Paulinus.

'Going missing didn't help, and I have unfinished business in the north. Top that with the offer of Camp Prefect in the Glorious 2nd and I couldn't refuse. This is my son, Marcus, whom I spoke of. He has returned with me to join the 2nd Augustus cavalry. You'll be amazed at his skills, he's had the best teachers,' said Artorius.

'So, you're Scipio's replacement. He's replaced Brachus in Mogontiacum after his retirement,' responded Julian.

*I'm thankful Scipio took the offered post*, pondered

Artorius as he received congratulations from the three, calling for a celebratory jug of wine. Paulinus wasted no time in fetching the required intoxicant, the best he could find from his own special collection. The first beaker had barely touched the sides before Brunhilda appeared, babe in arms.

'You have returned? Mother said you would when the time is right,' she said, speaking in her own local dialect.

'I need to discuss my return with you. I've received mixed messages,' Artorius responded in the same dialect. Marcus looked to his father, confused.

'We will eat first, and then we can discuss our respective news,' suggested Paulinus.

Having sated their hunger, Artorius and Marcus were invited into the kitchen by Paulinus and Brunhilda, while the two soldiers accepted an invitation from others who were gambling outside. The family group discussed the happenings surrounding Gigantrex and Ilona well into the night. Marcus was entranced by the talk of Ilona and her wolves, despite the reservations he still had because of his mother's memory. They said that the village had returned to normal, and that Breda remained as queen with the council, but Gigantrex had disappeared. There had even been talk of him heading for the coast, but no one was saying why, and that was if they even knew.

'The village and my mother have become notorious, thanks to Ilona's wolves. Rosevetha is accepting enquiries for her potions and predictions,' boasted Brunhilda.

'We will visit your village on our way to my Legion and discuss a few ideas I have had, including returning Ilona north to her old home, or perhaps to a new one – who knows. I'm sure either your mother or Rosevetha will know.'

Paulinus and Brunhilda smiled at the comment.

*

The following morning's sun was still in its ascendancy as father and son left Octodurus, taking the forest path. The steaminess of the woods made both sweat as they reached a small stream, with Artorius reflecting that there had been more water on his previous visit. The water was warm but welcome as the pair sampled it and the horses drank their fill. The forest was alive with birdsong and an occasional deer ran in fear at being disturbed. Marcus reflected on how beautiful the area was and how fresh the air tasted.

It was late afternoon when father and son emerged from the forest overlooking Breda's village. The pair sat back in their saddles, surveying the activity within the palisade, the gates being wide open, when a growling noise caught Artorius' ear from behind, followed by howling from a lone wolf who was camouflaged in the forest.

Artorius' eyes scanned the trees before calling out to Donor. The village below suddenly came alive, watched by an intrigued Marcus. People were shading their eyes to look up as Artorius again called out to Donor, slipping from his horse and handing his reins to Marcus.

A dark shape moved stealthily through the trees towards them, Artorius walking towards it. A howl came from the village below and the beast moving towards them responded. Marcus had all but lost his father in the forest darkness, when Artorius and a wolf walked back towards him, causing the horses to twitch with nerves.

'Son, this is Donor,' Artorius said, running his hand along the beast's back to Marcus' amazement.

Donor scrutinised Marcus carefully, but refused to allow

any closer proximity. Artorius took his horse's reins and remounted, pointing it towards the palisade where two women now stood outside the gates.

Ilona, watching, knew there was only one other who had that rapport with her pet. Her heart pounded in her chest and her head spun in euphoria: Artorius had returned.

Donor ran alongside Artorius' horse down the slope and towards the palisade, to the two waiting women. Breda stepped forward and welcomed the guests. Artorius quickly introduced Marcus to her as he slipped from his horse and strode towards Ilona, whose belly appeared to have doubled in size since he last saw her. Their arms reached out for each other; tears filled Ilona's eyes as Artorius returned her talisman and the couple melted together.

'I am sorry for your losses,' whispered Ilona.

'I return your father's talisman. It has a number on it, you must tell me about him,' replied Artorius.

'My father died the year I was born, so you'll have to ask Mother. Your son is like you, and the fates haven't been kind to him either, have they?'

'It's a long story, as I'm sure you know. Come and meet him. I didn't think he would come, I'm sure he still thinks I betrayed his mother. I have returned to fulfil my promise and then we travel north to Argentoratum. I have a few ideas, which I hope you will welcome,' suggested Artorius.

The conversation between Marcus and Breda flowed easily. Marcus stared past her to the beauty walking beside his father. Her hair was like beaten copper reaching down to her waist, her green eyes like emeralds, but it was the softness of her welcoming smile that radiated the most. He felt embarrassed and awkward. This lady carried his brother within her, and when Marcus took her offered hand, she drew him close and held him.

In that moment, he saw two youths walking with wolves. Marcus drew back sharply. *Ilona was like Tia, but she could also project the future…* For the first time he felt frightened and pulled away.

'What are you, a witch or a goddess?' he demanded.

'She is neither, and as for myself – well! She should not have let you glimpse the future, since you are still struggling with the emotions of the past,' responded Rosevetha, smiling.

'What are you talking about and who are you?' demanded Marcus, as Artorius grabbed him by the shoulder.

'I am Rosevetha, grandmother of your brother-to-be,' she laughed. 'Strong willed, clever and a born leader – you are a force to be admired by many. You will break many hearts, but there will only be one in time.'

'I have lost my only love,' he spat.

'Marcus, control yourself,' demanded Artorius, spinning his son around to face him.

'No, he is right, Artorius,' said Ilona, taking Marcus' hand in hers. 'He will not need witchcraft, just guidance to make him the great man he is to become. Winning hearts is not all about finding love. He will buy his and set her free.'

Marcus' anger drained away as Ilona gazed into his eyes. The world around them didn't exist until Marcus felt something lick his hand. There beside him was the wolf Donor. Marcus' hand slipped instinctively for a blade at his shoulder as Ilona gently ran his hand through the beast's fur. His heart stopped. *Had he entered a land of dreams, or was it nightmares*?

'Only three men will ever achieve this, and you are one of them,' whispered Ilona, smiling. She tried hard to reach the pain inside him. It would come. Grasping an arm each of father and son, she waddled into the compound and the waiting feast.

Marcus was introduced to the village youths, who tried to goad him. Artorius, seeing Marcus' hackles rise, encouraged a display of his sword craft and archery. A village youth, not wanting to be outdone, stepped forward with a large broadsword roughly the size of himself. His movements were slow, but would be lethal. When Marcus sprang forward with both blades rotating in front of him, he was met with rapturous applause from the older men. The village elder stepped forward to inspect the swords. Taking Egorix's, he ran a finger over the symbols, and holding it aloft he spoke in his own language.

Marcus turned to his father, who had paled at the old man's speech. 'I never knew where Egorix came from, but now I do. That is his elder brother.'

'He was out hunting the night a star fell to earth and what he found was crafted into this sword,' said the old man. 'I haven't seen him in fifteen years. Pray, tell me about him?'

Artorius related what he knew of Egorix, the man and friend, finishing with how he met his end at the hands of Victus' henchmen and bequeathed his sword to Marcus. The village leader agreed that it now lay in the hands of another great warrior, as foretold by Breda, and much to Marcus' embarrassment.

Artorius felt awkward that when the hosts were pre-occupied, Ilona led him away. They walked hand in hand outside the hall, their absence went unnoticed. They entered a warm hut, where the floor was covered with animal furs and a small fire burned in the central hearth. Ilona sat on a low cot where Artorius was bade to join her, which he did without hesitation.

They spent the night hours wrapped tightly in each other's arms, talking of the future, a discussion that was interjected by the occasional kick from within Ilona.

*

Artorius employed his time in the village discussing his plans and rebuilding the relationship with Ilona, who wore an almost perpetual grin. Plans to return north were welcomed by mother and daughter, especially with the talk of building a new home near the garrison. Breda felt the village had lost faith with her following Gigantrex's disappearance, and asked that she might join the party too. Artorius began to think less of his return to the Legion and more to his retirement. His plans were somewhat dashed temporarily, when he was informed that Ilona couldn't travel till after the birth, which was barely two months away.

It was with great reluctance and a flood of emotion that the following day Artorius, drawn by duty, set off for Argentoratum. Amid a tearful departure, Ilona blamed her heightened emotions on her pregnancy.

Breda took her chance and eased Marcus aside. 'Your father was warned about Gigantrex. He is dangerous, greed dominates his mind. I know it hurts to see your father with another woman, but fate decided that a long time ago. Your brother and his mother will be safe. Now, go safely and take this...' Breda took a droplet of amber inscribed with strange signs from her neck and placed it over Marcus' head. 'It was a wedding gift from Egorix many years since. A young lady watches over you,' she whispered. Tears filled Marcus' eyes and he whispered Tia's name as Breda drew him to her.

Artorius and Marcus wasted no time in shortening the

distance to Argentoratum. The fort stood proud on land, with a great loop of river flowing around it. Four bridges crossed the river, having passed through the canabae that led to the garrison. Artorius felt a great sense of pride to have Marcus riding close beside him as they approached the southern gate bridge. The salute from two veterans was crisp and there was obvious pleasure at who they saw before them. Both punched the air with their pilus.

'Welcome back, Camp Prefect Civilis, your Legion awaits your return,' exploded from their mouths in unison.

As father and son entered deeper into the garrison, cheers rang out from all quarters. Artorius flushed in embarrassment, and Marcus felt a deep pride in his father. While Artorius reported to his new Legate, Sextus Aquila, the primus pila sent messages out to every cohort – the air was alive with the sound of cornua. Officers and soldiers alike came running and gathered outside the administrative building. Artorius went to speak to them, but was stayed by his Legate.

'They need a moment to assemble without you, Camp Prefect,' suggested the Legate.

Aquila led the way to the entrance then moved aside, offering Artorius the honour of stepping through the door first. As he walked out into the late afternoon sun, cheers erupted from the gathered Legion, followed by the deafening beat of thousands of gladii against scutum. Artorius raised himself to his full height and, straight-backed, Aquila stood to one side, his hand on Marcus' shoulder.

'You have a lot to live up to, young man, but I am sure you will,' related Aquila.

Artorius quickly embraced his new role as Camp Prefect, and it was decided that Marcus belay his enlistment until he had settled into the army way of life and its customs. The Legion having been without a Camp Prefect since Scipio's departure, Artorius was buried in paperwork and meetings with his officers, some newly promoted after the demise of the conspirators. Every day Artorius woke with a vision of Ilona, and despite reassurances of her well-being in a weekly message from Breda, he still worried. Father and son had visited Ilona's home in the forest en route, but a tree had been uprooted in a storm and crushed it. Artorius' thoughts turned to providing her with a new one.

Marcus was left to explore the military base on his own. Male friends came easily to him – some naturally and some encouraged by their military fathers – and his presence hadn't gone unnoticed by the local young girls, despite the ravages of the plague. The latter went unnoticed by Marcus, but not by the Legate's son, who was jealous of this newcomer and his instant popularity. Marcus' ability with weapons raised his status, even amongst the older soldiers.

Through his friends, he was shown the ideal location for a new home. A well-worn track led from the south canabae into the forest, leading to a meadow watered by a stream that fed the great river. On the first day he had seen it, wild deer had watered at the stream, which was abundant with fish. Acquiring an allowance from his father and monies he earned from running errands and teaching weaponry skills, Marcus had soon arranged the start of the new home. He sought help from the architecti, who offered their free time, most said, to repay Artorius for past deeds. Marcus created a killing zone around his home, and trees were felled to provide for the palisade boundary. The home was of wood now, but in time he knew it would be replaced with stone walls. Artorius was oblivious of where his son was or what he was doing, having engrossed himself in his role to distract him from thoughts of Ilona, and failing abysmally.

The Legate's son Rufus Aquila, was dark haired, shorter than Marcus by a head, and was a spoilt, arrogant, unruly bully who harboured jealous thoughts against Marcus' popularity. Rufus' friends were mostly locals, half-witted like himself, and enjoyed inflicting pain on animals or humans smaller than themselves. Rufus could not afford to confront Marcus openly – he had too much support, but Rufus was sure there would be a time when he was on his own.

# Chapter 25

As the Kalends of Iullius approached, life around the Villa Aphrodite changed dramatically as Naomi's pregnancy approached its full term. She had women proficient in childbirth and a wet nurse amongst her staff, and as the day approached, Victus found himself pushed away with free rein – much to his satisfaction, that was what he intended.

He spent his days around the Genua docks, where he cultivated prospective businessmen to invest in the growing wealth from the villa. He was a shrewd businessman, never risking his own money unless he had to. Money poured in, achieving large dividends which Naomi knew little of. He reinvested a small percentage back into the estate, even proposing the building of their own private residence. Naomi agreed to expanding the facilities within the extensive grounds, but was content with occupying the luxurious top floor of the villa.

*

Gigantrex had found life hard since leaving the village. His size frightened people and when he approached Romans for information, he was often set about by bodyguards. The only people he drew to him were the undesirables, thinking he was after vengeance on the Roman he sought. Heavy drinking, diminishing money and the frustration of getting nowhere led Gigantrex to slip into the bad company of a money lender. The men swayed between recovering money from lenders, to relieving the wealthy of their goods on the open road. Easy money and wanton women were easy to come by, resulting in Gigantrex's promotion to leading the band.

The money lender Christos was of Greek origin. A thin wiry man in his late forties, formerly a slave and then released, he hated Romans with a vengeance on the outside, but his true feelings were hidden from all. During a drunken night of debauchery, Gigantrex disclosed his story to one of Christos' prostitutes about the man he sought: Victus Claudian.

The name stirred a memory for Christos when he was informed and rifling through his scrolls, the name Victus Claudian appeared before him. 'Wanted for treason' the document said, but that was nearly a year ago. *I need to establish if he is still wanted*, Christos thought, slipping the document into his satchel.

Using the secret network few knew of, Christos' information soon hit a dead end with details of an estate in Genua that was used as an exclusive brothel, where an Antonius Porta was the owner. Gathering the best description of Victus Claudian – a man missing two fingers and having a slight limp – Christos set off for the three-day ride to the Villa Aphrodite, accompanied by Gigantrex.

Christos and Gigantrex arrived in Genua and settled for two rooms in an understated inn outside of the town. Christos posed as a trader in luxurious goods to the rich and famous, while Gigantrex was his body guard, a role he enjoyed.

'I know Porta very well,' said the innkeeper. 'I supply him with the best of wines for his business, know what I mean? He is well liked locally, though he has a vile temper when crossed. He is always on the lookout for a good business deal, though he strikes a hard bargain and I should know. He is currently looking for a good bodyguard – I don't know why, because he has no enemies hereabout that I know of.'

Christos had to be sure that Porta and Victus Claudian were one and the same. He wanted to question the innkeeper further, but decided on an alternative. 'How would I meet this Porta? At his villa, or somewhere more conducive to talking business?'

'Never talks business at the villa, he keeps that from his mistress, Naomi,' responded the innkeeper. 'You can usually find him at The Anchor Inn, next to the port office. An ex-soldier, I'd say – good looking, with a slight limp, and he always wears gloves. Rumour has it that they hide an injury, though no one dares to ask.'

Striding towards the quayside, Christos stopped alongside an alley and, checking they weren't being watched, pulled Gigantrex into it. Gigantrex looked suspiciously at Christos.

'You wanted the services of Victus Claudian, who I believe is Antonius Porta. He needs a bodyguard and I need to make business contacts with him. Take yourself to The Anchor Inn and make it known you are available as a bodyguard. Contact Porta and find out who he really is and then come back to me.'

'Why are you so interested in him? If you're thinking of double-crossing him, I'd think again from what I know of him,' replied Gigantrex.

*He doesn't know what dangerous is*, thought Christos, watching Gigantrex walk away. Slipping from the alley, Christos headed for the port office.

The Anchor Inn was very much like any other wharf-side hostelry; seagulls circled overhead as the ships bobbed about in the harbour. The smell of fish permeated the air and scantily clad females of all shapes and sizes paraded outside, calling out to prospective new arrivals. The size of Gigantrex caused a veritable buzz among the prostitutes along with some wary looks from the locals. An attractive and mature female brushed her competitors aside, addressing Gigantrex in his own tongue, causing him to look twice at her in shock.

Peter Baggott

'Surprised to find one of your own, handsome? I'm a widow and my body is all I have left. Maybe I could entertain you?' Gigantrex declined. 'What brings you here anyway? she enquired, her tone changing.

'I've been told a man called Porta is looking for a bodyguard and I believe he frequents this inn.'

'I'm Sabina. He's inside, though he's no easy man to work for. Maybe I could introduce you and you could see your way to helping me.'

Sabina stroked Gigantrex's arm before slipping hers through it. She walked him to an outside seat and called for a drink. With the drink's arrival, Sabina disappeared into the dingy interior, giving some of the other prostitutes a chance to try and steal him.

Victus sat at his usual table facing the only entrance, surrounded by business sycophants who were vying for his sole attention. Sabina slid in, giving Victus the eye. Acknowledging her, he stood and moved towards her.

'There's an extremely large barbarian looking for work as a bodyguard and he has your name,' she whispered.

Victus cupped her face with his gloved hand. 'You're wasted here. I could arrange far more comfortable surroundings at the villa if you'd let me? Where is he?'

Sabina led him outside, to the surprise of those at his table.

Seeing Sabina reappear, Gigantrex brushed his female admirers aside who, in turn, suffered the lashing of Sabina's tongue.

'This is Porta. I didn't get your name,' she said to him.

'You never asked it. I am Gigantrex.'

'You certainly are,' responded Victus, laughing as he offered his hand, which Gigantrex gripped firmly. 'Walk with me?' invited Victus, as his hand slipped to the pugio on his belt, a movement that did not go unobserved by

232

Gigantrex.

'You'll not need that. I have information I am sure you will want to know of.'

'So, you're not after a job. Who sent you?' snapped Victus, stepping back and drawing his pugio.

'Artorius Civilis lives!'

The blood drained from Victus' face as he stared in disbelief at the giant before him. *Why should this man seek me out, and how does he know of my connection with Artorius Civilis?*

'How do you know this, and why come to me?' Victus recovered his composure and pushed Sabina away out of earshot.

'Porta is not your real name, is it? I have come looking for Victus Claudian, who is hated by the Civilis family, and I know of his attempts to kill them. I am willing to help him complete that enterprise,' replied Gigantrex.

Gigantrex watched the populace scuttle about the wharf, carrying and collecting goods from small boats, and unloading larger ones at anchor while his words sank in. He related his involvement in finding Artorius alive in the hut of a seer and her daughter outside Argentoratum.

Victus remembered the old hag and her daughter. *Could they have saved him? How could they have found him?* He was still pondering this when Gigantrex informed him that he had recently heard Artorius was returning to the 2nd Augusta with his son.

'I am Victus Claudian, as you believe, but why are you offering your help, and what's in it for you?' demanded Victus.

Gigantrex explained that Ilona was pregnant by Artorius. With Artorius dead, he was sure he could persuade Ilona to accept his offer of marriage and then he could return to his village with her and her wolves. Gigantrex suggested that with Victus' help, they could wait for Artorius' return and kill both father and son.

Victus strutted around the wharf deep in thought, still shocked to find that Artorius was alive. *Could this be the chance to finally finish the Civilis family? The unborn must die also. I could use this giant then cut all ties...* He flicked his hand across his own throat, as a sneer creased his face.

'One further thing: I was helped to find you by a Greek called Christos from Rome, a money lender who claims to hate all Romans, but he seems particularly interested in finding you.'

'I need to sort some unfinished business. Sabina, whatever Gigantrex desires you must see to it. I'll be back shortly. Sabina can be very accommodating, can't you?' suggested Victus, reaching under her shift and grabbing her buttock without her flinching. 'Make sure he doesn't disappear before I return,' Victus whispered.

Victus limped away, leaving the couple talking over some frothy beer. It was only a short walk to the harbour office, where the port Centurion was trying to make sense of the harbour records presented to him by the senior taxes clerk. Catching his eye, the Centurion gladly left the clerk to respond to Victus. Checking there were no observers, Victus limped down the jetty, followed by the Centurion.

'Caelia, have there been any unusual visitors today?' he enquired.

'Funny you should say that. We had a Greek making enquiries, asking about holding facilities for a prisoner. He said he was hoping to arrest someone wanted for treason, but didn't say who, and he provided authority for me to supply all he needs. Why, do you know who it is?'

'Just heard a rumour and had to find out for myself. Where is the Greek now?' asked Victus.

'He's staying somewhere on the edge of town and said he would be back when he had confirmation of the subject. All hush-hush, by the look of it – politics, no doubt.'

'I am sure it is. Will we see you at the villa tonight? We have a troupe of exotic dancers arranged. Do be my guest – I know how you enjoy female gymnastics.' Victus laughed as he slapped the Centurion on the back, leaving him nodding acceptance.

Victus made for a hovel on the riverside just beyond the moorings, where he spoke to his facilitators, led by Udo, about a new target. Udo's men slipped along the water's edge, mirroring Victus' movements as he returned to The Anchor where Sabina and Gigantrex were deep in conversation. Victus approached Gigantrex from behind, watched by Sabina. Victus' pugio slipped easily from his belt and was placed at the base of Gigantrex's neck, Sabina being waved away with a quick toss of the head.

'Don't move or this knife will be projected through your neck. What is this Christos to you?' snapped Victus.

'Nothing. He needed heavies and, well... look at me.'

'Did you know he is a spy and bounty hunter?' enquired Victus, forcefully pushing the blade deeper against Gigantrex's neck.

'Why should I? He was my employer and he said do, so I did.'

'Kill him, and when you have, come to the Villa Aphrodite. Do this and I'll make it worth your while. We can then begin to plan the Civilis project, and don't even think to double-cross me. Now go!'

Gigantrex stood without looking behind him and headed back to the lodgings which Christos had vacated for the Centurion Inn on the coastal road, east of the docks.

Gigantrex felt his hairs prickle on the back of his neck. He knew he was being followed, but this was just another inconvenience. Seeing a dark figure partially hidden in a doorway opposite the Anchor Inn, he made straight towards him. Udo tried desperately to withdraw further into the gloom, but couldn't.

'Can you tell me where the Centurion Inn is on the eastern coast road?'

Udo stepped out of the shadows nonchalantly. 'Follow this road. Don't lose sight of the coast and you can't miss it,' replied Udo, trying to walk around Gigantrex, who grabbed him by the throat and pinned him against the wall.

'You can walk with me and see the job done. I know you're one of Porta's men and you can call your friends if you like.'

Udo released, he slid down the wall, choking. When he could manage it, he whistled, summoning two males from a side alley with swords drawn, who were promptly waved away. Gigantrex laughed at the pathetic sight, not even considering their chances against him. Explaining why he sought the inn, he suggested they accompany him, which was quickly agreed. Two slipped back into the shadows while Udo, still rubbing his throat, walked alongside Gigantrex.

Reaching the inn, Gigantrex sought the entrance on his own, while Udo and his men filtered out of sight.

Christos was sat with his back to the wall inside the relatively clean and quiet hostelry, planning his next move, when the doorframe blacked out at the arrival of Gigantrex. Christos called for more wine, inviting his large companion to join him. Gigantrex assured Christos that Porta and Claudian were one and the same.

'Why the interest in him?' questioned Gigantrex.

'I'll need your muscle and the support of the authorities. There is a sizable bounty for Victus Claudian, dead or alive. Are you interested? Help me with this and I'm sure I can make Artorius Civilis disappear for you.'

'How? Who are you really?' asked Gigantrex.

Christos looked carefully around the room and leaned forward. 'I am one of the Emperor's agents and a bounty hunter,' he whispered.

Gigantrex leaned back and stared at him. *You could have helped me without us having to come here. You deserve your just desserts*, he thought. 'I'm with you.' *You snivelling rat*, thought Gigantrex, offering his spade-like hand.

'No time like the present then. First, we need some of the port authority's troops, then to the villa.'

Christos stood and led the way out into the bright light of the late afternoon. The day's heat had yet to dissipate and was still uncomfortable; sweat oozed from the pair as they set out at speed towards the dock. The streets were empty at this hour, most people enjoying the cool interiors of their homes.

Gigantrex eased the knife from his belt and strode up behind Christos. 'What's the hurry in this heat?' he called.

Christos turned to answer but a blade swept forward into his stomach, ripping into his intestines, and a giant hand across his mouth stopped him from screaming. Gigantrex caught him before he fell, dragging him into a side alley which led to the water's edge. Relieving Christos of his money belt and jewellery, Gigantrex pitched the body into the sea. As it hit the water with a splash, Gigantrex turned to find Udo standing behind him.

'Follow the coastal road back through the town and take

the left fork. You'll see the villa,' stated Udo, and with the task completed, he and his men scurried out of sight, leaving Gigantrex alone.

*

Even before Gigantrex presented himself at the villa gate, Victus knew of the completed task, answering the call to the gate himself. Taking Gigantrex to the villa kitchen, the staff were instructed to see to his every need.

'We have much to discuss. In the meantime, enjoy the pleasures of my house,' invited Victus.

A group of half-naked females fawned over Gigantrex as Naomi's maidservant approached Victus.

'The mistress is in labour, master, and asked for your attendance at the birth, but I thought you might need some company while you wait?'

Victus held the maid's head roughly from behind and crushed her lips against his. She submitted willingly before being dragged across the ground floor of the villa to a private room Victus had absorbed as his own. Drawing his pugio as the door clicked shut and grasping the maid's dress, he ripped it open, throwing the torn fragments on the floor. The maid knelt before Victus, who had discarded his toga, and took his manhood firmly in her hand. Victus forced her mouth down on to it, almost choking her with the force. The maid was used to his violent ways and, like her mistress, she enjoyed them, biting gently on his penis. Bending down, he lifted the maid into his arms as her legs clung tightly round his waist, the dampness between her legs pressing against him. Parting her labia, he drove his manhood deep inside her, making her squirm, and strode towards the sole piece of furniture in the room: a bed. He did not break his pace, but launched himself on to the bed, driving himself deeper into her as she screamed out and pleasure filled her face. Another higher pitched scream from another part of the house caused the pair to stop momentarily.

'That'll be the mistress, she must be giving birth. I should go to her,' suggested the maid as Victus drove hard and deep into her.

'You can go when I say.' Victus pulled out and turned the maid over, spread her legs and slid easily back into her.

The maid moaned and screamed into the soft bedding she was forced into. Each scream from above spurred Victus on to drill the maid deeper till, soaked in sweat and spent, he rolled on to his back.

'You can go now. Call me when it's born,' ordered Victus.

Rolling on to her back, pleasure covered the maid's face. Sliding from the bed, she gathered up her tattered garment to cover her nakedness and, bowing, she left. The screaming from above continued as Victus lay in momentary post-coital pleasure, his mind quickly changing to more important matters: the Civilis family.

Victus, awaiting the inevitable birth, sought out Gigantrex, whom he found being entertained by three females. Victus stood and watched as the three cavorted around Gigantrex, taking pleasure in him and themselves.

'Leave,' ordered Victus, and the three scattered from the room, leaving Gigantrex with the biggest erection he had ever seen. 'Enough fun, down to business.'

Victus struggled to think with the screams still emanating from the upper floor, but plans were laid and Gigantrex was dispatched immediately with funds to gather intelligence on what was left of the Civilis family. As Gigantrex departed, the house was shattered by the loudest of screams followed by deadly silence.

Victus bounded up the stairs to Naomi's bedroom, and as he opened the door the silence was broken by crying – that of his new-born son. Naomi lay in drugged euphoria, her job done: the child was born. Victus looked down on his son with mixed emotions as he was wrapped and presented to him. *I need a name, and I owe my father for the sacrifice he made for the family. So be it.*

'Welcome to the world, Victorius Antonius Claudian.' Victus raised his son into the air, Naomi oblivious to her son's naming.

*

*Victus' aid will ensure I regain my village after the deaths of the Civilis', though I doubt he will allow any witnesses to survive. He may think me a simpleton, but I am not the fool he thinks I am*, considered Gigantrex as he rode away.

It was the early hour of night some days later, mist covering the ground and hiding all but the roofs of the town buildings, when Gigantrex slithered into Octodurus unseen. This would be the starting point of his enquiries. Hobbling his horse on the outskirts of the town, he had to know what his sister knew and he was sure she wouldn't want to see him.

Avoiding his sister's inn, Gigantrex headed for the Bear Pit, an inn visited by the town's lowlife and a source of manpower, at least until he regained his rightful place in his estranged village. The local gang leader, Audo, was present. He controlled movement through the town, offering unhindered passage to merchants for a small gratuity, a profitable side-line. Gigantrex offered him a proposition, which Audo accepted eagerly and left without question moments later, directing Gigantrex to a nearby barn where the subject would be brought.

Audo and three of the roughest and ugliest men you could imagine approached the Bear Inn from the rear.

Brunhilda had slipped out of its rear to fetch water from a trough and as she was about to fill her jug, she was seized from behind, a knife placed to her throat.

'Any sound and you are dead. A friend wishes to speak to you. Play nicely and you'll be home before dawn,' Audo said to her in a deep makeshift voice.

Brunhilda tried to struggle as three further hooded figures approached her from the front. With heads down to avoid recognition, she was tied, gagged and blindfolded and quickly marched away from the inn. It was a short walk to the barn where Gigantrex was pacing the floor, and seeing his sister, he pointed to a small stool. Gigantrex gestured to Audo to remove the gag, which he did with the same dire warning as before.

'Who's there?' she pleaded. 'I have a baby at home that needs me. Who needs to do this to talk to me? It could only be you, Gigantrex, brother that was and bastard you are.'

Gigantrex stood still, aghast that she had guessed. 'Right as always, sister. I need information that only you can provide about our mother.'

'She's no longer your mother, she has disowned you and shortly she will leave the village for good,' replied Brunhilda.

'And where would she be going at her time of life?'

'She's leaving with the seers when they return north, and the wolves will return to their old hunting ground.'

'Well, I've returned to stop that happening. When do they leave?' demanded Gigantrex, but silence was his sister's reply. 'Well, maybe I'll have to keep you prisoner until I find out. The choice is yours. How is my Roman nephew?' he asked, laughing.

'You wouldn't dare do anything to my child,' Brunhilda screamed.

'Gag her unless she has an answer,' said Gigantrex.

'Wait! I don't know exactly. They're awaiting Artorius' return after the birth, which should be any day now,' pleaded Brunhilda.

'I thought you'd see reason. Gag her and leave her at the inn's rear door. I'll require your services again shortly,' ordered Gigantrex, tossing a bag of coin at Audo.

Brunhilda was deposited a short while later, still trussed. Audo and his friends dispersed as they heard Paulinus calling for her. Paulinus opened the rear door, and the poor interior light leaked out on to a body, trussed by the trough. In an instant he knew it was his wife; she sobbed and shook in fright as he released her.

'Who did this and why?' demanded Paulinus.

'Gigantrex is back and he is intent on preventing Ilona leaving. We must warn her,' replied Brunhilda.

'We will visit the village tomorrow. I'm not leaving you here on your own if he can do this to you,' responded Paulinus.

# Chapter 26

In that same moment of Gigantrex's arrival in Octodurus, the wolves filled the forest edge surrounding Gigantrex's old village. Inside, Ilona went into childbirth, overseen by Breda.

Rosevetha sat by her fire, casting powders into it and chanting in some long-forgotten language. Ilona had desired Artorius' presence, but Rosevetha withheld word, knowing the child would be waiting on his arrival.

Ilona crouched on all fours, Breda holding her hands and encouraging her. They knew the birth would not be easy. Rosevetha approached her daughter from behind. Now that her cervix was dilated, Rosevetha eased her fingers into her daughter, gently manipulating the child within. The child had to be turned or it would die, but that was not going to be an option for this child. The boy's head filled the opening, and Rosevetha's work was done.

Ilona howled rather than screamed, and the forest echoed like the sound of hell in response. It calmed her as she felt her body forced open. Rosevetha ran a commentary as the child was expelled, bloodied and for a moment lifeless, before erupting into crying, having drawn its first breath. Breda moved quickly to secure the cord and assist the expulsion of the afterbirth, which she gathered in a bowl.

Ilona collapsed, sweat glistening on her body. Her swaddled baby was returned to her by Rosevetha, in tears, something Ilona had never seen before.

*

Artorius, deep in sleep, awoke suddenly.

'*Your son awaits you*' echoed in his brain as he tried to make sense of it all.

'Father, did you hear that?' enquired Marcus from the

doorway, still rubbing sleep from his eyes.

'Did I hear what?' replied Artorius.

'It was like someone whispering in my ear, that Ilona has given birth.'

'So I wasn't dreaming,' Artorius responded. A smile covered his face and a deep longing filled his entire body. 'We need to make plans to finally bring them north. I have the option of an ex-senator's house by the river.'

'I have a surprise for you' said Marcus. 'I haven't been idle since we arrived and you have been too busy to notice my absence. Have you time for me to show you something today?'

Artorius looked quizzically at his son. 'What have you been up to?'

'Meet me as the sun reaches its highest point at the east gate and I'll show you,' replied a beaming Marcus.

*

At the suggested time, Marcus awaited his father by the east gate. Rufus had been made aware that Marcus was there alone and, seeing this as the opportunity he had waited for, he gathered his misfits.

Artorius had spent an easy morning and as the sixth hour of day approached, Legate Aquila appeared at his office door demanding a status report. Aquila was usually happy for Artorius to keep him updated, but a post rider had arrived from Rome that morning, which never boded well. Calling for the senior clerk, he arrived with arms full of scrolls and tablets. *This is going to take a while, but I'm sure Marcus will understand*, Artorius thought.

Back by the east gate, Rufus accepted the guards' grudging salute as he passed through, his cronies following shortly after. Marcus was passing time with the duty Optio, discussing the origins of his swords. The

Optio was trying out Egorix's blade for himself, remarking on its quality.

'Shouldn't you be doing your duty inside the camp, Optio, instead of gossiping?' remarked Rufus.

'If you weren't the Legate's son I'd thrash that arrogance out of you, you ignorant little shit,' the Optio snapped, returning Marcus' sword.

'I'm sure my father would love to hear your comments,' remarked Rufus.

The Optio's face coloured with anger, Marcus grasping his arm and shaking his head.

'You're right, Marcus, he isn't worth spit,' the Optio whispered as he marched back through the camp gates.

'Not giving lessons today, Civilis?' remarked Rufus sarcastically.

'I'm free if you'd like to learn some simple skills?' responded Marcus sharply.

'Why not? Maybe you could teach some of my friends as well.' Rufus called forward his four sycophants, who had slipped through the gate unnoticed, quickly surrounding Marcus.

He stepped back, his hands reaching for his swords.

'Don't even think about it. Walk towards the river and keep your hands where I can see them. It's about time we had a talk and a lesson in respect from your senior,' barked Rufus.

Marcus' arms were seized and tied from behind. He was quickly marched away from the camp walls and through the canabae side streets. Marcus assessed the streets as they went: they were no different from Rome, the buildings occasionally of brick, but the majority were made of mud, a local style. The streets tended to be little more than muddy walkways in the wet, and once away from the main arterial routes, the edges filled with life's expulsions. Rufus and his friends knew the backstreets better than Marcus, and he was soon lost for direction. It was almost as if they were trying to shake off a tail. The edge of the village was soon reached, the river appearing before them and a small clump of trees below a bank hiding the group from view. Marcus felt his swords being removed and watched them being handed to Rufus, who assessed each one.

'Where did you get this heathen weapon with the symbols on it?' demanded Rufus.

'What does it matter to you? It's mine,' replied Marcus, struggling to free himself.

'Bring him to me. Let's start his lesson in respect,' Rufus sneered. 'Force him on to his knees. I am the Legate's son, and as such I am your superior, so you will treat me with respect. You have accumulated a large gathering, all of whom appear to have forgotten who I am. By the time I have finished with you they will see me for who I am: their true superior.'

Marcus was forced to his knees, the rope cutting into his wrists. 'You mean an uncouth bully leading a team of ani—'

Marcus' head spun sideways with the force of the punch Rufus inflicted on him. Marcus spat the blooded phlegm at Rufus, who shrank back. 'Can't stand blood either?'

'Tie him to a tree and teach him a lesson, but don't make his face any worse than it already is,' ordered Rufus of his friends.

One by one they set about Marcus, levelling their punches at his body. Marcus struggled with the pain. The training he had shared with Tia had hardened his stomach, but he wasn't as fit as he had once been. Rufus oversaw the beating, picking his nails with a short blade.

*

Rufus and his friends' actions hadn't gone unnoticed by the gate guards, who sent for the Optio. He decided the situation required Marcus' father. In seeking out Artorius, he found him still in the company of Legate Aquila. Artorius' office door was ajar and the Optio could hear the two talking about their respective sons, Aquila decrying his own child's behaviour. The senior clerk went to stop the Optio, who barged his way in. Relating what had been reported, Artorius stood, begging his leave of Aquila, who tried to play the incident down as just a boy thing.

'Five to one is not a boy thing, and I suspect they intend Marcus injury. There will be blood spilt,' suggested the Optio.

Aquila agreed reluctantly, and accompanied Artorius. Passing through the gate, they were directed towards the town. Artorius and Aquila marched through the town to shocked faces, making enquiries as they walked. On reaching the canabae centre, Artorius was informed of a group leading a youth with his hands tied down towards the river's edge. Aquila's face paled at the news and his footsteps matched Artorius as he increased his pace.

As they reached the town's edge, and with the wooded clump in front of them, Artorius observed a group of youths walking towards them. Artorius and Aquila slipped into a doorway out of sight, and as the youths led by Rufus neared they could be heard laughing. Rufus was swinging a sword in front of him. As the gang came within twenty paces, Artorius stepped out, stopping them dead. Rufus passed the sword to one of his friends and attempted to walk past Artorius, but his way was blocked.

'I demand you get out of my way or else, Camp Prefect,' demanded Rufus arrogantly.

'Or else what, son?' The Legate stepped from the

shadows.

'Nothing, Father...' responded Rufus awkwardly.

'Where is my son Marcus?' demanded Artorius, now face to face with the arrogant youth.

'Why should I know? We haven't seen him, have we, lads?' Rufus looked at the smirking group.

'Don't lie to me. You were seen marching a restrained youth towards the river,' stated the Legate. As Rufus' friends sensed trouble, they started to edge away from the two adults.

'Stay where you are,' ordered Artorius, his spatha already sliding freely from its scabbard.

'We won't need that, Camp Prefect,' suggested the Legate.

'I'll ask nicely one final time: where is my son?' demanded Artorius, grabbing the nearest youth by the throat and shaking him, causing him to choke.

'We left him tied to a tree, it was all Rufus' idea,' the boy spluttered.

'Show me – and hurry.' Artorius released the youth's throat, but retained him firmly by the arm.

Aquila, puce with rage, struck his son hard across the face, knocking him off his feet. Grabbing him by the collar, he dragged the boy after Artorius.

The local youths grew more nervous as they neared the place they had left Marcus, and on finally seeing him still tied to the tree, three of them ran. Artorius' youth struggled, until his legs were kicked from under him. Artorius dragged him forward and threw him at Marcus' feet, while Rufus too was propelled towards the tree by his father.

'Cut him down – and gently, don't make the situation worse,' barked Aquila.

As Rufus' knife cut away Marcus' bindings, Artorius caught his son and lowered him to the ground. Marcus flinched as he was settled on the floor – *a sign of injuries*, thought Artorius, as he lifted his son's shirt to reveal a torso covered in red marks.

Rufus cowered behind the tree as his father looked down on Marcus.

'By the gods, what have you done? You have gone too far this time!' Aquila seized his son from behind the tree and struck him harder than before, blood trickling from the boy's cut lip.

Artorius scooped his unconscious son into his arms and headed back towards the barracks to seek the help of the clinicus. Rufus and his one remaining associate were dragged behind them by Aquila. They were both assured that retribution would follow.

*

Paulinus and his family, ensconced on a cart, arrived at Brunhilda's village just as the sun peaked. Upon seeing her mother, Brunhilda hailed her with a wave. Breda was surprised to see her daughter and family.

'What brings you here? By your look, it is important.'

'Gigantrex is back,' replied Brunhilda simply.

Paulinus assisted his wife and child to the ground and they disappeared with Breda.

Reaching the great hall, Brunhilda explained to her mother and Rosevetha about her abduction and her brother's intention to prevent Ilona from leaving.

'We were too busy with the birth to see the signs. Not a word to Ilona, but we need to warn Artorius somehow,' exclaimed Rosevetha, looking to Paulinus, who had just entered the room.

Following a heated discussion over much beer that night, Paulinus volunteered to warn Artorius.

*

Artorius sat beside Marcus' cot in the infirmary, and as the signal for the fourth hour of night sounded, Marcus stirred. His body was a mass of red and purpling marks, eased by cold wet blankets to draw the bruising.

Marcus looked sideways at his father with pain-filled eyes. 'Why me, Father? What did I do that was so wrong?'

'I don't know, son. Just rest, I'll have some hot food fetched,' answered a troubled Artorius.

*

Two days later Artorius was summoned to Aquila's office. The outer office was full, where Rufus' friends were present with their fathers. Artorius and a bruised Marcus were waved into the Legate's private office. Aquila was sat at the desk with his head buried in paperwork, and to his right stood Rufus, looking extremely awkward. As the door shut Artorius saluted, and Aquila looked up, indicating two empty stools in front of him. Artorius removed his cassis, retaining it under his arm.

'I have a problem to resolve and I have asked you both here for your opinion,' said Aquila. 'If this had been a simple fight between boys, whoever they were, I'd have left it there. However, having seen what was so senselessly inflicted on your son, out of what I have established was mere jealousy, needs serious action. Rufus is my son and needs to learn a severe lesson. You will have seen that my son's associates are outside with their fathers. They will all be required to enlist, and as for my son, he will be subject to the same training. When I am informed that he is fit enough, I will request that he be allowed a Junior Tribune's posting, but not in my Legion. I thought it only fair that your son should decide the whole gang's further punishment. I had considered flogging the local youths for assaulting a Roman citizen, but my son was the main culprit and I intend to set an example with him. Firstly – Marcus, isn't it? How's your recovery?'

Marcus looked first at his father, then Rufus, before responding to the Legate. 'Sir, I had done nothing to warrant a beating. If I had fought one and lost, so be it, but I know not what to suggest. I would like to undertake training alongside them, if I may?'

'A commendable request. I presume you are aware, Camp Prefect?'

'I knew he would want to join the 2nd Augusta. Three generations of his family have lived and fought amongst it. He is of age shortly and very accomplished for his years.'

'I have heard a lot about your son, and all of it good, especially his skills with double swords, which is quite a feat. Marcus, you mentioned that if it had been a fair fight, regardless of the outcome, you would have been happy?' Marcus nodded. 'Might I suggest – with your agreement – a contest between you and my son with practise sword and shield?'

Marcus looked to his father, who shrugged his shoulders, offering Marcus the choice. 'I agree to an open fight,' he replied, 'so that all may see justice done at your convenience, sir?'

'Excellent idea. The training ground at the first hour of day tomorrow after parade,' suggested Aquila, looking at his son, whose face was a picture of hate. 'The Primus Pila of the 1st Cohort will referee, with your agreement, Camp Prefect?'

Artorius nodded his agreement, a smile lighting his face as he reached out for Marcus' shoulder.

'Would you bring the others in, Camp Prefect, and the clerk to interpret?' requested Aquila.

Artorius rose from his stool and, opening the office door, invited in the contents of the clerk's office. The facts of the incident were related to those gathered. Two reacted violently, flooring their sons with punches, but Artorius blocked any further action. The four boys were informed by the Legate that they should be flogged for assaulting a Roman citizen, if it hadn't been for his own son instigating the assault. They were ordered to attend the camp at the start of the following morning, where they would witness the contest between Rufus and Marcus.

The Legate stood to his full height, stern faced, and addressed the group. 'Each one of you is old enough to enlist, and so following the contest, you will be enlisted into the Legion. Refuse and you will be flogged for the assault.'

One of the fathers who had previously assaulted his son stepped forward. 'My son is a coward, but he will be proud to join the Roman army. It will make a man of him, like it did me. May I be so bold as to ask what will happen with your son?'

The Legate squirmed at being put on the spot, but informed the gathering of his decision on Rufus, which was met with nods of agreement. Two of the fathers tried to appeal against the decision, citing that their sons were required on their respective farms. The Legate reiterated the alternative punishment, and silence followed as the group was told to leave.

'Rufus, get out of my sight. I think you should take the time you have to practise for tomorrow – and stay out of any further trouble,' ordered Aquila.

The Legate offered Marcus his hand as father and son made to follow the rest. 'Don't go easy on him, boy. I would be proud to have you in my Legion and I believe that, like your late brother, you ride well. We always have vacancies in the cavalry.'

Artorius' face lit up: it was the option he had hoped for.

\*

Gigantrex woke early, dispatching a messenger to Genua with a message for Victus. He didn't expect him to arrive before Artorius had been and left the village, but it was worth a try. Gigantrex was later met by Audo in company of one of his men, who was sweating profusely; both looked nervous.

'Fredenand has been watching your village and he saw what he believes to have been an ex-soldier leave via the forest trail to the great north road,' explained Audo.

Gigantrex had underestimated how fast his sister and husband would react to his interrogation. He could only surmise that it was Paulinus who was heading north to warn Artorius. He couldn't let that happen.

'Do your men ride?' enquired Gigantrex. Audo nodded in the affirmative. 'Are their horses any good?'

'Some of the best. They were gifted, if you know what I mean?' replied Audo.

'I need three, plus your man here, to go after the one that left the village this morning. I want that man stopped, by any means, before he reaches Argentoratum. Go!' demanded Gigantrex.

Audo and his man scuttled away.

\*

A cold and damp mist crawled from the river as Marcus stepped outside to look for his father. Artorius was in the mess hall with some other senior officers, devouring a bowl of oats in warm milk. Seeing Marcus, he bade him join them.

A plain cassis with a face guard sat on the table, and Artorius offered it to Marcus. The officers were discussing the upcoming contest between the boys as the first hour of day sounded, at which everyone rose and departed for the parade ground.

As per their daily routine, the Legion were mustering, the parade ground echoing to the sound of barked commands and abuse of the slow or poorly turned out. The Legion's buccinators sounded their horns and Aquila approached on horseback, trailing his son, who was on foot carrying his cassis and face guard.

Artorius marched smartly to the front, calling his Legion to attention. The parade ground echoed to the sound of caligae driven on to hard ground, pluming dust into the air and obscuring the rising sun. Formalities completed, the men were dismissed to their duties, with many trying to find a reason to be working on or near the parade ground, hell bent on seeing the Legate's son get his comeuppance. Betting, though illegal, was rather one-sided: Marcus' prowess was well known, but there were always a few who would bet on the outsider.

Marcus stood facing Rufus, who scowled back at him, as their fathers spoke with the adjudicating Primus Pila. The moment was broken by Rufus' four accomplices, who were dragged by their fathers on to the Legion's hallowed ground, some displaying signs of a beating.

Two practise swords and round shields were produced and presented to Artorius. The weapons were tested by the adjudicator and offered to the two boys. Marcus accepted a wooden sword with Jorgan's warning ringing in his head: *Never underestimate your foe.*

Rufus stood motionless, watching Marcus going through warm-up exercises. His wooden sword was heavier than Marcus', but it rotated easily in his hand. The adjudicator called them both together, Marcus calm,

Rufus angry and agitated. With helmets secured and tested, Rufus pushed Marcus away, with Marcus instantly adopting a low stance.

Rufus glared at Marcus and advanced on him. The first contact echoed for all to hear. Shields punched forward, it was then that Marcus realised Rufus was stronger than he looked. He rolled sideways, leaving Rufus alone, which did nothing to help his temper. Rufus charged at Marcus, but again Marcus rolled away.

Rufus roared like a mad bull, charging and slashing at Marcus, now facing him. The blows were easily deflected, but the reverberations brought pain back to the bruised muscles of Marcus' arms. He swept low at Rufus' legs, sending him crashing to the floor and jolting his shield arm, and Marcus stepped back into a low stance as Rufus erupted from the floor. He wasn't going to be made a fool of again as he followed Marcus, slashing at anything that came within range.

Marcus calmly parried and side-stepped, rolling away from pressure to the applause of the gathering observers, a red mist descended on Rufus driving him forward. The veterans admired the fluidity of Marcus' movements as Rufus' strikes became fast and furious. Time and time again, Rufus was sucked in by Marcus' feints, only to result in a strike against him.

Marcus slipped on a piece of damp ground and Rufus charged, kicking Marcus in the ribs, and as he rolled away in pain, Rufus struck at his legs, drawing first blood. Cheers rang out and Rufus' confidence soared as he beckoned Marcus to him. Rufus wiped the sweat from his eyes, whereas apart from the minor cut, Marcus' energy was as fresh as when he had started.

Marcus drew Rufus to him. Every breath caused pain, but he was still in control. Kneeling with his head dropped, Marcus pulled his shield in tight to his body.

Rufus charged, striking down, and Marcus punched his shield with full force at his charging opponent. Rufus' shield was rammed against him, its rim bending his face guard. Marcus struck home at the exposed stomach with the flat of his sword, and Rufus recoiled backwards on to the floor, the wind knocked out of him.

Rufus discarded his sword and shield as he clutched at his stomach. Dropping his own shield, Marcus pinned Rufus' arms to the floor and placed the tip of his sword on his throat.

'Yield, you are beaten,' demanded Marcus.

'Never,' spat Rufus as he tried to dislodge Marcus, but he had tired himself out.

Marcus looked to the adjudicator, who stepped forward and raised Marcus' arm. Marcus stood, releasing Rufus, who rolling away, his hand slipping behind him. Sun on metal caught Marcus' eye, and grabbing his shield from the floor, he rammed it full force into Rufus' face, sending him staggering backwards.

Blood poured from Rufus' broken nose and he dropped the small blade he had hidden in his waistband. The gathered crowd looked shocked as Marcus struck Rufus with his shield, but when the blade fell, there was uproar.

Artorius rushed forward, seizing the blade, closely followed by Aquila. The red-faced Legate punched his son in the stomach and turned to the adjudicator.

'Centurion, take my fucking son to my apartment and instruct his mother that he is to be locked in his room till I return.' He turned to Rufus. 'You are a disgrace to your family, that was the last straw! Now take him away,' ordered the Legate.

'Step forward, you four, you are about to be sworn in,' demanded a fuming Legate of the shaking accomplices. 'I presume you all speak the language of Caesar's Rome?' They all nodded in agreement.

'*Clinicus*, step forward and ensure they are fit to serve,' ordered Aquila.

The Legion's senior *clinicus* saluted and marched forward. Each youth was called forth, ordered to strip and examined from head to foot. All were passed fit, despite protestations from two, which were overruled. The Legate recited the *sacramentum* and the eldest of the four repeated it, while the other three responded as one, '*Idem in me.*'

'Clerk, enter their names on the Legion's rolls as auxiliaries, to be trained here and then assigned to a Legion as required. March them away and assign them a billet,' directed Aquila.

The youths looked to their fathers; they now belonged to Rome. The Legate, calming, looked at Artorius and his fist punched out a salute as he and Marcus were about to leave.

'For a youth you are commendably skilled, Marcus. Taught by your father, no doubt?'

Before Marcus could answer, Artorius replied: 'I wish I could take the credit, but it was a joint effort of my father's freedman, who taught me, and my son's late Scythian girlfriend. He is well skilled with a bow as well.'

'A bow has its place amongst our auxiliaries, but not with a legionary,' replied the Legate.

'I still have the surprise to show you, Father, when you are free?' offered Marcus.

'Take some time with your son – he deserves it, Camp Prefect. I have my own to deal with,' responded Aquila darkly.

As father and son passed through the barracks to the

accolade from soldiers young and old, Marcus collected his twin blades. Artorius questioned where they were going as they left the barracks to knowing winks from the guards. *It appears I am the only one not to know about this mysterious secret*, thought Artorius.

Marcus led his father on to the even more well-worn track towards the forest. A swirling mist lingered in the trees as a wooden wall loomed up before them on the edge of a meadow. The meadow had been extended to provide a considerable killing ground in front of a palisade. Tree stumps were the testimony to that palisade. A thatched building greeted Artorius as he stepped through the gateless gap, and he looked at his son, who beckoned him forward.

Stepping through the building's latched door, Artorius found a large room built around a central stone fireplace and chimney. Three rooms led from the main one, large enough to sleep two, and in the largest sat a wooden cradle. The abode needed furniture and Artorius knew someone who could fill it, as he immediately imagined Ilona and his new son. Marcus waited outside. An amazed Artorius stepped out into the improving light of day.

'There are fresh fish in the stream which feeds into the Rhenus, and deer still visit despite our home being here. I thought the forest could house Ilona's wolves and their presence would add to our security. What do you think?'

'I don't know what to say. I know how much you loved your mother, as I truly did. To create this is overwhelming.' Artorius hugged his son to him.

'When will you fetch Ilona and my brother?' enquired Marcus.

'I need to beg leave from the Legion to do that, and now might be a good time,' responded Artorius.

\*

Paulinus had taken his time through the forest. It had been a long while since he had travelled this route, but then he didn't know he was being followed.

Audo travelled with his men, all ex-Legion scouts, and utilising the great north road they sped towards Aventicum. Audo dispatched Fredenand forward in an attempt to overtake Paulinus if possible.

Paulinus reached the forest's edge and the great north road, but held back in the cover of the trees as a horse that was being ridden at speed passed in front of him, heading for Aventicum. As Paulinus prepared his own horse for the road he wondered what mission the rider was on. *No doubt something political, nothing else ever warranted that kind of speed these days.*

Audo was only a couple of hours behind his man, oblivious that their target now lay between him and his scout.

Fredenand reached Aventicum's outskirts without sight of the target, his horse lathered in sweat. Retracing his steps, he eventually led his horse off the main highway, where a stream ran alongside, and whilst he chewed on dry meat he allowed his horse to drink and munch on an apple he carried with him.

A little way behind, Paulinus was taking the journey more leisurely, while the rest of Audo's gang closed the gap unknowingly.

Fredenand, believing he had missed his target, decided to save his horse and await Audo's arrival. He aimlessly sat on the streamside, watching what little traffic there was and dozing as the sun's warmth got the better of him. It was more luck than chance that, on hearing a lone rider pass, he opened his eyes. Not believing what he was seeing, he rubbed his eyes as his target trotted past. Deciding luck was with him, and with the day drawing in, he followed his target.

Paulinus felt the hairs on his neck rise as he heard a rider behind him, and guessing it was the one by the stream, he brought his horse to a halt and faced the traveller, his hand slipping to his sword pommel.

'Heading for Aventicum?' Fredenand enquired, stopping in front of Paulinus and offering both hands as a sign of no weapons.

'Where are you headed? That was you by the stream back there, wasn't it?' responded Paulinus.

'Only as far as Aventicum. I gave my horse a rest and took the chance of a snack. I don't suppose – with yourself being ex-Legionary, if I'm not mistaken – that you would fancy company? I was a scout for the 14th Gemina myself, what Legion were you with?' Fredenand enquired. *If I can slow him down, Audo and the rest will catch us up*, he thought.

'There is only one Legion. I was a Centurion in the glorious 2nd Augusta, of course,' insisted Paulinus.

'A fine Legion; I have friends who still scout for them, but in times of relative peace there is little to do and many men leave,' added the scout.

'Join me. There is always strength in numbers and you seem reasonable enough,' offered Paulinus, turning his horse alongside Fredenand's as he advanced.

The pair began to build up speed, Paulinus insisting they needed to reach Aventicum by the last hour of day. Fredenand couldn't think of a reason to counter the suggestion. What neither had seen was Audo closing in on them, and as the gap closed, Audo recognised Fredenand, whom he presumed was in company of the target.

Fortuitously, the roadside was frequently heavily

wooded. Audo and his accomplices slipped from the road on to a well-worn track that ran parallel, but was hidden by the trees. Overtaking Fredenand and the target was no mean feat, but within a couple of miles it had been achieved and Audo lay in wait on an incline and a blind bend. He sent another scout ahead to warn of their impending arrival. Reining in his horse, Audo considered a well-practised head-on charge led by himself, hoping that Fredenand would then attack Paulinus from behind and success would be guaranteed.

They didn't have to wait long as the lookout signalled the pair's arrival and ran back to his horse. Taking the centre of the road, Audo led the charge around the bend at a gallop, with spears in hand.

Paulinus reacted slower than he would have years before, and out of the corner of his eye he saw his fellow traveller reach for his sword. His own sword slipped easily from its scabbard and with his head down, he galloped at his aggressors.

Audo closed on his target, and Fredenand struck his sword across Paulinus' back. Paulinus pulled his horse up suddenly and it reared, discarding him on to the floor badly. Head and stone made contact with a loud cracking sound.

Audo pulled up short of the inert figure and, jumping from his horse, he approached Paulinus. Feeling under his jaw, there was only a faint pulse. Paulinus was dragged unceremoniously into the edge of the forest and left there.

'If he's found he'll be dead and it'll look like an accident. Otherwise, the elements or the wildlife will see him off. Get his horse,' ordered Audo, but Paulinus' horse had other ideas and bolted. 'Leave it, let's get out of here.'

Audo and his men galloped back towards Octodurus,

leaving a camouflaged figure watching their departure.

Junius crawled from his hiding place as Paulinus' horse returned to its master. Approaching the beast stealthily, Junius seized the reins as the horse shied. Junius soon had the horse under control, and hobbling it, he checked on its rider's condition. *Alive, but only just. Mathilde will save him if anyone can*, he thought as he lifted the body on to the horse and started his walk back through the forest to his farm, collecting his day's kill on the way.

Mathilde, a native with long black tied-back hair and piercing blue eyes, was bent over a bubbling cauldron when Junius entered their home carrying a man across his shoulders.

'Who's this and where did you find him?' she enquired.

'He was ambushed and left for dead. He's in a bad way, but I couldn't leave a fellow comrade of the Legions,' answered Junius, lowering Paulinus on to a fur on the floor.

'You and your old ways. Is there anything for the cauldron?' she asked.

'It's outside, I've had a good day,' responded Junius as he stepped outside, returning with a full sack and dumping its contents on the hut floor to a smiling Mathilde.

Mathilde turned and assessed the deathly white body before her. The man's senses were minimal as she pinched and squeezed at his skin. 'He's barely alive, as you say, but apart from the cut on his back and the large lump on his head, there's nothing broken that I can tell. Where was he going?'

'He was headed towards Aventicum when they attacked him; he appeared to have befriended one of his attackers,' replied Junius.

'I may need miracles to save this one, but as always, I will do my best.'

\*

Returning to Octodurus in the early hours of night, Audo found a restless Gigantrex and related the news of Paulinus' demise.

Gigantrex was troubled on where to go next. *Should I take the initiative and stop Artorius before he gets to my village, or wait for his departure and oversee Audo and his men finish him off?* He pondered over his options, his mood darkening with every thought.

Fredenand was ordered to watch over the village and warn of any departure, and he left begrudgingly. Gigantrex had decided to engage Artorius when he left, whether Victus' help materialised or not. He prayed that the new child would cause a delay.

## Chapter 27

It had been a long and hard journey with the carriage, as Artorius and Marcus trundled off the highway into the forest towards the village. A cacophony of birdsong tantalised their ears and both surveyed their surroundings.

Fredenand watched their arrival from his roadside cover, unobserved. Mounting his horse, he hastened to find Audo and then both sought Gigantrex's counsel to decide what to do next.

Dark shapes moved between the trees as father and son entered deeper into the forest. There was a flash of white, and two wolves slid from their dark surroundings followed by a pair of pepper-coloured cubs, causing the horses to shy.

'It appears we have a welcoming committee,' remarked Artorius as he spotted Donor, who continued to approach.

Artorius handed the reins to his son and jumped to the ground, calming the horses as he stepped forward to greet Donor with an open hand. The she-wolf, followed by her cubs, was cagey, sliding alongside Donor. Artorius reached out to her, but she avoided his touch; the cubs, however, wove in between his legs.

Marcus was encouraged to join his father. Donor never flinched, but the she-wolf withdrew further, followed by the cubs. Leaving Artorius, Donor brazenly walked up to Marcus and brushed against him. The sensation for Marcus was mind-blowing as he felt the fur run through his fingers. The wolf sat in front of him, staring up and enjoying the attention, and after a few moments the she-wolf and cubs joined them. Marcus knelt on the ground and the cubs ran to him without fear, their mother sitting alongside her partner as Marcus fussed over them.

'You've obviously been accepted. Ilona said you would be. I'm almost jealous that the she-wolf accepts you! Let's go, Donor, I am sure your mistress awaits.'

Donor gave a howl and his family moved away at a walk, followed by Artorius and Marcus, leading the carriage into the meadow.

The gates were wide open and a lone female stood with babe in arms. Flowing red hair shone like copper as the sun broke through the mist, and even the child's head displayed a copper sheen. The young woman wore a tight-fitting gown of grass green, tight against her milk-laden breasts, and a garland of flowers adorned her hair. Artorius' heart jumped a beat – Ilona looked more beautiful than he had ever seen her. Both walked towards each other, their eyes locked, the world around them stopped in time.

'Your son greets his father and his mother is blessed by your return. We are packed and ready for our journey,' remarked Ilona in a whisper as the couple melted together.

Marcus entered the village, leading the carriage, to be met by Breda who hugged him to her. Though shocked, Marcus enjoyed the moment. Rosevetha hobbled forward aided by a stout rod. She appeared to have aged in the short while they had been in the north. She eyed the couple's reunion.

'There was never any doubt your father would return,' she said to Marcus. 'He is a man of honour. Don't impugn him for your new brother – the fates decreed it long ago. The gift you have prepared is testimony to your greatness. You will achieve fame and distinction from all you graze. Did you receive our warning about Gigantrex?' enquired Rosevetha. Marcus shook his head.

Artorius and Ilona walked hand in hand to join the villagers who were gathering around Marcus. Breda stepped forward to greet them. 'A final feast is prepared in your honour, as you will never see the village again,' she volunteered.

Artorius looked shocked and turned to ask Ilona, who smiled and answered 'Later' as she led him towards the great hall.

A large fire burned within, a spitted boar rotating above it. The long tables were adorned with bowls of wild fruit and enough jugs of frothy cold beer and amphorae of wine to quench any thirst. Breda took the head table, inviting Artorius and Ilona to seats on her left, with Marcus, the village elder and Rosevetha to her right. Villagers entertained their guests with music and dance and the talk was light-hearted, but Artorius and Ilona were in their own moment; their son lay asleep throughout. Breda engaged Marcus with enquiries about Argentoratum and his new home by the river. He was astounded by her knowledge, but he knew he shouldn't be.

While the party were occupied, Artorius and Ilona slipped away. Like lovers in their first flush, they made haste to Ilona's hut, where a fire spat and furs covered the floor. Their son was placed into a wicker basket beside their cot as Artorius and Ilona stripped slowly.

Ilona lay back naked, inviting Artorius to join her, but it was the first time he had been truly able to appreciate her. Her skin was as white as snow, a red triangle of pubic hair stood proud between her legs, and emerald green eyes sparkled from the pillow between thick red locks of hair. Artorius' passion was obvious by the large erection in front of him.

He knelt beside her and ran his calloused hands over her soft skin. He traced his finger around her erect dark

266

nipples, skimming over her stomach, his fingers brushing through her pubic hair and squeezing her pubic mound gently. Ilona emitted a soft moan and opened her legs, begging him to take her. Artorius climbed above her as she clutched his member and guided it into her wet warmth. The two slid together with an ease of familiarity and the only sounds were their own breathing intensifying as their coition continued to finality.

Sated and sweat covered and wrapped in each other's arms, sleep swept over them.

*

Artorius woke the following morning to find Ilona suckling their son. Pride radiated in her smile as Artorius ran his hand across his son's face.

'Have you thought of a name?' enquired Ilona.

'Not really, I thought we would choose together – perhaps our father's names? Do you know your father's?'

'My father was a Roman soldier from the lost legions. I never knew him. I was born the year he died,' said Ilona, and Artorius looked shocked.

While Ilona gathered herself together, Artorius was handed his son. He had never held any of his children as babies and felt extremely awkward and nervous, but Ilona was having no excuses.

The couple found Marcus, Rosevetha and Breda deep in conversation.

'Paulinus is missing. He was coming to warn us of Gigantrex's return. He plans to stop us leaving,' stated Marcus.

'How long ago?' enquired Artorius.

'About the time we set out from Argentoratum. He took the forest route, but that has been checked with no sign of him. Enquiries at Octodurus have proved negative as well,' Marcus countered.

'I have to return to Argentoratum, but I owe it to Brunhilda that we look for him as he did me,' responded Artorius.

'Today I sensed him nearby,' added Breda. 'There is a healer who cares for him, but she has blocked our ability to see him. I will search with some of our young warriors.'

'I will go with Breda – I owe him a debt for your life,' offered Marcus.

Artorius nodded helplessly. 'We need to leave as soon as we can.'

'Your son is ready. We must leave in the morning. My wolves are already returning north and they will protect us on route,' suggested Ilona.

*

A weakened Paulinus opened his eyes to find a strange woman staring down at him and his head bandaged. The room around him was warm and filled with tempting food aromas, but he couldn't tell what hour of day it might be.

'You have a hard head, Roman – you were lucky my husband found you. Someone seeks to find you, but I have blocked them for now,' said Mathilde.

'I don't remember anything and I don't know who I am or where I'm from. Why would a seer be interested in me?' replied Paulinus.

Mathilde shrugged, wondering what might happen if she let the searcher in.

Junius was surprised to find the patient awake, but more surprised when Mathilde explained he didn't know who he was. Junius had seen comrades with head injuries lose their memories, sometimes permanently, and while Paulinus slept, the couple discussed the alternatives, which weren't many. Mathilde knew the seer would come looking, but when? And how could she guarantee her patient's safety?

*

Mist clung to the forest as the village woke to the sound of wolves howling. Ilona was already awake and standing by the open gate as Donor, his mate and cubs emerged from the mist. Donor's mate approached on her own and sniffed at the baby's hand that was offered to her. Ilona felt a strong bond between two mothers as the she-wolf rubbed herself against the hand, but seeing Artorius, the she-wolf growled.

'She accepted Marcus yesterday, but she's wary of me?' he said.

Ilona shrugged.

'I will prepare the wagon and we can leave. Breda and some of the village youths are accompanying us to Octodurus,' stated Artorius.

A short time later the sun had started to burn off the mist, though it still clung to the treetops as the large party set off towards the great north road. The whole village gathered to say a final farewell to the wolf queen, but with Breda leaving as well, there was a leadership void which none wanted to fill.

Ilona insisted on sitting beside Artorius at the front of the cart, the baby secure in a wicker basket beside its grandmother. Marcus took point while Breda, dressed every bit a warrior, shouldered a bow and took the rear with a half dozen tested youths. The forest either side of them moved with shades of black and white as Ilona's pack shadowed the group.

When they reached the forest edge and the road, Ilona called a halt and climbed down, Donor approaching her. The two became almost as one as Donor stood on his hind legs, placing his paws on her shoulders, and she whispered to him. Dropping to the ground, Donor raised his head and howled, and the forest resonated as he disappeared amongst the trees.

The party resumed its journey watched by Fredenand who, in turn, had been observed by Donor. A portion of the pack detached itself and followed him as he retraced his steps. Artorius' party were too far away to hear it when the screams pierced the forest silence. Gigantrex would be waiting in vain for news.

As the party started up a slope with wooded sides, it was Breda who called a halt at the spot where Paulinus had been ambushed. She looked around her, to quizzical looks from the party.

'Paulinus was taken from here and is close by. His carer is a powerful healer and she questions our trust. She is well known and feared in Aventicum. The sooner we prove our trustworthiness, the sooner we will recover Paulinus.'

Aside from that, the day had been long and uneventful and the party eventually reached Aventicum in the early hours of the evening, seeking food and lodgings. Marcus and Breda secured the carriage and horses and went in search of information.

They learned that a healer by the name of Mathilde was well known and equally feared, but none were sure where she lived. Her husband and guardian, an ex-soldier, occasionally visited the town to sell furs. Greasing palms, a request was made to notify them if Mathilde's partner reappeared. Marcus related such to his father, assuring him that he would follow once Paulinus was found. Space was limited and Marcus opted to sleep in the inn's barn with the village youths.

*

Audo was roused from his sleep by loud knocking at his

door. Rolling his lover from his chest to muffled grumblings, he stepped towards the door as it rattled again.

'What is it?' he demanded.

'Fredenand's horse has returned without him and it's covered in blood.'

'Wait, I'll be right there,' ordered Audo.

Still dressing as he left, he found the caller ashen-faced. Both made towards their stables where Fredenand's terrified horse was hobbled. The saddle was torn and blood covered the animal's flanks.

'Someone must have hacked him to pieces with this amount of blood,' observed Audo as his colleague clutched an amulet around his throat. 'I need to speak to Gigantrex immediately. Clean the horse,' he ordered, striding away.

Gigantrex didn't respond to the knock on his door until it was flung open.

A blade touched Audo's throat in the blink of an eye.

'What do you want at this hour?' Gigantrex demanded.

'Fredenand's horse has returned covered in blood and the saddle is torn to shreds,' related Audo.

'The wolves, no doubt?' responded Gigantrex.

'What wolves?'

'Ilona's wolves, didn't I mention them? Artorius and Ilona must have left the village if the wolves are moving. Round up as many men as you can – we're going after them.' Gigantrex's face twisted with anger.

'You never mentioned any wolves,' Audo responded.

'Never mind that,' Gigantrex snapped. 'Your men will be well paid. We'll stick to the road, they don't need to know about the wolves, do they?'

Audo drew a deep breath and left. Barely an hour later,

he and a half-dozen men he had dragged from their beds at the promise of a good reward, met with Gigantrex and set off towards Aventicum.

*

It was still dark when Marcus awoke. Hearing voices, he went outside to investigate.

He spotted the innkeeper, carrying a lantern and talking to an unknown male. The second male was grey-haired, sun-tanned and powerfully built, and must have been about his father's age. He stood with his legs slightly apart, hands on hips, back straight, a spatha in his belt and a bow and quiver over his shoulder.

Marcus heard snatches of the conversation, and it soon became clear that the innkeeper was talking about their group. The other man turned in Marcus' direction, but didn't see him in the darkness. Slipping a coin to the innkeeper, the male slipped back into the shadows, and Marcus followed.

The unknown male glided through the town's side-streets with familiarity, checking regularly for anyone following, although he did not spot Marcus, who slid in and out of dark doorways with ease. Reaching the town limits, Marcus was distracted by a hobbled horse and in that moment, he lost his man. He instinctively withdrew as deep as he could into the shadows of a doorway, his eyes piercing the surroundings for movement.

Junius knew he had been followed. Propelling a stone at a door nearby, he waited for the movement he expected. As Marcus turned, Junius slipped behind him, placing his pugio into the young man's back.

'Why are you following me?' Junius demanded.

'I am looking for an ex-soldier married to a healer named Mathilde. They may know the whereabouts of my father's friend, Paulinus,' replied Marcus hesitantly.

272

'Can you describe him?'

'I have never met him, but his wife's mother is with us. She is a seer and has seen Paulinus with Mathilde,' he answered.

'Turn around, but keep your hands where I can see them. Take me to this woman,' ordered Junius.

'I can't, I'm lost,' said Marcus bluntly, and Junius laughed.

Turning Marcus around and removing his swords, Junius ordered him to walk up the road in front of him, keeping his own blades at his back. The return journey to the barn was a much shorter one. Junius instructed Marcus to send for Breda and cautioned him about bringing others.

He dared not turn around and entered the inn by the rear door, startling the innkeeper. Finding Breda's room, Marcus knocked gently and entered. Breda was sat on her cot, dressed and waiting.

'You've found the healer's man and he wants to see me? Lead the way and be quiet.'

Marcus nodded, leading the way back to the barn. He searched the early morning light for his man, but couldn't find him. Breda looking questioningly at Marcus, who shrugged, and just then Junius stepped out of the shadows behind them, making Breda start.

'So, you are the seer Mathilde spoke of. Why do you look for this man?' snapped Junius.

Breda explained: 'Mathilde has done well to keep him from the shades, but is it true that he remembers nothing?'

Junius ignored the question. 'How do we know if you wish him well or ill?'

'Only Mathilde can decide that, but I wish to return him to his wife's care if he can travel,' snapped Breda.

273

'Marcus, go to your father and bid him wait till I return. I will go with this man alone.' Her voice resumed its usual calmness.

'You can't go alone,' pleaded Marcus.

'If what she says is true then she will be safe. Take these fine weapons back with you. Go,' ordered Junius.

'If anything happens to her, I will find you and kill you,' stated Marcus, reaching for his swords.

'Go away, puppy. You are hardly a threat to me, a seasoned ex-Centurion of the 2nd.'

Marcus snatched his swords, rotating them in front of Junius and ending his display with Junius' head held between them. 'You may know my father, Camp Prefect Artorius Civilis, also of the 2nd. I am his son, Marcus.'

'Impressive. Artorius Civilis, there's a name from my past… Bid your father greetings from Junius Germanicus. This way, lady – you have a horse?'

Breda nodded.

'You must have known Paulinus yourself, he served with my father,' suggested Marcus.

'Many fine men did,' replied Junius.

Breda disappeared into the barn, to get her horse. She secreted a blade into her saddle, her only protection. When she came back out, Junius made to cover her eyes.

'There's no need, I can describe where you live, but not how to get there.' Breda's eyes burned into Junius, who turned away and led off down the main street.

Marcus tapped gently on his father's door, which Artorius opened almost immediately. He was partially dressed, and in the dim light of a lamp, Marcus could see his brother at his mother's breast. He turned away in embarrassment. Artorius looked back and pulled the door to as Marcus related the encounter, mentioning

Junius' name.

'He was a fellow Centurion some years back and is now retired. Funny how no one ever travels far from the Legion. Breda will be safe with him, although it looks like we'll have to wait till she returns,' stated Artorius.

\*

Junius led Breda just beyond the limits of the town, then followed a well-worn track into the forest. Breda cast her eyes around her, wondering if Ilona's wolves were close, but she saw nothing. The birds were in full song, and she even heard an eagle calling somewhere above her.

'Always a fortuitous sign, the eagle?' prompted Junius.

Breda nodded. 'We are close, I sense, and Mathilde is aware.'

'In all my years in the army I have never known a place where so many women see without looking,' suggested Junius.

Breda laughed as she overtook him, entering a clearing with a lone wooden hut, where a raven-haired woman stood waiting. 'Mathilde, I presume? How is my daughter's husband?' enquired Breda as she slid from her mount.

Mathilde nodded and pointed to the open door, following Breda inside. Paulinus lay on a fur-covered stretcher, his skin pale with a bandage covering his head.

'My husband witnessed the attack. He was left for dead and doesn't remember anything,' Mathilde related.

'I should know this man, it seems, but I don't recognise him,' stated Junius, who appeared at the door.

Breda was already kneeling beside Paulinus. He opened his eyes and looked up into her face.

'Paulinus, don't you recognise me? I am your wife Brunhilda's mother – Breda?'

Only a blank expression filled his face. Breda spoke to him softly about his inn and his family in Octodurus. Even mention of Artorius didn't raise a glimmer.

'Is he safe to move? My daughter is heartbroken at his disappearance,' enquired Breda.

'He is still weak, but I don't see why he can't be moved in a wagon,' replied Mathilde.

Junius drew his wife aside, relating all that had happened and the mention of his old comrade and the man who lay before them – all three of them from the 2nd Augusta.

'I see and feel no reason to disbelieve what has been said. He should return to his family, only they can mend his mind,' offered Mathilde.

On their return to Aventicum, Junius procured a wagon and enjoyed a beer-fuelled reunion with Artorius. After much discussion, Junius offered to accompany Breda and Paulinus back to Octodurus and then return with the wagon. Breda decided that her daughter would need help until Paulinus recovered – if he did, that was.

'Do you think he will recover?' enquired Artorius.

The three women looked at each other and shared the moment.

'There are always two paths, but only Paulinus can choose,' replied Rosevetha.

The air was sharp on the throat the following morning as Artorius and Marcus greeted Junius, steam emitting from both his horse and himself. The three stepped inside for some warmed wine to fortify them. The three women were deep in conversation, excluding all others in their whispers, which stopped abruptly as the men joined them. None of the men dared to ask what was being discussed; the knowing looks froze them.

It was with great sadness that less than an hour later,

Artorius' party bade Breda goodbye. Marcus was especially sad, who saw a grandparent in her, and she saw in him a grandson she would have been justly proud of. They clung to each other and tears fell easily.

'Tia will be your guardian, don't be afraid to talk to her. You will find your destiny in a lady from the Green Isle,' whispered Breda.

'No one could replace Tia,' insisted Marcus, his head filled with a deep longing.

'You are wrong. You will cross the sea on a new conquest and there you will find her, where you least expect it. Many will offer themselves, but you will know her in that first moment.'

'If you see it, it must be so,' accepted Marcus.

'No, there is always a choice. The right choice will be your life,' stated Breda, smiling.

'Will you re-join us?'

'I cannot answer that. I can see for others, but not myself. Take care of your family, now and in the future, and remember me occasionally.'

Rosevetha, Ilona and Breda shared a final moment.

'He comes towards you, nothing will stop him,' whispered Rosevetha.

Breda nodded, and with that she pulled away, smiling to Marcus. Junius' horse trailed the wagon he drove and as Breda mounted she was handed her bow, her quiver already attached to her saddle. 'Time to go,' she stated.

Ilona, in tears, held her swaddled son close as Breda left for what destiny held in store.

\*

Paulinus was awake but in a trance-like state when Breda saw him next. Placing Paulinus in the rear of the wagon, Breda attended to him. Her bow and quiver lay beside her.

'Junius, the men that attacked your friend head this way. Come back to me safe,' said Mathilde, offering him his bow and spear.

'Mithras protects me as he always has. Cast your mantle about me as you have before,' responded Junius.

These actions didn't go unnoticed by Breda. 'You know my son's coming, don't you? He means us harm.'

Junius nodded as he cracked his whip over the horses, and the wagon moved off.

As the group aimed for the breach in the forest and the great road, Breda called her warriors to her and warned them of an imminent attack by Gigantrex and others. Immediately Breda's warriors held back behind the wagon and an argument ensued.

*

Gigantrex, Audo and his gang were closing the gap, but they didn't expect to see a wagon pull out of the forest in front of them with Gigantrex's mother kneeling in the back of it.

'I want my mother unharmed, but any that oppose us, kill,' ordered Gigantrex.

Audo notched and dispatched an arrow at the arguing warriors at the rear. The argument abruptly stopped as the wagon struggled on to the road, when a whoosh and a thud unseated one of the warriors, an arrow embedded in his chest.

Breda reacted immediately and let fly two arrows, one after the other, one lethal and one fatally wounding. Audo was knocked from his horse by a backhand from Gigantrex, causing Audo's men to stop.

'You fucking idiot, now look what you've caused,' Gigantrex spat as he raised himself up. He slipped his left arm through the back of his round shield and drew his sword in his right.

Junius, seeing the hesitation and chaos, whipped the horses into a frenzy and aimed them at Gigantrex and his group. Only two warriors remained with them as they tried to bludgeon their way forward. The twang of Breda's bow filled Junius' ears with joy as horses and two more men recoiled with protruding arrows. Audo screamed at his men to retaliate as he remounted his horse, while Gigantrex was already in pursuit of the wagon, which jolted Paulinus and Breda in its hurried movement.

Two warriors turned to face Gigantrex, swords drawn.

'Stay, Gigantrex. Your mother is still our leader since you left, and we will defend her,' shouted the elder of the two.

Gigantrex stopped short. 'More fool you! I am the rightful chief and you will obey me or die.'

'Then in your father's name, we will defend his lady.'

Gigantrex charged at the two who tried to block his way. His shield rim took the full impact of a sword slicing down at him, buckling on impact. His sword punched out at the man on his right, gouging a deep cut in his thigh, and as his horse bolted an arrow took the rider's life.

Gigantrex continued after the wagon as an arrow thudded into his damaged shield. *My mother obviously has no feelings for me anymore, but I'll not have her killed*, he thought. An arrow whistled past him and he knew its target – Breda spun off her knees, clutching her shoulder, but not before dispatching another arrow which slammed into Gigantrex's horse's chest. It screamed in agony and collapsed, sending Gigantrex colliding with the road. Audo pulled up short of Gigantrex and let fly an arrow, taking the fleeing warrior in his back while his horse ploughed on.

'Do you want me to stop them?' he shouted.

'Who was in that wagon?' demanded Gigantrex.

'Your faithful warriors claim it was the man we left for dead.'

'You said you had killed him!' Anger was written large across Gigantrex's face as he reached up and pulled Audo from his horse. Gigantrex reached for the knife in his belt and embedded it into Audo's chest, his face a mask of horror. 'That is for the injury to my mother.'

Turning to his faithful warriors, Gigantrex looked to Audo's remaining men and ran his finger across his throat. They were no match for the warriors.

'To our village! I go to reclaim my rightful position.'

Junius drove as fast as the horses would pull them, and taking a careful look behind, he found the view empty. Breda lay injured in the rear. Stopping, he investigated her injury. The arrow-head had snapped off when she fell, which aided its removal. The injury was clean and, though shocked, Breda was surprised at the encounter's outcome. The remaining warrior's horse stood alongside the wagon, its rider sadly dead.

'If you're okay, let's see if we can make Octodurus without any further mishap,' enquired Junius.

Breda nodded and thanked him.

*

By midday of the fourth day, Artorius stopped the wagon. The high walls of the garrison stood above the native village that clung to it, just a few miles distant. He called his son alongside.

'Marcus, I think it only fitting that you lead the way to our new home.'

'But Father, we left it an empty shell?'

'We did, but I left instructions for a few comforts to be

waiting.' Artorius smiled at his son's shock.

Marcus led the way towards the garrison, then took the well-trodden path to the clearing and halted. There was still the same sound of birdsong and running water, and a set of gates stood closed, where previously there had been none. Finding them secured from the inside, he looked to his father, who called out. A bolt slid from inside and a gate swung open to reveal a middle-aged couple who nodded to Artorius.

'This is Octavius, an old colleague of mine, and his wife Klothilde. I found him on hard times, an old injury led to his discharge. Is everything sorted, Octavius?'

'There's no longer an empty shell and I've added a hut for ourselves, as you said – thank you. We've had a few wolves appear over the last few days. I've never known them here before, only further south where the wolf queen was,' replied Octavius.

'Let me introduce you then, to the Wolf Queen, Ilona,' said Artorius, taking Ilona's hand.

Shock filled the faces of the couple as they looked first at each other, and then at Ilona. She lifted her head and howled, the forest silenced, and then repeated the sound. New howls echoed around them as a dark figure loped out from between the trees.

Artorius helped Ilona down from the wagon as Donor approached the gathering. He looked round, assessing the new faces that edged back within the palisade. Ilona reached out, and Donor offered himself for the caress he loved and nudged the new born that was offered to him. A ghost-like figure trailing cubs exited the forest confines and joined Donor as father and son stepped forward.

Octavius clutched an amulet around his throat and took a sharp intake of breath, as Rosevetha's bent form slipped from the wagon.

Artorius looked at Octavius. 'And this is her mother, Rosevetha the seer.'

Klothilde stepped forward and knelt, gripping Rosevetha's hand to her bowed head. Rosevetha lifted Klothilde's face to gaze deep into her soul and she felt it, but feared not.

'You have chosen well, Octavius. She is a warrior queen, but then you didn't know that, did you?' Rosevetha smiled at a dumbstruck Octavius.

'Revelations as always,' joked Artorius to the merriment of all.

# Chapter 28

Gigantrex settled back into control of his village with little resistance. The village elder's son had assumed leadership following Breda's departure, and though young, he had proved himself and was popular. Encouraged by his father, he challenged Gigantrex against opinion from his friends, and the result was inevitable. The village elder succumbed to Gigantrex's right to rule at the cost of his son, and was found dead the following day in suspicious circumstances, which no one dared question.

Gigantrex had to re-establish himself and win back the men's respect, and calling the council together, he laid out his plans. They were not taken well, especially the part about bringing Ilona and her wolves back, and Rosevetha was certainly not to be part of the package. Gigantrex dispatched two of his most supportive men to Argentoratum to watch Artorius' movements, and others to Octodurus to await Victus' arrival.

Gigantrex's men in Argentoratum were surprised by how easy it had been to locate Artorius. Rumours were rife that Rosevetha the seer and her daughter, the Wolf Queen, were located locally. The men, however, declined to enter the forest to locate the home out of fear of Ilona's wolves.

Mother and daughter were aware they were being watched, but only Rosevetha knew the origin and for now she kept that to herself. The family group had gelled well, especially Marcus, who was warming to both Ilona and her mother, as well as doting on his new brother. Marcus was in awe of Rosevetha and what she could see, but she never gave anything away, believing there was always a right time to know and not before.

\*

The Villa Aphrodite woke daily to the sound of the baby crying, who was cared for by a wet nurse on the ground floor. It had taken only a few days of incessant crying, being woken at all hours, and most importantly the disturbances whilst enjoying the pleasures of Naomi, that Victus snapped. She had insisted on attending to their child herself, despite the chasm that was growing between them.

Victus spent his days on the wharf-side, playing the entrepreneur, and so successful was he, that obtaining funding at no risk to himself was easy. His leisure time was spent with Sabina, and though she was not as experimental as Naomi, she drained him with other skills.

It was late one afternoon and Victus was dozing, when Sabina responded to a knock at the door. Leaving Victus, she was summoned below. Gigantrex's message had found its way to the inn. Asking the innkeeper to see to the messenger's needs, Sabina crept back up to the room to find Victus already dressing. He cupped her face in his hands and kissed her hard on the lips, and as he was about to leave, she waved a scroll in his face.

'A messenger down below is being looked after, he has brought news from Gigantrex.'

Victus snatched the scroll and hurried down the stairs and outside, where he read the message. Returning inside, he interrogated the messenger about the time he had taken to get here. Sabina stood by the bar, trying to catch what was being discussed, until Victus realised he was being observed and sent her to fetch Udo. Placing a sestertius in the messenger's hand, Victus sent him on his way to tell Gigantrex that he was coming.

Udo was eventually found discussing fire protection for a new business. The owner wasn't initially forthcoming, however, once tied to a chair with a blade tickling his testicles he saw the reasoning. Once Udo was informed that his master required him, the final negotiations were left to a lesser colleague, with a severe warning.

Victus was unusually alone when Udo found him, and chastised his man for his tardiness. He related the news from Gigantrex and explained that he required good men he could trust, who were willing to travel for a worthy bounty. Sabina listened in, and the news of an escapade in her homeland gave her courage to address Victus directly.

'I was born a Helvetti and still have family near to Argentoratum. I know their language and there are always those who are keen to let Roman blood, at a price,' offered Sabina.

Victus hadn't considered using local talent, and he knew her people's reputation, his mind slipping back to the ambush of Cassius Civilis. 'I thought you loved it here? You have everything and your own little business, but if you want to return to your heathen wasteland, I could use your talents,' he said, winking at her.

But Sabina had her sights set higher – much higher, or rather taller: Gigantrex.

Leaving Udo still arguing about Sabina's inclusion, Victus returned to the villa. There he was advised that Naomi was sleeping, as the baby had been particularly tiring that day. *The fates are working to my advantage*, thought Victus as he set about packing, an activity which was cut short by the appearance of Naomi herself.

She stood at the open door and watched Victus, oblivious to her presence, packing saddlebags. She was starting to feel neglected, as well as troubled. *Has he grown bored with me? Was the child one step too far?* she deliberated.

'Where are you going this time, and who with? That harlot Sabina, no doubt. The wharf gossip says you're rutting her. You must have a tidy sum put aside! Yes, I know about your businesses and the profits that enhance our lifestyle.' Naomi indicated to all that was around them. 'But I'd rather have you.'

'I just want you too, but I need to finish with the Civilis family once and for all. With them out of the way, and with the money I have accumulated, we could return to Rome without fear of the past. We could buy the aristocratic life we deserve and live off the Villa's income, and have more time for each other,' suggested Victus.

Naomi looked at him; maybe she had been mistaken. He had always spoken of a return to Rome and buying equestrian status, but the Civilis family had prevented this and they had to be gone.

Smiling, she took his hand and dragged him towards their special room. He smiled back expectantly. *That was easily sorted without any more awkward questions about Sabina*, he thought.

The wet nurse was given strict instructions to deal with any eventuality before Naomi shut the door. Not an item in their special room lay unused before the day's end, when they adjourned to their bedroom, sweating from their exertions. Naomi called for food and wine before crawling up the bed, where Victus lay uncovered and naked. Red welts covered both of their bodies, Naomi displaying reddened ankles and wrists from her bondage. Her eyes sparkled with lust as she looked hard and long at Victus, before the moment was shattered by the knock at the door.

The maid was called in with no attempt made to hide their nakedness from her. Naomi rose from the bed and approached her. Taking her face in hand, Naomi kissed the maid hard on the lips. She ran both hands across the maid's body, caressing her small breasts and squeezing gently at her nipples.

Victus raised himself to watch as Naomi lifted the thin shift over the maid's head, exposing her nakedness. Naomi knelt before the maid, her nipples showing her obvious arousal. Naomi's tongue ran across the maid's stomach and over the hairless mound, where she parted her legs, exposing herself to Victus' eyes burning in the back of her head. Standing, Naomi took the maid's hand and led her to the bed, where Victus waited eagerly, his penis in hand. Their room resounded to the sounds of sexual abandonment all night.

It was an exhausted Victus who slipped from the bed some hours later, leaving Naomi and her maid wrapped round each other, oblivious of his departure. The ride to the wharf-side in the last hour of night was accomplished at a gallop.

The new day was barely an hour old when eleven horses – five ridden by hooded figures, five spare and a pack horse – left Genua travelling north. Victus found riding that morning particularly arduous. Everything that was in contact with the saddle was sore and painful, but he had enjoyed every moment of the previous evening. The days were long, from daylight to dusk, and the journey had to be as short as the group could make it, swapping horses frequently and eating as they travelled.

Eight days later, Victus' group – saddle sore, tired and argumentative – rode into Octodurus and seeking a good inn, they were directed to The Bear.

Paulinus held his new son, Maximus, as Brunhilda scuttled around the kitchen. Paulinus' memory had partially returned, though he couldn't remember the ambush and the headaches continued to plague him, but less so as time passed.

Breda served in the bar or tended the baby as required.

With the inn empty, she sat outside as a group approached. She was immediately struck with foreboding at the male limping towards her; something told her that this man was to be feared by all.

Sabina threw back her hood and stepped in front of Breda, addressing her in her own tongue and requesting board and lodgings for five.

'We'll only require two rooms, these three can share,' insisted Victus sharply.

Breda hesitated. 'I'll check with the owners.'

Slipping back inside, she took Paulinus aside. 'Many times, I have heard you mention a man with a limp, who tried to kill Artorius. Something tells me it is he who is outside requesting board and lodgings; would you remember him?' she enquired.

'I think so. Let's have a look, and I hope if it is, he doesn't remember me.' Paulinus slipped out of the back door and round the side, peering at the group who had their backs to him.

Paulinus' heart froze as Victus turned to face him.

'Are you the innkeeper? Have you two rooms or a barn for these three?' he asked.

*He obviously doesn't remember me*, thought Paulinus. 'Yes, we have two rooms. Secure your horses in the barn at the rear and come into the bar. Your name, sir?'

'My name is Victus Claudian and I am expecting to meet someone here in a day or so.'

'No problem, sir.' Paulinus, struggling with a growing headache, returned to the kitchen.

'You were right, Breda. It's the devil himself and he's expecting someone. I need to send a message up the line to Artorius, if I can?'

'We need to see who comes and then I will go – you're not

fit and my shoulder's healed. They might notice if you left,' she suggested.

Gigantrex's men had seen Victus' party arrive at the Bear Inn, and even though they knew Breda's family ran it, they were unaware of Artorius' association with them. Gigantrex's men stepped into the inn and occupied a table alongside Victus, who was deep in a conversation that was excluding Sabina. She made her own enquiries about Gigantrex's village with Brunhilda, who made to comment, but Breda turned her away.

'The village is about a day away. Your dialect is local, is it not? Why do you ask after him?'

'I was born outside Argentoratum, a soldier's bastard. I was to marry a chief's son, but my friend – his sister – sold me into slavery with a soldier. I escaped when the soldier drowned. I'm hoping to pick up with Gigantrex from when we last met.'

'Gigantrex is expecting you at his village,' whispered the senior of the two warriors to Victus.

'I'm sure he is, but why didn't he come himself?' enquired Victus.

'He's not welcome here, it's a long story. We'll meet you at first light tomorrow,' replied the older of the two, seeing Breda looking at him. With that and without a reply from Victus, Gigantrex's men left.

Breda watched the men leave, and being overly attentive in serving Victus' party, she eavesdropped by engaging Sabina in small talk, much to the annoyance of Victus. She had foreseen the confrontation between Artorius and her son, but she hadn't seen Victus in the equation. Back behind the bar, Breda volunteered again to warn Artorius and his family, and Paulinus agreed unwillingly, his health forestalling his involvement.

Leaving Udo and his men to enjoy the local brew, Victus

took a flask of wine and ordered Sabina upstairs. Her reluctance was well hidden, except from Breda. The room contained a reasonable-sized cot, a small table with an oil lamp, and clean bedding.

Victus didn't know what it was to appreciate a woman. Like most men, it was pain for her and pleasure for him. Draining him as quickly as she could, Sabina faked orgasms till he fell asleep. She recovered her discarded clothing and crept from the room, leaving Victus snoring. She heard a rider leave in haste and startled Brunhilda as she went inside the inn.

Waking in the last hour of night and provisioned, Breda had been seen off by Brunhilda, taking the north road for speed.

'Who was that leaving so early?' Sabina enquired.

'Just my mother heading back to her village. She helps us now and again, my husband hasn't been well,' responded Brunhilda.

*What can this woman see in my brother? She's not like the rest*, wondered Brunhilda as she returned to the kitchen.

Brunhilda served watered wine to Sabina, and then Victus appeared, full of arrogance and self-importance, demanding food and drink. With the group fed and watered, they were preparing their horses when Gigantrex's man re-appeared and they all left immediately.

*

Gigantrex sat in the great hall, forewarned of Victus' arrival; the messenger had been dispatched immediately to Argentoratum to obtain current intelligence. Victus was allocated Ilona's hut, whereas Udo and his men were expected to live as the village warriors did, on the great hall floor, which was not to their liking. Sabina ingratiated herself into Gigantrex's household and village, and Gigantrex couldn't help but notice her popularity while they waited for news. Victus spent his time with his men, hunting in the fruitful forest around them. The nights were spent in drunken revelry, allowing Sabina to get closer to Gigantrex, who drank sparingly. Victus had long since abandoned Sabina in preference of female captives.

Eight days' hard riding brought the knowledge Victus and Gigantrex craved, and it was better than expected. Enticements were offered to Gigantrex's warriors to join them, with the only stumbling block being talk of military repercussions for killing a Camp Prefect. *Artorius' death must be seen to be the result of a renegade band operating*, thought Gigantrex. The plan was to move north with a war party, living off attacking local and Roman farms around Argentoratum.

Victus wasn't happy with the obvious delay, but he had waited this long – what was a little more time?

*

Leaving the main road, Breda was drawn into the forest around Argentoratum by the presence of Rosevetha and Ilona. The smell of smoke tickled her nostrils as her horse stepped out into the cleared ground around the palisaded home. There was no sign of any wolves until the gate was opened by Marcus at Rosevetha's bidding.

Marcus' face beamed when he saw the visitor. Donor strolled beside him, a beautiful and surreal sight. Breda slipped from her horse to be taken into Marcus' strong embrace, her horse becoming skittish at Donor's proximity until Breda calmed it. Holding Marcus at arm's length, she saw that he seemed taller, thinner, bronzed and toned. He was a son any mother would be proud of.

Ilona was enjoying the afternoon sun, overseeing her

baby and surrounded by wolf cubs.

Rosevetha appeared at the door. 'Welcome, how is Paulinus? What news do you bring?'

'Paulinus is recovering, but the news I bring is not good. Victus Claudian was heading for my husband's village when I left,' replied Breda.

'Victus Claudian? Where?' demanded Marcus, overhearing the name.

'Gigantrex summoned him. He still wishes to seize Ilona after the deaths of you and your father. Haven't you warned them, Rosevetha?'

'All is not clear to me and we both know what that means,' replied Rosevetha. Marcus looked between the two for an explanation, which wasn't forthcoming. 'We need to consolidate our gifts.'

Scooping up her son, Ilona appeared to glide across the ground that separated her from the gathering group. Octavius and Klothilde were introduced to Breda – neither had ever seen such a gathering, and the combined power of the three women was felt by all.

Marcus took Breda's horse to the barn, Donor trotting alongside like a pet dog.

'You were right about Marcus and your son being accepted by the wolves, Ilona. It's unbelievable how domesticated they seem,' observed Breda.

'The pack are happy to be back near their old hunting ground, and as for Donor and his partner, they spend every day here. I've never known them enjoy human company so much. So, you bring us news of Gigantrex's coming. It is time to prepare, my wolves will be our eyes. Come, you must be thirsty. Artorius will return later and I know he will be happy to see you,' replied Ilona.

'He won't be happy with the news. We must prepare for Victus' final confrontation,' responded Marcus, returning to the three women.

'Nothing is ever sure,' interjected Ilona, and both her mother and Breda nodded agreement.

*

The last hour of day sounded as Artorius walked his horse through the barrack gates to crisp salutes from the late guards. Returning the salute, he bid the guards a good night and mounted. It didn't take him long to breach the dark of the forest in front of his new home, but unusually, the gates were barred.

With trepidation, Artorius reined back his horse and looked around the forest edge, but nothing moved. Moving into the shadow of the gate, he called out to Marcus, who slid the bar across and slipped out through the narrow opening. His son stood with his double swords drawn and Breda followed to kneel in front of the gate, an arrow notched to her bow. Two sets of eyes scanned their surroundings as Artorius guided his horse through the gate and was greeted by Octavius. Breda and Marcus followed, backing their way inside.

'What's happened? I take it Paulinus has recovered, Breda?'

'He is better, but I bring bad tidings, hence the precautions,' she replied.

'We have urgent plans to discuss, Father, over a full stomach.'

Artorius dismounted, leading his horse to the barn.

Everyone gathered for the shared meal and the discussion soon turned to one subject: Victus. Artorius and Marcus recommended that they withdraw into the barracks – it would be cramped, but they would be safe. It was thought unlikely that anyone would dare to try to kill the family within those imposing walls.

Past arguments surrounding his family's move to and

from their estate to avoid Victus filled Marcus' thoughts, but Victus had still inflicted heavy losses on family and friends regardless. His eyes misted as Tia filled his mind, and everything around him ceased to exist once again.

*Rosevetha has the message*, resonated in his head.

As if prompted, Rosevetha, who had sat deep in her own world until now, took Ilona and Breda's hands in hers. 'We cannot escape this devil. We must face him here, where Ilona's pets are, here in the forest.'

Artorius tried to argue against the suggestion. 'I'll not have Ilona and my sons put at risk out here. How long do we have to prepare, do any of you know?'

'Wherever you and Marcus are, so will our son and I be,' said Ilona.

'We will know as they get closer,' Breda responded. 'I wish to stay if you allow it. I offer my skill as an archer to the conflict.'

'I too am an accomplished archer, though a little rusty,' added Klothilde, to a surprised Octavius.

'So we have four archers, Marcus with his double swords, and Octavius and myself with spear and sword. Hardly a great number,' calculated Artorius.

'But you have forgotten Ilona's pets, and we will know when they are coming. Beware of a raiding party, don't be drawn out to them,' added Rosevetha.

*

Victus' group swept north, living off the land and stealing where necessary to survive. Gigantrex was continuously on the lookout for a base to strike from, close to Argetoratum. Finding a semi-derelict farm south of the last mutatione before Argentoratum, the group set about repairing it.

They took it in turns to ride daily, to forage and

occasionally raid other homesteads. Victus left Gigantrex to organise the raids; the aim was to become a nuisance. Victus knew this would lead to local demands for action from the Roman authorities. Sabina's time was employed to fraternise with the locals, gathering intelligence relating to Ilona's location. She was happy to be away from Victus' clutches.

Being back amongst her own, Sabina became a part of the scenery without anyone really noticing her. The talk of the canabae outside Argentoratum's fortress was of the sudden appearance of a large wolf pack, but strangely, no one seemed to fear it – in fact, they felt protected. They were aware that the 'Wolf Queen' had returned. So famous was Ilona becoming, that some talked of her as a deity, but there were none who claimed to have seen her. None knew where she was living, apart from somewhere in the forest south of the fort, and all knew of her Roman lover, the Camp Prefect. (Names meant little to the locals, just titles.) Sabina was in awe that such a woman could exist and she immediately understood why Gigantrex wanted her as his queen – but that was a position she intended to fill, if only she could persuade him to think of her in that role. She needed something to turn his mind away from the Wolf Queen, but she dared not challenge her.

# Chapter 29

Romans and locals alike appeared at the fortress gates, demanding the Legion's actions against a renegade band who were raiding local farms and ambushing travellers. Artorius had approached the Legate Aquila, who was disinterested in small raiding parties that didn't impinge on the military machine. On his own initiative, Artorius dispatched daily scouting parties with explicit instructions not to engage unless attacked, and they weren't, often arriving just after the attackers had left.

At first there was nothing to suppose that the raiding party was anything but that, until they attacked an ex-legionary's farm while he was away. He returned to find that his headman and two slaves had been killed when they tried to stop the raid, and two young female slaves had been abducted. His wife, who had hidden, described a giant of a man who appeared as the raiders killed the headman. He had berated the raiders for the murders and struck one of them, causing an argument within the group. Artorius was approached directly and a description was related. *It can only be Gigantrex... Time for action*, thought Artorius, though there was no mention of a limping man.

Artorius marched straight to the Legate's office, only to be informed that he was dealing with a private money matter. Artorius was about to return to his own office when Aquila stomped out of the room, head down.

'I need to have an urgent conversation with you about the raiding party, Sir.'

'They are just scrounging, don't waste my time,' replied Aquila angrily.

'They have killed a freeman and two slaves, and abducted two females belonging to an ex-soldier from the Legion. Intelligence suggests that one of the raiding party is Victus Claudian, wanted for murder and treason.'

'What intelligence?' demanded Aquila.

'Victus Claudian was identified at Octodurus recently and he is in the company of a local man known to me as Gigantrex. A man fitting the description of Gigantrex was seen at the raid on the ex-soldier's farm today.'

'How do you mean, "he is known to you"? What dealings have you had with him? Come into my office and we'll finish the discussion there, seeing as we seem to be gathering an audience,' snapped Aquila.

Artorius turned to find the head clerk and two soldiers behind them, trying to look inconspicuous. 'Get back to your work or I'll find you other employment,' he growled. The group dispersed rapidly as Artorius followed the Legate into his office, and with a final look, shut the door.

Artorius related how Gigantrex and his father had joined his friends to search for him after he was reported lost, presumed dead.

'When my friends found me, I had been saved by my now-partner, Ilona. Because of my family in Rome, Gigantrex offered Ilona and her mother a place in his village. However, things didn't work out and Ilona left with me when I returned, as you know. Victus Claudian stayed at my friend's inn recently and made it known that he was meeting Gigantrex, for whatever reason that may be. Gigantrex's mother, who has disowned him, brought the news to us a few days ago.'

'You lead a complicated life, Camp Prefect, and I'm sure I'm not privy to the full story. If Claudian is amongst this group then we have a duty to secure his arrest immediately. Do we know where they are hiding?' replied Aquila.

'The whole story is too long and complicated. We are not certain where they are, but we believe it to be local, Sir.'

'Use what you need to secure Claudian's apprehension – and this Gigantrex, dead or alive,' ordered Aquila.

Artorius saluted, and leaving the Legate's office, he called for the junior clerk and sent him to find Marcus, who was in the barracks going through the paces with the new conscripts.

Marcus was easily found on the practise ground, stripped to the waist and sweating with a wooden sword and shield at his side. He sat against a practise pole, sharing water with the youths who had been Rufus' friends, Rufus and his mother having since returned to Rome on the insistence of Aquila's parents-in-law. Marcus' expertise with sword and shield was both easily taught and accepted by his audience. The group had gelled well and Artorius was content that his son had befriended his previous attackers.

Receiving a message from his father during the day was unusual for Marcus. Collecting his shirt, he set off at a run for his father's office, where Artorius related the latest news and the need to set their plans in motion for an immediate attack from Gigantrex and Victus.

'Everyone is talking about this renegade band; have you thought how we can increase our numbers against them?' enquired Marcus.

'If the news got out then we wouldn't be able to accommodate all the volunteers. We need a select few, a turma of cavalry would be the best. It's all going to be about timing,' added Artorius.

'Rufus' ex-friends are more than proficient with a bow, and some are good with swords. A single tent would be enough and we could practise in the clearing by day,' suggested Marcus.

'Archers would certainly be an asset. I'll speak to the Legate and suggest their training off camp. Maybe Octavius could help with their scutum skills.'

*

The last hour of day had passed, and the darkness of the forest surrounded father and son as they slipped off the metalled road on to their home track. The smell of wood smoke filled their nostrils, with Marcus, as ever, looking for signs of Donor and his pack. Gripping his horse between his legs, Marcus cupped his hands together and gave a howl that received an instant response from beside them.

Donor strolled towards them, the yellow of his eyes looking from Artorius to Marcus before he made for Marcus, who slipped from his horse and handed the reins to his father. The beast nuzzled into Marcus' hands like a domesticated dog before Donor stood on his rear legs against Marcus' shoulders, their faces meeting in an unbelievable stare. Another howl from a short distance away caused Donor to look away momentarily.

'Your mistress calls. Go,' said Marcus, pointing in the direction of their home as Donor dropped back to the ground, turned and was lost in the blink of an eye.

'I can't believe your link with Donor. Long may it last,' said Artorius in awe.

Mounting again, the two proceeded to the edge of the clearing where torches brightly lit the palisade corners, another held by Ilona who stood alone by the open gate to welcome her men. Artorius vaulted from his horse, scooping Ilona into his arms as Marcus walked the horses past them. Marcus had grown to love Ilona and he knew the love between her and his father was strong, but deep inside he still had only one mother, Amoria.

Breda and Rosevetha were deep in conversation in front

of a bubbling cauldron over a crackling fire, when father, son and Ilona breached the threshold.

'Victus' men are nearby and they have a female looking for us. She has an ulterior motive for being here – she wishes to return to these, her own lands, as the queen she should have been. I must find her and see if we can turn Gigantrex. We may yet save the day and take Victus,' Breda offered.

'How many are we talking of, can you see?' enquired Artorius as he unclipped his spatha, placing it by his bedroom door.

'Victus is buying local warriors with silver,' whispered Rosevetha, trancelike.

'He will dispose of Gigantrex and his warriors, whatever happens. He doesn't believe in having live witnesses,' remarked Artorius.

'Then that is the way to Gigantrex. I must find this Sabina tomorrow before it is too late,' responded Breda.

'I dare to ask of the outcome, or when,' said Artorius.

'You know better than to ask such a question after what you have seen and heard. When? When the wind blows on a moonless night,' responded Rosevetha, chuckling.

'You make fun of me?' he replied.

Rosevetha took Artorius', Marcus' and Ilona's hands, placing them one on top of the other, and wrapped them in bark. Sitting as straight as she could and closing her eyes, Rosevetha raised her head to the roof and began chanting in a forgotten language.

'How do you know the old language?' enquired Artorius.

'I know many things,' replied Rosevetha without opening her eyes.

'You forget that my father was one of you, not a true Roman,' responded Ilona.

'Like the tree from which this bark was taken and now encapsulates your hands, you will live long, though the future is filled with blood.' Rosevetha collapsed into a heap on the floor.

Ilona cradled her mother as she repeated only one word, a name: 'Cloelius'. Rosevetha slipped into a deep sleep as father and son lifted her gently and laid her on her cot. Tears streamed from Ilona's eyes, and Breda and Klothilde tried to comfort her till Artorius took her in his arms.

'That was your father, wasn't it? What has she seen?' begged Artorius.

Ilona nodded.

'I cannot see what Rosevetha has seen,' remarked Breda. 'She is the most powerful seer I have ever known and she is using that power to block Ilona and me. We only see what she wants us to see.'

The family ate without thinking, each with their own thoughts of what might lay ahead. Ilona asked to care for her mother through the night, but Breda brushed this aside, offering herself while Ilona looked to her son.

Artorius tried desperately to comfort Ilona, but she was inconsolable. She sensed without saying it that her mother's days were almost spent, but why now? She eventually settled on to Artorius' chest as he stroked her hair, and she succumbed to sleep. Their son slept, oblivious to the night's revelations.

*

Marcus opened the single gate the following morning in company of his father and Breda, to be met by Donor like a ghost emerging from the swirling ground mist. Marcus' hands ran through the beast's thick damp fur and he whispered into Donor's ears: *Protect the household.* Donor looked towards the palisade and seemed to smile

301

as the three mounted and headed for the canabae.

Slipping into the canabae like three spirits, the river mist swept before them, curling around every corner. Leaving Breda in the market place, which was already a hive of activity, the two men proceeded to the barracks entrance. Fists thudded against breastplates in salute of the Camp Prefect and his son, not only out of respect for his rank, but especially the man that bore the rank. Pride beamed from Marcus' face: he had never heard a bad word said or whispered about his father.

Rank and file were already spilling out of their barracks as the buccina sounded the first hour of day. The sounds of morning were all around them: jingling metal of lorica, nailed caligae crunching on the hard parade ground, cough-ejected phlegm, the moans and groans of latecomers, beaten and berated at the tops of their voices by their officers.

Artorius slid from his horse, passing the reins to Marcus as the melee settled into conformity, a light breeze catching the Century flags behind their sacred Eagle at the centre of the gathered. Centurions dressed the frontage of their Centuries, calling out their attending numbers. A trumpet sounded as a lone horse entered the parade ground.

'Legio II Augusta, attention! Legate on parade,' commanded Artorius.

The ground shuddered with thousands of stamping feet, and the sound of scutum and pila forced firmly into the ground. Artorius marched briskly up to the advancing Legate, his salute proud and confident, unequally returned. *The hierarchy never learn to salute with a soldier's pride*, thought Artorius.

'Legio II Augusta, present and correct for your inspection, Sir,' recited Artorius.

The Legate nodded as he walked his horse along the expectant columns, picking out minor misdemeanours and leaving their Centurions to deal with them, or addressing individuals for whatever reason he felt the need. With the first Cohort – the elite – reviewed, the Legate returned to the frontage and played out his daily message of duty and honour in the best Legion in Germania before dismissing them to their duties. *Just another day*, thought Artorius.

As the Legion was marched away to their various allocated duties, Legate Aquila disappeared to his office, followed by Artorius.

Marcus stabled the horses and sought the training ground, and his recruit friends.

# Chapter 30

Breda shuffled her way around the market, not really seeing any of what was offered as she sought out Sabina. The hours slipped away as the mist cleared and the warmth of the day required the shade of a tree for Breda, wondering if Sabina would appear at all.

It was the third hour of day, with Breda sat deep in thought, when she recognised Sabina from the inn: dark hair cascaded down her back to her waist. She looked in her early thirties, was strikingly handsome, and Breda guessed from her look that her life hadn't been easy.

'You were at the inn in Octodurus, weren't you? It was you I heard leaving early,' suggested Sabina.

Breda nodded.

'I seek a local seer, and her daughter, the Wolf Queen. I wish to know my fortune,' responded Sabina.

'I can tell your fortune for you as well as any. You have set your eyes on a giant of a man who craves another for her gifts. It is for you to offer your life to win him. He supports a man of evil who will kill him when he has achieved what he wants.' Breda watched Sabina's reactions. Her dark eyes gave little away, but Breda felt her pain. 'Who are you that was sold into sexual slavery long ago out of jealousy, when you were destined for a high place?'

'I was Sunnhild of the Marsi, once destined to marry a chief's son, but his sister had other ideas. I am known only as Sabina now. What else can you see? Are you Rosevetha?'

Breda laughed. 'You haven't had the lady described to you, have you? Or you would know I am not. Will I not do?' Breda offered an open palm for payment.

'You are good, I'll give you that, but I have been told to

ask for Rosevetha and her daughter,' replied Sabina.

'Your master wishes her harm and all those around her: man, woman and child.'

'So you do know her, and you are toying with me?' snapped Sabina.

'I know what you seek and for whom, but I have an offer for you to consider from the mother of Gigantrex. He is a fool to crave Ilona and her wolves. He will never have either, though in you he might have a future. Does he know your past? I think not.'

Sabina stepped back in shock, stumbling over a tree root. Breda reached out and steadied her and in that moment, Breda saw her son kneeling over a wounded Sabina.

'Rosevetha, Ilona and I saw you coming. I can take you if you wish, but I must blindfold you,' offered Breda.

'I hate Victus, but he was the only way I could reach Gigantrex. I hoped that he would see me for who I was and can be again. I wish no harm to anyone, and if Ilona doesn't want Gigantrex then there is hope for me.'

'Walk with me, Sabina.'

Breda led the way from the market watched by the stallholders, some of whom were clutching at amulets around their throats, thankful they hadn't given any secrets away. Reaching the edge of the canabae and with the metalled road heading south, Breda turned Sabina around, and taking a scarf from her neck, she bound it over the young woman's eyes. Sabina hesitated, but with Breda taking her hand, she allowed herself to be led.

Walking around the edge of the village, Breda walked through the forest to the stream and followed it to Artorius' home. Ilona stepped beyond the palisade with babe in arms and Donor running beside her as she sensed Breda's closeness. Passing her babe to Breda, Ilona faced Sabina and removed the scarf.

The two women stood face to face. Ilona offered her hand, and the moment of touch was electrifying. Sabina saw herself wounded, being cradled by Gigantrex, and shuddered.

'I see why Gigantrex desires you, your beauty, your gift and the creature beside you. What have you just shown me?'

'I have told you that you will have to offer your life for his, for him to truly see you. Only fate will decide if this will mean life or death,' responded Breda.

The three women walked towards the open gate through cultivated ground and into the compound to await the return of Artorius and Marcus. Sabina looked around the palisade interior – three buildings, simple and secure. She liked what she saw, imagining a large hall and having Gigantrex as her man.

Rosevetha stood at the house door, bent and dishevelled. 'You brought her. Maybe with our combined efforts she will see the sense of what we propose. Welcome, Sunnhild of the Marsi.'

\*

Victus and his men were tiring of inactivity. Sabina was always moping around Gigantrex and was feeling useless: not an inkling of information had she scratched from the locals. Gigantrex, on the other hand, was enjoying his position with his own men whilst increasing their numbers from the local disaffected and keeping all fed and watered by their raids. Arguments increased between Gigantrex's and Victus' men.

Gigantrex had returned in the last hours of day, full of himself for having relieved a couple of well-to-do Roman businessmen of their wealth and goods, but Sabina hadn't returned. Victus wasn't overly worried and was considering her as a liability, and anyway, he had other female dalliances. Gigantrex and Victus began to argue about her mission.

'I didn't realise you were looking for Rosevetha and Ilona,' interjected a newly recruited local youth. 'I know where to find them.'

Victus spun round, grabbing the youth by his collar. 'Where are they?' he demanded.

'The Camp Prefect's son has had a home built on the edge of the forest, south of the canabae near the stream. The forest has been cleared around it to build a wooden palisade. It will be hard to approach unseen and, of course, there are the wolves. We hear them, but you don't see them.'

'How many do we number now, twenty? Enough to handle any problems from the wolves, but I must see the compound at first light tomorrow,' ordered Victus.

'What about Sabina?' enquired Gigantrex.

'She is expendable, and what does she matter to you anyway? I thought you'd set your sights on the Wolf Queen?'

'I have, but Sabina is a kindred spirit who wishes to return to her people and I would offer her my village if she wished it,' snapped Gigantrex. *Is this how he deals with those who help him*, he pondered.

\*

Artorius built a back-up plan with the cavalry, requiring a turma on duty overnight, every night, whilst continuing with daily scouting parties for the renegades.

Father and son left the garrison in the last hour of day, taking their time to pass through the canabae and on to the track that took them home. Marcus felt the four-legged company long before Artorius did; he was deep in thought. The forest darkness sucked them into itself before expelling them out into the clearing around their home. Ilona met Artorius, explaining they had a visitor who might be able to tilt the balance of the expected attack. Entering his home, Artorius was met with a house full, awaiting his return. Hot meaty broth bubbled in the cauldron over the fire and the table was set.

It was a night of hard talking. Sabina was open minded, welcoming any suggestions to win over Gigantrex, but they would need something powerful to turn his head. The recurring theme was Victus, who didn't like witnesses. Unfortunately, Gigantrex was blinded by his own ambition. Would he believe a prophecy involving Sabina in his future?

\*

It was the last hour of night when Victus, Gigantrex and the local youth came within sight of the canabae of Argentoratum and turned into the forest.

'The track to Ilona's home is about a half mile further on, but if we follow the stream we won't be seen,' related the youth.

Victus knew they wouldn't go unseen: Ilona's wolves were around them somewhere. The forest was densely wooded with barely enough room to slip between the trees on occasions, and the sound of running water soon filled their ears. The stream when they got to it wasn't wide, but it was fast flowing. Victus asked if it could be approached from the other side, but the youth didn't know. Walking stealthily, wood smoke soon invaded their senses followed by the smell of food cooking. The youth pointed to the mass of trees in front and crouched down, looking around him. Gigantrex followed suit, whereas Victus remained upright.

'The Wolf Queen's home is there,' the youth pointing to a shaft of bright light piercing the trees.

Using the leafy cover, the three moved forward towards

the light. As they closed on the cleared space, the palisade stood proud in the landscape, nearly twice the height of a man. Nothing could be seen of the palisade interior, and only a single wide gate allowed entrance from the track.

Victus circumvented the cleared space under tree cover; the site was flat in all directions except one, a rock outcrop. Struggling with his leg injury, he had to be assisted to reach the top, and even here the trees and some of the rocks had been cleared. However, from there he could see into the palisade, where there was little movement.

A gravel bank high enough for a man to stand on slotted up against the palisade interior. The space contained three wooden buildings, the large one he presumed to be the home, a smaller hut and a barn. Movement caught Gigantrex's eye and he motioned to Victus as Sabina appeared from the largest building. She was accompanied by three women: Ilona and Rosevetha were known to Victus, but not the third, and there were two males – the youth had to be Marcus Civilis.

'What is Sabina doing in there? I told her to find the location, not visit it. Who are the other man and woman?' snapped Victus.

Gigantrex hesitated. He didn't want Victus to know his mother was there, so he shrugged his shoulders. 'It could be part of her plan to gain their confidence, she is clever enough.'

Gigantrex didn't believe what he said even as he said it. Three powerful women – surely, they will have seen through any façade Sabina had created?

'We can't take this place by night,' muttered Victus. 'It'll be risky, but it will have to be early morning, as they wake. I require four of your best archers, Gigantrex, to position themselves up here where they can fire into the stockade. My men will remain on the forest edge and stop anyone trying to break out. With fire arrows aimed at the roofs we will draw them out so they can be picked off. Meanwhile the mercenaries can dig out the gate posts. We'll need shields.'

'I will advise my men against killing the women,' injected Gigantrex.

'If they are killed, so be it,' responded Victus sharply.

'I want Ilona and the child out of there alive, that was our deal!'

Victus looked up at him. 'Whatever happens, happens, as long as all the Civilis' are dead.'

*He didn't question that, the fool, because I mean the child as well*, thought Victus as he turned away from the outcrop and headed for the horses.

\*

Marcus opened the gate, allowing Sabina to leave alone, and as he did so the sun reflected off a glint of metal on the outcrop above them. 'There's someone up there. Fetch Father, Octavius?' he said, scanning the outcrop for any movement.

'We know, we felt them earlier. Don't make the parting seem too familiar, Sabina,' insisted Breda. 'Tell Gigantrex what we told you: that there is no way to stop them coming. Our futures depend on the capture of Victus.'

Sabina slipped through the narrow slit in the gate and followed the track back to the canabae. As she walked, the prophecies filled her head and she prayed to Turan. *I will have to offer my life to save Gigantrex, but Breda told me it was the only way. It is my destiny, and without Gigantrex I have no future.* All around her the forest appeared to move, dark figures slipping between trees heading towards the palisade.

\*

Artorius joined the group, Marcus pointing out where he had seen the reflection. 'It is unlikely they will try to attack at night, with the forest and the wolves on our side. Early morning would be my guess, and on a moonless night. We must build up our stocks of arrows and sharpen our swords if this will be our final confrontation. Why didn't Rosevetha warn us, Ilona?'

'We cannot answer that question yet. Even my pets can observe without being observed. Open the gate, Marcus,' replied Ilona, smiling.

First Donor and then his partner, followed by their cubs, reached the gate. Looking outside, Marcus called his father. There before them the killing ground was covered by furry movement, black, grey and pepper coloured: the pack was expanding. Ilona sidled up beside Artorius and slipped her arm through his, smiling.

'An impressive army – one I wouldn't want to face again after my experience in the snow. I must counsel Aquila about the recruits and arrange for some cavalry shields,' added Artorius as Donor and his partner sought Ilona's caress and the cubs ran to Marcus.

As Artorius headed through the canabae he saw Sabina, deep in thought, heading south to rendezvous with Gigantrex. She knew she had been seen and an excuse had been devised.

Once back in the barracks, Artorius sought immediate permission from Legate Aquila to train the new recruits at his home with suitable sleeping accommodation and spare weaponry. By midday all had been agreed and with a wagon loaded, Artorius marched his new recruits through the canabae and into the forest. Being aware of the wolves Marcus had repeatedly told them of, the recruits were sceptical of their safety.

*

Sabina was reflective when she was met by Gigantrex on his own, hailing her from a stand of trees at the side of the road.

'I wondered where you were and if you were okay, though Victus didn't seem bothered. Where have you been?'

'I was looking for Ilona and Rosevetha when a woman, Breda, approached me. I said I was looking for my fortune to be told and Breda took me to their home in the forest. I had a good look round while I was there,' responded Sabina.

'Who told you your fortune?'

'All three of them, and when Ilona touched me I was given a view of the future they spoke of and it involves you. They named you. Breda said you have lost your way, but you could find it again in a new and stronger love built on sacrifice. I understand why you want Ilona, she is beautiful and her child is an angel, but she is happy with her man. Her control of the wolves is amazing and they have taken to the soldier's son. We are friends, aren't we, Gigantrex? Can I be honest with you?'

'Why do you ask?' queried Gigantrex.

'I came from this area and my real name is Sunnhild of the Marsi.' Sabina then related her story, tears trickling down her face as the memories of her past flooded her brain.

Gigantrex stood still, not knowing what to do, then drew her to him, consoling her. Sabina was confused. Did he have feelings for her or was it just a friendship between two?

'Ilona told me that the two of you would never be, that fate has placed you with another. They guessed that I have feelings for you which I have never spoken of. Forgive my honesty, but if you must still try for her then I will help you,' related Sabina.

'I love you too, but as a sister and friend. I intended to offer you a place in my village when this situation is sorted. I will have Ilona as my bride, and her pack of wolves; she will see sense.'

'Ilona will forever hate you for what we are about to do, because the fates are against you. They said to beware of Victus' treachery,' she pleaded.

'I don't fear Victus and his men. I took my village back, what can they do? Did they tell you what the outcome would be?'

Sabina shook her head.

'Come,' said Gigantrex. 'We must get back so that you can tell Victus what you know.'

*

Marcus welcomed his returning father, trailing the recruits who in turn followed a loaded wagon. Donor strolled alongside him. The recruits, seeing the wolf, stopped dead in their tracks as Marcus ran his hand through its fur and Donor gave them all the eye.

The next few hours were spent unloading the wagon while everyone got to know each other. Marcus was surprised at the large number of buckets until his father answered the question by pointing to the straw roofs. Under Artorius' instruction, the new recruits were made aware of the plans and the ulterior motive of their being present. All appeared happy at the move, even when being supervised by Octavius.

'What are these, Father?' asked Marcus, picking up a spiked metal object from the bottom of the wagon.

'They are calthrops, anti-personnel weapons. Grab as many as you can and follow me. Are you joining us,

Octavius?' Artorius indicated to the recruits to follow suit.

The group walked through the gate and along the outside of the palisade. Artorius and Octavius instructed the youths in laying the weapons in a pattern, returning to the wagon to get the rest until it was empty.

'Anyone approaching the palisade under cover of dark will almost certainly find one with their feet – or worse if they are crawling.' Artorius congratulated himself on the forethought. 'Don't forget that they are out there if we have to engage their attack in the open. Ilona, you must show these to Donor,' he added, pointing to the calthrops as Ilona strolled over.

Donor was already sniffing around this painful weapon, carefully following the line around the palisade.

'The pack will know of them, you can be sure of that,' stated Ilona, as Donor re-joined her. 'A nasty surprise for the unsuspecting.'

'Added security. I don't know what Victus' plans will be, but I would have men against the wall to prevent any escape, which means having them in situ in the dark hours. The biggest threat will be us being overlooked from the rock outcrop. Archers up there would have to be good to pick off targets, but fire arrows at the roof would be an easy shot. We need to cut the trees back further. Octavius, take the lads up there and sort that, please.'

'Certainly, Sir,' replied Octavius jokingly, punching his fist into his chest in salute, an action resulting in a coughing fit.

'Fetch the axes and some water, it'll be a warm task. Move,' ordered Octavius after he had caught his breath.

The youths, including Marcus, marched back into the compound, returning with axes and water bags. Octavius set off at a fast pace and the group were soon scrambling up the outcrop. It was not long after that, that the sound of chopping trees could be heard. Breda appeared from the house in response to the noise, the crying child in her arms, to find Artorius and Ilona looking towards the outcrop.

'Added precautions,' responded Artorius as Ilona reached out to comfort their son. She stroked the child's head as the bright, tiny eyes searched everyone's faces.

'Our son is destined to see like Breda and I,' stated Ilona, noting Artorius' look. 'He will lead Marcus to a destiny that Rosevetha forecast long ago.'

'There is no moon in three days,' related Breda.

Artorius nodded. 'How many will they bring?'

'We collectively see many,' interjected Ilona.

'Have you all done enough to turn Gigantrex?' enquired Artorius.

'Rosevetha will reach to him on a plane that Ilona and I can only dream of,' replied Breda.

*

The compound was bathed in crimson light as Octavius returned, his sweating youths bragging about who had chopped the most. The mood was light hearted, but Octavius knew that the coming days would define how the recruits would survive the future. *I have no doubts about Marcus and I envy him his youth, but then I would never have been a match for him*, thought Octavius.

The same crimson sky bathed Victus, Gigantrex and their men as they sat around the crackling fire with a boar roasting over it. Sabina described the interior of Artorius' homestead as she had been instructed to do. Their appetites sated, Victus drew Udo and his men away. Gigantrex's men enjoyed the fruits of their spoils, drinking deep of the stolen wine.

Gigantrex himself sat alone, deep in thought, and for the

first time Sabina was unsure of her own existence. Should she believe the prophecy, or should she disappear into the darkness? She knew she could survive, but surviving wasn't enough. Gigantrex wrapped himself in his blanket by the fire and settled into a troubled sleep, with dreams that were invaded by his mother. Sabina waited till his snoring started and then lay down beside him.

Meanwhile, Victus, Udo and his men held their own counsel in whispers. 'I want no survivors, either on the homestead or with Gigantrex's men. When Artorius comes out to fight, as he surely will, you will all remain at the back and on my signal, no witnesses. We go in three days, and there's a gold aureus to each one that survives after the job is done,' said Victus. All nodded assent.

# Chapter 31

For two days Victus and Gigantrex prepared their men, running over the plan again and again. The only sorties into the countryside were to provide food and drink, and Victus' mood grew darker as the day of reckoning advanced towards them. Sabina struggled from day to day, reminding Gigantrex of what she had been told, but eventually he could take no more of it.

As the sun drifted towards the horizon in a bloody sky, and with alcohol drunk and their stomachs full, the group set out for Argentoratum across country.

'Sabina, go back to Octodorus and follow this map to my village. Tell them I sent you and that I will return shortly,' insisted Gigantrex out of earshot of Victus.

'But I need to fight alongside you, I said I would support you,' she pleaded.

'No, I would never forgive myself if I lost you as a friend, and where we go, you are at risk. Do as I ask.'

With that, Gigantrex took Sabina's hand and offering his map, turned and raced off to join the others. He informed Victus that he had sent Sabina back as she was no longer needed, and Victus shrugged it off, mentally noting to find her afterwards and kill her.

Tears filled Sabina's eyes. *But you don't know I have a destiny to meet*, she thought. Slipping the map into her saddlebag, she headed for the north road. The red sunset turned the metalled road into a pathway of blood, a look Sabina worried over as she raced her horse. Finding the track to the homestead, Sabina eased back as her horse reared, and a wolf howled nearby. The response echoed around the forest. With her skittish horse, she proceeded nervously until she breached the forest, stepping out into the killing ground. The palisade was well lit and she could see movement around the interior of the walls.

'You are very brave, Sunnhild of the Marsi, to have returned to face your destiny. May it end as you wish,' said a stern female voice.

The voice appeared as if beside her, but she saw no one and, shaking her head, presumed she had been hailed. At the fireside within Artorius' home Rosevetha sat trancelike, her eyes closed. 'Sabina who once was Sunnhild returns.'

Breda exited the home, calling Marcus down to the gate. 'Sabina returns. Open the gate and I'll beckon her in.' With the gate open, Breda called out: 'Come, Sunnhild, you are expected.'

Sabina walked her horse down to the palisade, and Breda took her in her arms as she dismounted.

'Gigantrex wouldn't listen. He sent me to his village, but if I go I am lost forever. I have come to face my destiny, whatever it offers,' stated Sabina, crying on to Breda's shoulder.

Marcus stepped momentarily outside the gate, surveying the killing ground and to be met by Donor on his own. Kneeling, he ruffled the creature's fur and took Donor's head between his hands. He stared into the yellowed eyes that appeared to smile back at him.

A howl rent the air behind Marcus, and Donor responded as Ilona glided towards them. Light shone around her; she looked like a spirit. Marcus blinked to confirm the reality of what he saw.

'Tomorrow will decide who stays and who walks with Lainth, but your lady will see you safe,' said Ilona.

Marcus felt a coldness down his side and a hand on his shoulder as Donor looked above him and howled gently. 'Does Donor see her?' he asked.

Ilona nodded and helped Marcus stand, while Donor

walked away, momentarily glancing back.

Marcus felt a breeze pass him by, following in Donor's direction. Ilona howled, then encouraged Marcus to do the same. He struggled to begin with, but his third attempt was returned with multiple howls. The edge of the killing ground moved, the palisade lights catching the eyes of the pack as they stepped forward as one, led by Donor. Marcus didn't know whether to laugh or cry as a light appeared amongst the wolves and a voice drifted on the breeze. '*I'm always here.*'

Ilona drew Marcus to her. 'Mother was right. I once had no one and now I have three men,' and with that she turned Marcus back into the palisade.

Sabina was being comforted by the fire as the couple returned inside the home. Artorius looked to his ghostly white-skinned son and went to comment, but was stalled by Ilona with a smile. 'It's okay,' she mouthed.

'There are more of you than last time. You've tricked me,' snapped Sabina.

'They are raw recruits, here to train with Octavius and Marcus,' replied Artorius.

'The dark moon rises; my time has come!' shouted Rosevetha, pointing to the door with wild eyes, and then she collapsed. Her breathing was heavy and stuttered.

'Mother!' cried Ilona as she rushed to gather her in her arms.

'What is it she sees, Ilona?' asked Marcus.

'We don't know, but I am sure all will be revealed soon,' replied Breda.

'Octavius, Marcus, recruits – with me,' ordered Artorius, exiting the home. 'Right, we are seven and we need to patrol the palisade tonight, this being the first moonless night, and after Rosevetha's outburst we can only presume our time has come to fight. There will be three shifts: two recruits with my son, one with Octavius and myself, and two-hourly changes. Octavius, first stag please, and you follow Marcus. I want to be on the last shift – and prepare to be roused at any time. Make sure the fire burns all night and I want two fire arrows in the direction of the barracks as soon as they attack: that will summon a turma of cavalry. Make the most of your sleep. Go.'

Octavius chose his buddy for the shift as the other three disappeared towards their tent. Marcus remained with his father, watching Octavius. His first check was the fire, then the gate, before he mounted the rampart, dousing the torches as he went.

'Rosevetha worries me with her predictions, she is implying this will be her end,' stated Artorius, placing his hand on his son's shoulder.

'Victus must be insane to enter the forest knowing Ilona's wolves inhabit it,' added Marcus.

Artorius, deep in thought, simply nodded.

*

Victus and Gigantrex had reached the track they had used the previous day by the ninth hour of night, when all was in darkness. A light breeze ruffled the trees around them, apart from which the night was as still as death. All around them, eyes watched their every movement.

'Gigantrex, take your six warriors to the outcrop. They must not light a fire until sunrise and it must be shaded from the compound. Then, and only then, I want the buildings set on fire and you are to kill anyone who exits them.'

'But no women are to be killed,' interjected Gigantrex.

'If they bear arms, kill them,' Victus snapped back.

'That was not our agreement!' spat Gigantrex, standing

over Victus.

'Then you had better hope they don't bear arms, shouldn't you?' The anger in Victus' face at being challenged was evident, but Gigantrex didn't back down.

'When you have positioned your men, return here and take the rest down to the palisade walls. My men will cover your backs,' said Victus, smirking.

Gigantrex part walked, part ran his men to Artorius' track and followed its course using the trees as cover. Donor and a portion of his pack paced alongside the group without being heard or seen. As Gigantrex and his men reached the tree line, they followed it towards the outcrop of rock, which stood like a sentinel before them. They soon scrambled up the slope to find that fresh trees had been felled. Gigantrex could only just see the compound from their new setting, and reviewing the orders, he countermanded Victus' order to kill any armed woman. His men shrugged their shoulders in resigned agreement: he was their leader, not Victus.

Wishing his men good luck, Gigantrex retraced his steps. As he did so he noticed that the palisade torches went out and everywhere appeared unnaturally still, until a lone wolf split the night air with a howl. The only reply came from inside the compound. *Ilona*, thought Gigantrex.

Victus was in close counsel with his own men on Gigantrex's return. Doubt was invading Gigantrex's head; he questioned having involved Victus. Maybe Sabina had been right about him, but it was too late now. The mercenaries followed Gigantrex like sheep back down the track to the tree line. The group crawled towards the palisade, where once again a lone wolf called out, causing the group to falter.

'Keep moving, you cowards! You're being well paid for

this, and don't forget that whatever Victus said, no women are to be killed or you will answer to me,' ordered Gigantrex, moving forward and followed hesitantly by the others.

It seemed like an eternity of crawling when one of the men screamed out in pain, a calthrop piercing the palm of his hand. Gigantrex moved quickly to him and gagged him. 'Bastards! They've laid caltrops, but how many? It can't be the only one. Move quickly and carefully.'

*

Artorius was about to relieve his son and the two recruits. Marcus peered carefully over the palisade in the direction of the scream that was quickly cut short. He wasn't sure, but he thought he could see some prone figures.

'We didn't expect an attack in the dark, Father.'

Artorius looked puzzled. 'Relight the torches immediately, and rouse Octavius and his recruit. I want two by the gate at all times.'

On the palisade, Ilona, wrapped in a fur, floated towards her men, a quiver protruding from the fur and a bow in one hand. 'They are here, aren't they? Can you see how many?'

'Not yet. How's Rosevetha?' enquired Artorius.

'I gave her a sleeping potion. She's calling for my father and I fear what that means,' she replied, stepping into Artorius' open arms.

Inside and out, the waiting game started. Unseen by those outside, the homestead occupants were soaking the buildings with water. Ilona and Breda, both armed, passed among the men and boys who were scattered around the palisade embankment with hot drinks and reassurances. Five faces looked carefully over the palisade edge for any movement, but there wasn't any.

*

On the outcrop, Gigantrex's men looked at each other, confused as the torches were relit. The questions on each tongue was the same: 'Why?'

Gigantrex and his mercenaries were up against the palisade. Victus, Udo and his men had followed and watched the whole episode played out before them from the tree line. Victus cursed, especially when the torches re-lit the palisade and the surrounding ground. The forest behind them filled with both dark and light four-legged phantoms.

Gigantrex led his men along the palisade wall to the gate. 'We need to weaken the footing of the gate posts with our swords, and try not to make too much noise,' he whispered.

Gigantrex's men frantically dug as best they could at the base of the gate posts, while Victus slept against a tree and his men took what sleep they could.

As night faded, those on the outcrop watched for the first signs of daylight and the decision was made to light their fire. With the flames burning, the four plunged arrows into it, lifting them skywards, and four shafts split the sunrise. Two thudded into the wet house thatch, extinguishing almost immediately, while the others wasted in the ground. Within the blink of an eye, four more took flight, and this time the tent fell victim. It burnt all too quickly before being soaked. The barn hadn't been dowsed enough and the roof begrudgingly caught fire. Flaming darts rained down on the interior of the palisade as Gigantrex and the mercenaries dug for their lives to loosen the posts.

*

Inside the compound people reacted to wherever the arrows fell and as one of the recruits tried to stamp out the tent fire he fell face down, an arrow protruding from his back. There was no way of retaliating, because the bowmen couldn't be seen. Seeing the youth fall, Ilona looked to the outcrop and, cupping her hands, let out a howl. The multiple response was followed by screams of terror and anguish as six archers were torn apart.

The mercenaries looked to Gigantrex, in shock at the noise, then dug frantically. Donor appeared on the rock edge, dragging a torn body which he let fall to the ground to be further crushed and broken. Lifting his head, he howled for all the world to hear, and Ilona responded in salute.

'Marcus, the fire warning. Now!' ordered Artorius.

Two arrows in quick succession were fired for height in the direction of Argentoratum.

*

On the walkway of Argentoratum garrison, the guards were counting the final moments of their stag. One who was a little more awake than the rest was aimlessly leaning against the parapet when the night lit up in the direction of the Camp Prefect's homestead. Calling for the Optio, the guard was initially berated for seeing things, but he was adamant. The Optio dispatched the guard to the Decurion's office, where he found the man dozing in company of two unknown youths.

'Sir, I have to report seeing lights in the sky in the direction of the Camp Prefect's homestead.'

The Decurion rushed from his office, the youths following towards the stables where the turma were sat playing bones or sleeping.

'Everyone up and mounted! Our Camp Prefect needs our assistance.' Amidst the jingling of metal, the turma mounted and headed for the gate.

'Open the gates now,' ordered the Decurion. They were

agonisingly slow to open, the horsemen slipping through the growing gap as soon as they were able.

*

Marcus, hearing a noise from below the palisade, peered over and looked down at several men by the gate posts. Shouting an alarm, Breda reacted first, mounting the embankment and dispatching two arrows into the men below; screams of pain guaranteed her victims. As they leaned against the gate post it dislodged, causing Breda to fall heavily on to her shoulder.

Hearing the crash and seeing a breach, Artorius ran towards it as a man pushed his way through the gap in front of Breda. Marcus jumped off the embankment to protect her, reaching behind him to withdraw his two blades and ploughing them forward on to the man's shoulder, smashing bone and ripping flesh in a shower of blood.

Breda was dragged clear, pain etched on her face and her left arm hanging limp. Others tried to widen the gap as Artorius, Octavius and the recruits, all carrying shields, arrived at the breach.

Gigantrex grabbed the side of the gate and with all his strength widened the gap, allowing some of the mercenaries to push through. Six shields confronted them – blades clashed, sparks flew, and the first two mercenaries lost their lives quickly. Gigantrex continued to pull at the gate posts, causing the gate to twist and half fall before charging through himself.

The first thing he saw was his mother, ghostly white, propped against a water trough and being tended to by Ilona. He bellowed a roar and charged against the shields, knocking the recruits backwards. His momentum carried him forward towards his mother. Ilona stepped back in terror and, dropping to her knee, she notched an arrow. The giant dropped to his knees by his mother and cradled her gently.

'Mother!'

'It is only a bone injury. She will survive if she gets out of here,' shouted Ilona over the growing noise of battle and the screaming horses in the barn with its roof alight.

'Son, do right by yourself, your destiny lies with another,' pleaded Breda.

Gigantrex's face was one of shock at being called 'son' again. He ran towards the barn and dragged the horses clear. Securing them to the trough bar, he turned towards the broken gate where only five fought the mercenaries. Gigantrex squeezed his mother's hand and strode towards the melee.

Klothilde knelt alone on the embankment, firing into the mercenaries' rear as they breached the gate. Sabina emerged from the home, aiding Rosevetha. Artorius' group were now fighting to protect Octavius, who had taken a blow to the head.

Gigantrex swung his axe, and a mercenary's head left its body in a spray of blood. He looked at Artorius and shouted, 'I am sorry, I am with you,' as his axe crashed down into another shoulder.

The mercenaries suddenly realised they had a fight on two sides and started to back away. Victus and Udo, seeing the confusion and the breach, ran forward. Victus halted out of reach of the gate, but having clear sight inside. He saw Gigantrex kill two of the mercenaries.

'Udo – your bow, now,' ordered Victus.

Udo, doing as he was bid, passed his bow and a shaft to Victus.

'Your time has come, Sunnhild, your destiny awaits...' said Rosevetha, pointing at Victus on the edge of the gate.

Victus raised the loaded bow and fired. Sabina knew its target and ran to intercept it. *My life or his*, she thought. She almost fell on to the arrow that swept her off her feet behind Gigantrex, invading her body without piercing a vital organ.

'Turn, Gigantrex,' screamed Rosevetha.

He did so to find Sabina with an arrow through her chest, her eyes closed, but he wasn't sure whether she was dead or alive. As he bent down to her, Victus let fly a second quarrel. It missed its target, but hit the one who knew to expect it: Rosevetha. She watched it fly, letting out an almighty scream as it punctured her battered body. Gigantrex scooped Sabina into his arms and laid her beside his mother, his eyes imploring his mother to save her. She half smiled in return.

'Ilona, the wolves...' croaked Rosevetha, blood seeping from her lips.

Ilona howled at the top of her voice. Donor and his pack, waiting on the forest edge, raced forward. She ran to her mother, tears cascading from her eyes, and she knew as she touched her that time was short. A tall soldier stood protectively in front of her mother with a hand outstretched.

Ilona had watched helplessly as the arrow left Victus' bow, and in that moment, she knew the truth. In less than the beat of her heart she had loaded and returned an arrow at Victus, and he fell. Udo ordered two of his men to drag Victus, an arrow protruding from his shoulder, towards the outcrop.

A mercenary broke free of the melee and, seeing Klothilde as a possible hostage, grabbed her arm, dragging her to the gate and using her as a shield. Ilona tried to sight the mercenary, but he used Klothilde to good effect, edging towards the gap.

Snatching up his fallen bow, Udo too observed the mercenary backing out of the damaged gate, dragging a woman with him. *Victus said no witnesses*, he thought, and loaded and fired, the quarrel piercing the unsuspecting mercenary's neck. The man faltered then fell forward on to Klothilde, spraying her with his blood.

Rosevetha's face had changed; it looked more youthful. 'It has been a long time, Cloelius. Look upon your daughter, the Wolf Queen.' Rosevetha took a deep breath and reached out to her lover. Their hands met once again; in that moment they were reunited and Rosevetha was no more.

The remaining mercenaries were being pushed back towards the broken gate. Udo, seeing the wolves, gave the order to make for the outcrop. His men faltered, turning their bows on the wolves and bearing down on them.

Donor ran for the gate and his mistress. Slipping out of the gate, the mercenaries turned to see a pack of wolves bearing down on them, saliva dripping from their mouths. Some of the men struggled back through the gate to the compound, while the rest made to run. The air was rent by screams as man and beast met in a clash of steel and teeth. Such was the savagery of the clash that both sides fought for their lives, with bodies torn and bloody scattered over the killing ground.

Ilona, cradling her mother, looked up through tear-filled eyes to see Artorius struck down from behind by the mercenaries fighting for their lives. 'Don't let him die, not now,' she screamed.

Gigantrex was covered in blood and gore, barely able to see, the battle so fierce, when he heard Ilona. He half turned to see Marcus ram his shield into his father's attacker, followed by his sword searching out the man's soft innards.

Ilona rushed forward to pull her man clear as Marcus, Gigantrex and the only standing recruit stood as a line of three. Marcus' voice rang out above the screams and mayhem.

'Left foot forward, ram shields, swords strike, again, left foot forward, shield, strike, again!' he ordered.

Such was the power of his voice that even Gigantrex found himself doing as he was told.

The mercenaries fell to the movement and the gap of escape narrowed. A trumpet sounded in the direction of the forest and a turma of cavalry raced across the open ground at a charge, scattering the wolves, who ran for cover. Looking from outside the compound, Donor raced towards the gap.

'Duck!' shouted Marcus as Donor leapt over the final battlefield, using Marcus's shield to propel himself into the compound.

Donor saw Ilona on the floor, still cradling Artorius, and ran straight to her and took up her defence as she reached out to him. She recoiled, finding blood on her hand from Donor's fur, but he didn't flinch. His eyes had caught sight of Gigantrex, and with teeth bared and growling, he made straight towards the giant.

'No, Donor, come back!'

Donor's steps faltered before returning to his mistress, where she tended to his small injury.

The final mercenary knelt before Gigantrex and pleaded for a quick end, but it was Marcus who stepped forward, knocking the sword aside and placing his own blade point against the man's throat. The man stared into Marcus's face and, ripping his shirt apart, took the blade in his hands, placing the point on his chest.

'Do it, you have the right. Never have I seen such bravery in one so young.'

'Bind him, Gigantrex, we will decide later,' said Marcus, withdrawing his sword.

Klothilde struggled to free herself from underneath the dead mercenary. Marcus, seeing movement, enlisted Gigantrex's help to extract her. She immediately made for her fallen hero, Octavius. Marcus looked round at the debacle inside the compound as the turma skidded to a halt outside. Rosevetha lay deadly still by the trough, while Ilona was administering a damp cloth to his father's head wound, his cassis nearly cleft in two. Octavius was having his arm placed in a splint by Klothilde and numerous cuts cleaned. Gigantrex knelt beside his mother who, despite her own injury, was tending to Sabina who was still alive, but barely. One of the remaining recruits, Bartold, stood alongside Marcus, his deathly white skin reddened with blood, while the other, Hatto, sat nursing mostly minor injuries. The air was full of the smell of death and bodily expulsions, and smoke swirled as Marcus noticed Octavius' home had burnt to the ground and the barn roof had collapsed.

'Marcus,' shouted a voice from outside.

He knew the voice but his brain wouldn't function as he turned to find Cezar clambering over the bodies that blocked the gate. The two friends hugged each other and their eyes watered as Marcus collapsed to the floor. Gigantrex strode over and scooped Marcus into his arms, taking him to the trough, which ran red with blood. Everyone looked on as Ilona wiped away the blood that covered him from head to foot, but apart from minor cuts there were no injuries.

'He's exhausted, and not surprisingly – he fought like a man possessed,' remarked Gigantrex as Marcus opened his eyes to worried looks around him.

A fist rattled off uniform as a Decurion stood in front of Artorius. Artorius tried to return the salute but failed.

Marcus reached up with a hand and was helped to his feet by Cezar and saluted the Decurion, who smiled back.

'I have sent riders to find Victus and his men, a few of whom escaped towards the outcrop,' reported the Decurion.

'I know I hit Victus, I saw him fall,' Ilona responded. *And now I know who will face him in the future. Your gift is now fully mine, Mother, as you said,* she thought.

Gigantrex and Breda looked down at Sabina. With the arrow removed and her injury cleaned, they packed it with herbs and moss. The weapon had missed every vital organ, but she still had a survival battle to win.

'She was always your destiny, Gigantrex. She knew that to win you she had to offer her life, which she did. We will do what we can, but her life is in Lasa's hands now,' offered Ilona. 'We have the dead to honour. The ground is awash with blood, as Mother predicted.'

Everyone looked upon Rosevetha. A smile filled her face; she had found her peace at last.

*

Victus passed out again as Udo snapped and removed the arrow, packing the injury with moss to stop the blood flow. Finding a lightning-struck tree with a burnt-out centre, he propped Victus inside it, covering him with fallen foliage. The only other survivor, he clambered up a tree alongside it and hid in the branches as the turma hunted them. The outcrop and its surrounding trees were searched diligently without finding him or his master, before the troops retraced their path to the compound.

Happy that the searchers had all gone, Udo slid down the tree and crawled to the outcrop's edge and peered over it. Only the main house stood intact. Bodies littered the floor, and the living were gathered around a trough of water. Three bodies – two male and one female – had been formally laid out. The mercenary dead had been dragged outside of the damaged gate by Gigantrex, who had obviously betrayed Victus. Udo knew that Victus would return and seek Gigantrex's death, but for now he, Udo, had to secure his master's escape.

Victus moaned, still unconscious as Udo dragged him through the forest, resting frequently till they found the hobbled horses. Securing Victus as best as he could to his horse, Udo decided to take the rest, walking them slowly along the forest edge that mirrored the Roman road until he could find help.

*

Artorius stood shakily, held by Ilona who clasped their son, and they surveyed the stockade. It had survived the test. Marcus and Cezar stood shoulder to shoulder with the surviving recruits, saluting their dead friends. An unknown youth who looked to barely be in his teens, stepped forward, offering his hand to Marcus.

'I am Rebellious. I met Cezar at Placentia and I have come to join the 2nd Augusta.'

'How old are you, son?' enquired Artorius.

'Seventeen, four days after the Ides of Augustus, sir,' responded Rebellious.

'Do you have anyone who can confirm that? You don't look old enough,' asked Artorius.

'My family are all dead. I am fully skilled in weaponry,' responded Rebellious, and his eyes watered at the memories and nightmares he carried.

Ilona reached out and took Rebellious' hand, juddering at the touch, which didn't go unnoticed by the gathered. Artorius was about to ask what it was, but Ilona shook her head. 'Welcome, Rebellious, to a better life.'

She took the hands of Marcus, Cezar and Rebellious and placed them together. 'These two and another will travel to foreign shores with you, Marcus, and the great bond of friendship will tie your lives together.'

'Don't ask, she probably saw you coming,' joked Marcus to the others. Ilona smiled and nodded.

The day drew on and with the turma's aid, the damaged barn roof and the remnants of Octavius' home were removed and used as Rosevetha's pyre outside the compound. Ilona had prepared her mother, wrapping her in her best skins. Darkness crept from the forest, with Donor leading his pack from it into the killing ground, the sky blood red above them.

Father and son carried Rosevetha towards the pyre, led by Ilona carrying her son. Tears soaked her face. Her family was all gone and a new one started. She stumbled, deep in thought, Breda taking her arm.

'I must not cry, she wouldn't have wished it. She stands with my father, reunited at last before me. Her power is now mine. Farewell, Mother and Father.'

Rosevetha was laid on the pyre with her potions and mixtures alongside her. Ilona gave the eulogy, telling of her father from one of the lost legions and how her mother had been crippled for fraternising with him. Ilona never mentioned the curse on the perpetrator – that was for another time.

Artorius took their son from Ilona and held him towards the pyre. 'Rosevetha behold your grandson Cloelius Civilis.' Cheers broke freely from the gathered accompanied by many in tears.

Ilona took Cloelius, tears ran freely as she thanked Artorius. Artorius handed Ilona a firebrand, which she plunged into the pyre's base. Flames surrounded Rosevetha, and as they reached her potions and mixes, they exploded in a myriad of colours.

Donor stepped alongside his mistress and, raising his head, he howled, the pack's response echoing around the forest wall.

Father and son stepped forward, heads bowed, raising themselves to their full height. They looked at each other and, facing the pyre, saluted the memory of a lost soldier who was once more reunited with his love.

———

# Authors' Notes

All Germanic names in this novel are taken from Ancient High-Born Germanic names.

The old Roman year started on the 1st of March. The days were counted as days up to the Ides, the Nomes or the Kalends of each month.

## Quintus Naevius Cordus Sutorius Macro:

21BC – 38AD served as leader of the Praetorian Guard from October 31AD – 38AD. He was a supporter of Caligula and was said to have turned a blind eye to Caligula when he had an affair with his wife Thrasylla. He was also thought to have given the order to smother Tiberius. Tiberius was believed to be dead and Caligula assumed control to then find Tiberius asking for food, Tiberius was smothered. Macro was arrested at Ostia Antica in 38AD on the order of Caligula, but he took his own life.

## Gaius Julius Caesar Augustus Germanicus:

otherwise known as Caligula: 31/08/12AD – 24/01/41AD (assassinated). Emperor between 37AD and 41AD.

## Publius Gabinius:

was one of Sejanus' conspirators and avoided execution. He was incarcerated in the Mamertine Prison from where he was later released and recovered the final missing Tuetoburg Forest Eagle from the Chauci tribe in 41AD.

*Acknowledgements:*

Thanks once again to my editor and proof reader Jessica. You have turned my story into a novel once again.

Thank you to all at Michael Terence Publishing for continuing to believe in my vision.

*More in the Series from Peter Baggott:*

VICTUS
The Civilis Saga Part 1

Rome 31AD.
Victus Antonius Claudian, sadist and rake seeks fame and fortune from his new mentor the Praetorian Commander and Ruler of Rome, Sejanus. With his only sister Porcia, he plans to elevate himself in Rome's society through a well-placed marriage.

The Civilis menfolk consist of a Senator, Lictus, his only son Artorius, Primus Pila of the 1st Century 1st Cohort of the 2nd Augusta Legion, and two grandsons Cassius and Marcus.

Fate or fortune brings Cassius and Porcia together with an inevitable consequence. On the same day as Victus is sent north by his mentor Sejanus to raise support amongst the Northern Legions for his cause, to become Caesar, he finds his sister is pregnant. In his search for the father of his sister's child he takes revenge on him and is protected by his mentor.

The Civilis' turn to Tiberius for justice, as does the senate against Sejanus' rule. Sejanus is denounced by Tiberius, who demands that the Senate sentence Sejanus.

Victus' world implodes. He has his fortune, but now he is a hunted man and the only way back out of his exile is to remove the Civilis family and friends.

More at: www.civilissaga.com

CAY – Rosevetha's Curse
The Civilis Saga Part 3

8 AD.

Hatred of Rome continues to fester in Germania Superior, but the innate mistrust between rival tribes prevents unification against the might of the Roman Legions.

Witold, a child of nature, has had a vision of a Chieftain's son uniting the tribes under a single banner to destroy Rome's Legions. Does he exist her parents ask, or is it a dream?

A year later Hermann der Cheruskerfurst (Arminius) unites the tribes against his Roman friend, leading to the decimation of three Legions and the seizing of three prized Eagles. Would the Romans return after such a defeat?

Five years pass without Romes revenge. Germanicus finally responds to Hermann's insult, leading five legions into Germania Superior, leading a young Optio Artorius Civilis and his Centurion friend Corvus Verelii to recover the lost Eagles. Will the tribes reunite under Hermann?

Agi, a Chauci chieftain, seeks Witold's help in his barren marriage. He is informed that he will have a son to be proud of, in the year of Hermann's death, but he is given a severe warning against injuring a fellow seer.

Losing his wife to Germanicus' early raids he leaves his tribe and joins Hermann to take revenge on all who fraternize with the Romans. As the Romans retreat over the Rhenus to their winter camps Agi is rigorous with his revenge on Roman supporters, exacting severe punishments. He hears of a young woman Rosevetha, with a daughter of a Camp Prefect from the lost legions and seeks her out. Having beaten and crippled her, Rosevetha in her last moments of consciousness curses Agi's son. Rosevetha predicts that in the moment of Agi's death he will see his son fall captive to a Roman who will change his life forever.

Seven years later as prophesied, Hermann is murdered and in that same year, Agi's son Cay is born. Agi pledges his life to reverse the prophesy by protecting Witold's sanctuary and the remaining Eagle, hers.

Eleven years later from the ashes of their compound outside Argentoratum, attacked by Victus Claudian, Artorius and Ilona prepare for his final years in the 2nd Augusta Legion. Ilona foresees danger for her husband and Marcus as they try to recover the last of the missing Eagles. In trying to recover the Eagle, Marcus will face the son of the man that crippled her mother.

Will Cay submit to Rome or suffer its revenge?

More at: www.civilissaga.com

# PETER BAGGOTT

Peter Baggott is an author with a deep interest in Roman history. He has served in three uniformed employments and is very familiar with Roman tactics which are still used in everyday life: shield tactics and skills – testudo being much used in the Police and Prison Service.

Peter chose for his writing this historical genre because of his innate interest in the subject and having been born in the Roman city of Lindvm, modern day Lincoln.

In his teens, on a daily basis, while delivering newspapers, Peter traversed the exposed Roman remains from The Steep to the Newport Arch, the only full Roman archway in Great Britain.

While working in a local hotel close to the ruins he utilised this knowledge to become a self-appointed guide to visitors from far and wide and has continued to keep up to date with local finds. There are many stories surrounding the infamous Legio IX Hispana, who were based in Lindvm, their disappearance has inspired his continuing interest in all things Roman.

Peter has also visited numerous Roman sites, both in the UK and in Europe and has used original Roman historical sources of Tacitus, Suetonius and Dio, Google Maps for distancing and location, Wikipedia and several archaeological online sources. Thus, he tries to keep abreast with new finds upgrading his work accordingly.